# THE FICTION OF ALICE MUNRO

# THE FICTION OF ALICE MUNRO

## An Appreciation

*Brad Hooper*

**Westport, Connecticut**
**London**

**Library of Congress Cataloging-in-Publication Data**

Hooper, Brad.
The fiction of Alice Munro : an appreciation / Brad Hooper.
    p.   cm.
  Includes bibliographical references and index.
  ISBN: 978–0–275–99121–0 (alk. paper)
  1. Munro, Alice—Criticism and interpretation.   2. Munro, Alice—Technique.
  3. Munro, Alice—Literary style.  I. Title.
PR9199.3.M8Z695   2008
813′.54—dc22      2008006940

British Library Cataloguing in Publication Data is available.

Library of Congress Catalog Card Number: 2008006940
ISBN: 978–0–275–99121–0

First published in 2008

Praeger Publishers, 88 Post Road West, Westport, CT 06881
An imprint of Greenwood Publishing Group, Inc.
www.praeger.com

Printed in the United States of America

The paper used in this book complies with the
Permanent Paper Standard issued by the National
Information Standards Organization (Z39.48–1984).

10  9  8  7  6  5  4  3  2  1

# CONTENTS

# Introduction

In a recent interview,[1] American fiction writer John Updike was asked about his role as editor of the anthology, *The Best American Short Stories of the Century* (published in 1999). He was asked, specifically, what he might have learned that was new about the short-story form after having read so many examples in the course of selecting stories for inclusion in that volume. In answering, Updike reaffirmed that the short story is not a moribund fictional form. "I can't give you a pocket summary of what's happening in the short story now," he averred, "except that people like Alice Munro and Laurie Moore and Thom Jones are writing larger, attempting to expand the short story and to let in a little more novelistic largeness, to get many things going. The form is far from dying."[2]

That Alice Munro would be mentioned in the pages of a distinguished literary journal that is read by the cognoscenti and mentioned by no less a literary figure of the magnitude of John Updike, is important to notice. Munro's career has been chiefly dedicated to the short story (only one of her dozen books has been a novel), which might seem to limit her appeal and name recognition to a relatively small readership, which would be readers of the *Southern Review*. After all, very few collections of short stories reach the bestseller lists; in other words, how many people can be observed in public places, on planes or public transportation, reading story collections? Or hearing them being discussed among even avid and discerning readers? Or, for that matter, chosen by book clubs?

The mention of Alice Munro in the *Southern Review* by a fellow writer who is obviously aware of who's who in today's literary firmament is one thing. It is another point (at a later point for her) to be the subject of an article in the *New York Times Sunday Magazine.*[3] And not simply mentioned in passing as in the Updike interview, and not simply mentioned in the pages of a limitedly read literary journal. But featured in an entire article in a newspaper reaching millions of readers. The article takes the reader to Munro's small Ontario town, sketching some vivid biographical details, while clearly identifying her literary objective: that she "has succeeded in putting this intractably rural, unhurried, and laconic region firmly on the literary map, rendering its human commotion—its gothic passions, buried sorrows, and forlorn mysteries—in dazzling plain-spoken stories that connect directly with her readers' interior narratives and histories of the heart."[4] And the following comment in the article corresponds with John Updike's *Southern Review* remark about her short stories: "As for Munro's playing fast and loose with the genre, it is an issue critics have raised from the start."[5]

That her accomplishments have become roundly and soundly accepted on a critical level—by literary critics, that is—both summarized and cemented into place by this quote found in a standard reference source, *Contemporary Literary Criticism*: "Munro's mastery of the short fiction form over the course of her career has drawn respect and has spurred many to consider her one of the most important writers working today."[6]

The central argument I will pursue through my close reading of all of Munro's short story collections and one novel, in the order of their publication, is that she has developed her own brand of the short story, one that permits her to get "many things going" and so she may enjoy "playing fast and loose with the genre." In many ways, a typical Munro short story, as the type has evolved over the course of her career, violates—at least at first glance—the standard definition of the form: which, traditionally, has the short fictional form, unlike its big sister the novel, *not* getting a lot of things going.

When Munro began writing, she rather upset the applecart. Her first stories found publication in such Canadian literary magazines as *Tamarack Review*, *The Montrealer*, and *Chatelaine*; and these first stories were collected in *Dance of the Happy Shades*, which appeared in Canada in 1968, and subsequently in the United States in 1973. It was obvious from the beginning of her career that she was after something different in her stories, and this striving for a difference has as its purpose suiting her own needs in telling the kind of story she wanted to tell. What exactly she was after and how she went about pursuing her goal was largely transparent in its execution, which is not to infer sleight-of-hand, but rather a process of lyrical subtlety.

From the beginning, Munro's stories primarily were character studies, the chief way of describing them. From the start, she strove to arrive at the best way to capture and delineate the essence of character. The result is the "going after something different" I referred to in the previous paragraph; Munro manipulated the form's traditional structure to accomplish an intense study of character. But she had no interest in *all* aspects of a character; except for the one occasion when she *did* write one, she did not write novels. Her stories are indeed *not* novels, nor do they even verge on hybridization as a "condensed" novel (which is not a real or viable fictional form, but a shortcut measure by a writer interested in, but not energetic enough, to write a true novel).

This, then, is the basic premise of my book: Munro's short stories are indeed that, not condensed or short novels. (A short story that goes longer than the usual number of pages must still retain the "single effect" quality or it simply flounders and has *no* effect; and a short novel must *still* do what a novel does, which is develop more than one aspect of a character's nature through a series of episodes and not just one or two isolated episodes, no matter how illustrative and exemplary the chosen episodes may be. If it fails to do that, then it, too, has no viability as a successful literary entity. Although one critic makes the assertion about Munro's handling of the two forms: "Ironically, although she had never written a 'proper novel' her short stories blur the distinctive between the genres."[7])

I will analyze how, for her, form has followed function, in somewhat of a fictional equivalent of Frank Lloyd Wright's guiding principle in his architectural designs—namely, his design tendency that came to be called the Prairie School. Munro's trademark fictional device is circling through time: her stories refracting past events through a narrator's perceptions and first-person voice, as these occasions from a character's past inform the salient traits of that character and *inform* the reader of those traits. (As one critic expressed it, her technique is to "hold past and present, not to speak of even more complicated zones of time in-between, in continual suspension."[8]) This, then, is the challenge she has chosen to take up; this is the risk she has accepted. The fictional form in which she has decided to spend basically all her energy working is not traditionally the place for much referencing of the main character's past. The "now" is what matters in a short story, traditionally speaking, and a vision of the now that is not clouded, encumbered, or weighted down by things that transpired before. The talent of a short-story writer is typically realized by how effectively—and expressly—the now of a character—again, the particular aspect of that character the author is not interested in capturing at this time—is communicated with a minimum of the past actually cited as possible.

The particular talent of Munro (not too strong to say "genius"), as we shall see in our forthcoming examination of her entire oeuvre, derives from an untraditional handling of the past. Her characteristic circling through time is *all about* the past; the difference she makes in her handling of the past is to arrive at a new way, unbound by traditional short-story moves and distinctions, of bringing the past into the frame of the story. In this pursuit, she avoids simple referencing of the past to actually equalize the past and the present in a layering effect that works its way down through time to arrive at the core, which is the present moment: the present situation Munro has selected to most readily, apparently, and tellingly reveal the essence of a character.

This complicated process is accomplished, I believe (regardless of the previously cited critic who insists Munro "blurs" the lines), with no compromise on her part to the integrity of either the short-story form *or* the novel. Her short stories, then, so I find, are not short novels, nor do they straddle both forms and result in being neither.

Munro has, as I shall explain and explore, achieved a middle ground. She had "birthed" her own variety of the short story. As a factor in defining the Munro short story, we will affirm that while her fiction aims first at character exploration and delineation, plot is not incidental; in fact, on frequent occasions she offers what for the short story would usually be considered complicated plots. Her plotting is controlled, reflective of her control over her technique in general. Thus we will, in forthcoming pages, discuss plot.

We will also explore Munro's abiding themes, including the state or condition of physical and mental isolation from one's own community; an off-shoot to that theme is the theme of individualism. Other themes include the degree to which an individual's present is a fabric woven from the past and the impress of family on one's conception of expression of individuality.

The weight given to setting in Munro's fiction will be given correlative weight in our analysis. Southeastern Ontario—Munro's stomping grounds—assumes an identity as strong and palpable as does the American South in the fiction of, say Eudora Welty; and what the lay of the land looks like and its place in determining character will be examined. (As an interesting aspect of setting that Munro does not employ is pointed out by E. D. Blodgett in the full-length study, *Alice Munro*: that she makes very little use of weather, which in Canada is a big determinant; and when she does it is "functional only as it bears upon character."[9])

But, of course, no analysis of Munro's fiction can be complete without discussions—and ample citing of examples—of her prose style. The direct, clean, limpid, subtle fashion with which she puts sentences together draws attention not to itself but to *what* she is saying, as "style" should do; thus, the overarching point of her stories—character analysis—is made not only possible but also elevated in effectiveness by her clear and clarifying writing style.

A brief biographical profile will prove helpful to readers inexperienced with her fiction as well as to those readers having delved into it but nevertheless remain curious about the basic facts of her life. Alice Laidlaw was born in Wingham, Ontario, on July 10, 1931; Wingham is a farming community populated by the descendants of Scottish-Irish immigrants. Her parents lived on the outskirts of the town, people of modest means.[10] She began writing short stories when she was fifteen.[11] She attended the University of Western Ontario (in London, Ontario) from 1949 to 1951.[12] She majored in English and her first short story was published while she was in college (in 1950, to be exact), titled "The Dimensions of a Shadow,"[13] in the student magazine, *Folio*.[14] She left college before graduating, marrying James Munro at age twenty (with whom she would have a twenty-year marriage and three daughters).[15] They relocated to British Columbia and there founded Munro's Books.[16]

Munro left her marriage in her early forties and went to teach at the University of Western Ontario; there she again met Gerald Fremlin (whom she had met previously when both were students there)[17] and they were married. Fremlin was a geographer and edited the *National Atlas of Canada*.[18] He grew up in the house where he and Alice currently reside, which is located in Clinton, Ontario, twenty miles from Wingham, where she was born. Clinton is a small town (of 3,500 inhabitants) southeast of Toronto and east of Lake Huron, "a three-hour drive from Toronto during which you pass nothing but mile after flat mile of fields punctuated by grazing cows and horses."[19] This has come to be identified as Alice Munro country, as familiar to her readers, non-Canadian as well as

Canadian, as the Mississippi of Eudora Welty's fiction. In fact, it would come as no surprise to her readers that the "authors for whom she has expressed most admiration are regional writers of the American South—Flannery O'Connor, Carson McCullers, and, especially, Eudora Welty."[20]

Munro's first collection of stories, *Dance of the Happy Shades*, was published in 1968 and won Canada's highest literary honor, the Governor General's Award. Her one novel, *Lives of Girls and Women* (1971), won the Canadian Booksellers' Association Award. *The Beggar Maid* (1978, published in Canada as *Who Do You Think You Are?*) and *The Progress of Love* (1986) also won the Governor General's Award; the former was also shortlisted for the Booker Prize in the United Kingdom. *The Love of a Good Woman* (1998) won the National Book Critics' Circle Award from the United States and the Giller Prize in Canada. *Runaway* (2000) also won the Giller Prize. Munro also received the 2005 Medal of Honor for Literature from the U.S. National Arts Club.

Although no actual short-list of candidates for the Nobel Prize in Literature is issued preliminarily to the official announcement of the prizewinner (done traditionally on the first Monday in October), speculation always abounds as to which writers the committee is seriously discussing in any given year. In recent years the name of Alice Munro has appeared on the speculation list, which is a significant statement in and of itself. Although lacking any official force behind it, her mention as a likely Nobel choice indicates that Munro has earned the respect of readers and critics the world over to the level of widespread belief that she deserves the hallowed rank of Nobel laureate.

Who really knows what considerations actually go into the selection of the winner, and what the selection committee's deliberations actually consist of? Consequently, who can accurately foretell if Alice Munro will win one day. It is certain, though, that she, along with Margaret Atwood and Robertson Davies, have put Canadian fiction on the international map (aided and abetted in this successful campaign, of course, by Margaret Laurence, Mavis Gallant, and Carol Shields). Munro has endowed small-town life in Southeastern Ontario with a universality of tone and traits; the characters with which she populates the region are grounded in that soil, carrying in their blood if not in their genes, its easily given-over-to isolation quality, yet at the same time they lead lives and speak personal truths that share in consistency and attitude with the lives of ordinary folks everywhere else, in big cities or small towns, who know the frustrations of growing up, of ageing, of loving, and of finding one's personal endurance level of family ties that overbind: in other words, everyone.

## Notes

1. James Schiff, "A Conversation with John Updike," *The Southern Review*, 38(2) (Spring 2002), pp. 420–422.

2. James Schiff, "A Conversation with John Updike," p. 437.

3. Daphne Merkin, "Northern Exposure," *The New York Times Magazine* (October 24, 2004), pp. 58–62.

4. Daphne Merkin, "Northern Exposure," p. 60.

5. Daphne Merkin, "Northern Exposure," p. 62.

6. *Contemporary Literary Criticism*, Farmington Hills, MI: Thompson/Gale, 2006, 22, p. 129.

7. Coral Ann Howells, *Alice Munro*, New York: St. Martin's Press, 1988, p. 9.

8. E. D. Blodgett, *Alice Munro*, Boston, MA: Twayne, 1988, p. 11.

9. E. D. Blodgett, *Alice Munro*, pp. 153–154.

10. Daphne Merkin, "Northern Exposure," p. 61.

11. Catherine Sheldrick, "Alice Munro," *Dictionary of Literary Biography*, 53, Canadian Writers Since 1960, Farmington Hills, MI: Gale, 1988, p. 295.

12. *Contemporary Novelists*, 4th ed., edited by D. L. Kirkpatrick, New York: St. Martin's Press, 1986, p. 625.

13. "Author Profile: Alice Munro," *World Literature Today*, 79(2) (May–August 2005), p. 61.

14. Catherine Sheldrick, "Alice Munro," *Dictionary of Literary Biography*, Farmington Hills, MI: Gale, p. 296.

15. Daphne Merkin, "Northern Exposure," p. 61.

16. "Author Profile: Alice Munro," *World Literature Today*, 79(2) (May–August 2005), p. 61.

17. Daphne Merkin, "Northern Exposure," p. 61.

18. Daphne Merkin, "Northern Exposure," p. 61.

19. Daphne Merkin, "Northern Exposure," p. 58.

20. Catherine Sheldrick, "Alice Munro," *Dictionary of Literary Biography*, Farmington Hills, MI: Gale, p. 296.

# CHAPTER 1

# SHE BEGINS HER CAREER

Munro's first collection of stories—her first book, period—was published in 1968 in Canada and in 1973 in the United States, titled *Dance of the Happy Shades*. It gathered fifteen stories, several of which had been previously published in such Canadian periodicals as *Tamarack Review, The Montrealer*, and *The Canadian Forum*. In its most recent paperback edition, the book runs in length to 224 pages. Simple mathematics indicate, then, that the individual stories in this first collection average fifteen pages each—short in length, in other words, by what has come in recent years to be thought of as an Alice Munro story. This collection was well appreciated for a first book of fiction, winning the Governor General's Award, the highest literary prize given in Canada.

Some American reviewers, upon the book's publication in the United States, were supportive in their response to it. For instance, W. J. Harding, reviewing the book in *Library Journal*, offered this: "These are not stories that were written to make one catch one's breath. They are quiet and graceful and one reads on because one wants to share the effecting sensibility that Munro displays throughout."[1] Other American reviewers, however, were critical of the stories; for instance, in the following case, in an unsigned review in *The New Yorker*, critical in a way that, given the major components of Munro's reputation as it stands three decades after the review was written, rings strange to our ears in retrospect: "The background in these stories is beyond all doubt authentic.... The conversations also are extremely well rendered. It is only when she comes to deal with personality and character that this writer's hand becomes weak and her work faint, so that in the end the stories can be compared to a series of excellent, irreplaceable photographs in which every leaf, every thread, every stick of furniture is as clear and clean-cut as the day the camera clicked, while the human hands and faces have faded away into a blank place that is beyond recall."[2]

Hardly have the "hands and faces faded away," in my estimation. They remain indelible long after the reading of the stories in this debut collection. Munro's abiding interest in, and facility for, creating character, given its first exposure in *Dance of the Happy Shades*. Her power in depicting and defining character displays itself in each story; the collection as a whole stands as testimony to that strength.

The fifteen stories are of a piece; they fit well together as a collection, which imparts a cumulative impression: the narrow nature of small-town life, with events being related in most instances by an adolescent girl. Two themes provide linkage between the stories: a child/youth/young person (usually precocious and always female) learning truths about the adult world, and the behavior of the social outsider within the small-town milieu. (Rosalie Murphy Baum, in an article in *North Dakota Quarterly*, "Artist and Woman: Young Lives in Laurence and Munro," compares Munro's handling of female adolescence with another Canadian fiction writer, Margaret Laurence.[3])

Of primary interest as we analyze the stories in this collection will be the compositional techniques Munro employs in their construction; we will seek to establish where at this points she resides in the evolution of what will become the typical "Munro" short story.

The opening story in the collection, "Walker Brothers Cowboy," propels the reader into the action straightaway, with no preliminary background to the characters and without any contextual explanation of what is about to happen to them. This is, of course, a technique in short story writing so exceptionally— and nearly revolutionary—practiced in the early twentieth century by Katherine Mansfield and since then has come to be regarded as one of the features, if not requirements, of the short story. Munro practices it well.

"After supper my father says, 'Want to go down and see if the Lake's still there?'"[4] By this opening line, "Walker Brothers Cowboy" establishes itself as a first-person narrative. What follows is a story about an adolescent girl and her differing and contrasting attitudes toward her mother and father, with particular focus on the event by which she will gain adult knowledge about one of them especially and, correspondingly, the adult world at large. The story's second line places the girl's mother within her domestic environment, involved in an activity that traditionally defines the role of wife and mother: "We leave my mother sewing under the dining-room light, making clothes for me against the opening of school."[5] By the insertion of a single word in the next paragraph, Munro subtly but immediately recasts the perspective by which the story is being told: her mother "make[s] me stand and turn for endless fittings, sweaty, itching from the hot wool, *ungrateful* (italics mine)."[6] The word *ungrateful* suggests an adult view of events; that the narrator is recalling this incident as an adult. The setting is made concrete in the story's second paragraph. The location is cited as Tuppertown, "an old town on Lake Huron, an old grain port."[7] We are in what will come to be firmly recognized as Munro country. These initial details as provided in this first story conjure a rather bleak atmosphere. As the young narrator and her father set out from their house on a walk, they proceed "down a long, shabby sort of street"[8]; the narrator remarks, "[W]e pass a factory with boarded-up windows."[9] They walk further, "then the town falls away in a defeated jumble of sheds and small junkyards, the sidewalk gives up and we are walking on a sandy path."[10] Down at the lake, there are "grain boats, ancient, rusty, wallowing."[11] And "tramps hang around the docks."[12]

Tuppertown, obviously, is a neglected place, its shabby tone correlating to the mood of the narrator: the sense of her being trapped, which arose from the story's opening paragraph as the narrator indicates her discomfort with her mother making school clothes for her. The narrator, indirectly but distinctly, imparts an increased sense of entrapment—imprisonment, almost, from her point of view— as she and her father, on their walk to the lakefront pass a group of children. "I don't know them... because my mother keeps my brother and me in our own yard, saying he is too young to leave it and I have to mind him."[13]

Thus a double layer of drabness surrounds the narrator's life: the town and the restrictions placed on her movement and social contacts by her mother. The walk to the lakefront is a breach in the wall of containment surrounding her; being with her father offers an element of freedom, as limited as those moments are in time and substance. Her precocity comes to the fore when, at the lakefront, the father explains to her the geological background to the Great Lakes, as she reflects on how brief, in the great scheme of the planet's history, is one individual's life on earth: "The tiny share of time we have appalls me.... He [her father] has not known a time, any more than I, when automobiles and electric lights did not at least exist. He was not alive when this country started. I will be barely alive—old, old—when it ends."[14] These are the sentiments of an intelligent youngster capable of understanding time and maturity; there is nothing in this passage, no single word as cited in a previous passage (such as "ungrateful") that suggests this narrator is actually an adult looking back on these events and assuming—guessing, perhaps, or simply filling the blanks—what she was thinking at the time.

At this point in the story, the narrator informs the reader that her father is a traveling salesman working for the Walker Brothers, selling an array of health items and spices—and even rat poison. Even though the exact time period in which the story is set has yet to be determined, the father's occupation ("as peddler knocking at backwoods kitchens"[15]) certainly suggests a time gone by—gone by the middle of the twentieth century. The family obviously has come down in the world, for the father, until recently, owned his own business; and by this line it now becomes clearer that the time period is the 1930s, and it gains for the reader more insight into the mother's narrow nature: "... my mother has no time for the national calamity, only ours."[16] That she came down in the world is not easily accepted by her; and the narrator says, in reference to her mother's attitude, "Fate has flung us onto a street of poor people (it does not matter that we were poor before, that was a different sort of poverty), and the only way to take this, as she sees it, is with dignity, with bitterness, with no reconciliation."[17]

The narrator maintains a mental distance between herself and the image her mother attempts to publicly project. Her mother dresses up too much in the afternoon to walk past the neighbors to go to the grocery store; the narrator is certain that, when she accompanies her mother, "we have become objects of universal ridicule."[18] What the narrator most detests is the way her mother makes her dress on these occasions, her mother's "creation,"[19] all decked out and her hair in curls the narrator can't abide. She interjects, in the middle of this stated objection to her mother and how her mother makes her look, by citing a circumstance she obviously feels more comfortable being a part of: "This is entirely different from going out after supper with my father."[20]

The mother often likes to recall earlier days, when the family operated under better financial circumstances; but the narrator, in keeping with her lack of rapport with her mother, states that in response to her mother's nostalgia, "I pretend to remember far less than I do, wary of being trapped into sympathy or any unwanted emotion."[21] The mother often resorts to a traditionally female reaction to depressive thoughts and conditions: headaches, which necessitate a retreat to bed.

The father is in every way opposite to his wife, at least by way of the narrator's image of him and the nature of her time spent in his company. One day—and this is *the* event that *is* the story—when the mother is having a spell, the father takes the narrator and her younger brother out in the car, to accompany him on his afternoon sales route. The father sings while he drives, suggesting a more positive personality than his wife's—a more sanguine nature, or perhaps just more resigned to the current economic conditions raging globally as well as within his own household.

The three of them drive in open countryside: "the land is flat, scorched, empty."[22] These landscape conditions correlate to the economic ones, as well as to the desiccated atmosphere the mother creates around her despite her airs and overdressing when going out in public. A couple of lines then reveal both plot information and a technical gesture on the part of the author that is not so much a flaw in the story's execution as it is an unnecessary distancing taking the reader away from the story's immediacy. "The nineteen-thirties. How much this kind of farmhouse, this kind of afternoon, seem to me to belong to that one decade in time, just as my father's hat does, his bright flared tie, our car with its wide running board (an Essex, and long past its prime)."[23] The time period is anchored: the Depression, as indications have been proffered all along. But, more, this passage amounts to an even stronger indication than previous hints have suggested that the narrator is recounting this story from a later point in time; by these few words, she places the situation in a historical context: that of her own personal history as well as national history. By these few words the narrator is glimpsed standing at a window allowing her a view of the past.

They drive on, paying calls at farmhouses. At one house, someone pours the contents of a chamber pot down from the second floor, just missing the father at the door, and in yet another contrast between the father's and mother's personalities and outlooks on life, the father instructs the narrator and her brother to "Just don't tell your mother [about it]. She isn't liable to see the joke."[24] Further on, the children realize their father has driven beyond the boundaries of his sales territory. They stop to pay a visit at a house in front of which is "a short, sturdy woman . . . picking up washing."[25] She recognizes the father but indicates it's been quite a while since the two of them have seen each other. She is introduced to the children as Miss Cronin, and in the house is her blind mother, who recognizes his voice. The blind mother is informed by her daughter that Ben—his name—had, since they've seen him last, gotten married and had two children. Obviously, the father was somewhat of a regular caller here in his past; but in what capacity? The reader is, at this point, as uncertain about the history here as the narrator.

One thing *is* certain to the narrator: this household is "exotic" to her. Her provincialism shows itself in her reaction to the picture of the Virgin Mary hanging on the wall. "We have never known any Roman Catholics at all well, never well enough to visit in their houses."[26] Her exposure to new experiences expands when Miss Cronin and her father have a drink of whiskey. "One of the things my mother has told me in our talks together is that my father never drinks whiskey. But I see he does. He drinks whiskey and he talks to people whose names I have never heard before."[27] The father has a life outside what his wife knows and a past outside of what the narrator has ever known or even heard him tell about.

This is amplified, as it were, when Miss Cronin puts a record on and insists the narrator dance with her, and informs her how good a dancer her father was in his younger days. "Round and round the linoleum, me proud, intent, Nora [Miss Cronin] laughing and moving with great buoyancy, wrapping me in her strange gaiety . . . "[28] Thus a sharp contrast is set up between the atmosphere within this house and within the narrator's home; and a sharp contrast between the spirited Miss Cronin and the narrator's nay-saying, dissatisfied mother.

Then they have to be off, to return home. Miss Cronin asks the father if he will ever come again, with obvious sadness at the obvious unlikelihood of that happening. On the way home, the father assumes a grave demeanor. The precocious narrator understands she is not to mention this episode—this adventure—at home. She sees her father in a new light; she has an adult epiphany: that parents have a past and a side to their personality children can never fully realize and understand. "I feel my father's life flowing back from our car in the last of the afternoon, darkening and turning strange, like a landscape that has an enchantment on it, making it kindly, ordinary and familiar while you are looking at it, but changing it, once your back is turned, into something you will never know, with all kinds of weathers, and distances you cannot imagine."[29]

As they draw near to town, their hometown, "the sky becomes gently overcast, as always, nearly always, on summer evenings by the Lake."[30] The change in the atmosphere is symbolic of the return to the "temperament" within the narrator's household, at least as far as what the mother lends to the tenor of the house: a return, then, to "real" life after this unexpected and quite out-of-the-ordinary adventure.

The relationship between the narrator's father and Miss Cronin is left ever uncertain. But the vagueness is in keeping with the narrator's—a juvenile's—perspective and limited information and reluctance to disrupt the almost magical quality of this visit to another "land" by asking what might be taken by her father as impertinent questions.

This sensitivity of Munro's to make the narrator's incomplete picture of circumstances also ours—that is, it is also her reader's unfinished understanding—effects an immediacy with the story, draws a personal connection on the part of the reader to the narrator, her story becomes our story as well. One of the aspects of Munro's technique of which we will follow the development over the course of our examination of her oeuvre is not only her use of a strong narrator presence but also the distancing from events she may or may not employ in each story; meaning, as we have indicated at two places so far in this analysis of "Walker Brothers Cowboy," Munro occasionally "lapses" in presenting a story related by an adolescent narrator to reveal a moment of adult reflection/sensibility that, while not actually derailing the narrative drive, nevertheless casts a degree of doubt in the reader's mind as to the narrator's precocity in the first place and, in the second place, arouses in the reader's mind the question: Which is it? Are we in the mind of an adolescent seeing things in the adult world for the first time or witnessing an adult recalling what she experienced as an adolescent but her adult take on it "tidies" it up to an extent? (E. D. Blodgett in the full-length study, *Alice Munro*, sees these narrator interruptions as "formal strategies employed by the author to lend more credibility to the story simply by showing her narrator's efforts to arrive at a certain truth within the fiction."[31])

Other traits of the typical Munro short story that will come to be exhibited repeatedly throughout her oeuvre are present in this opening story in her first collection. Although "Walker Brothers Cowboy" is, as all her stories will be, a character portrait, it is not without a strong plotline. Her characters, as they reveal themselves, which is Munro's chief intention, do so by moving from point A to point B to point C (without, of course, taking themselves all the way to point Z, which would be a novel's purview). "Walker Brothers Cowboy" sets the pattern: external events lead to internal changes in a character—primarily a gain in awareness of the often-confusing adult world by a precocious but relatively sheltered adolescent.

The clarity, purity, and even lovely eloquence of Munro's writing style, her use of stirring and never vague metaphors, is a strong factor in this story:

> ... [M]aple trees whose roots have cracked and heaved the sidewalk and spread out like crocodiles into bare yards.[32]
>
> A very quiet, washing noise on the stones of the beach.[33]
>
> She is wearing a farmer's straw hat, through which pricks of sunlight penetrate and float on her face...[34]

(Munro's metaphoric yet exacting language itself poses a question, however: Is it in keeping with an adolescent's point of view, appropriate to an adolescent's voice; or is such radiant use of language another kind of technical "lapse"? Strictly speaking, yes.)

In structure, "Walker Brothers Cowboy" is a qualified example of Munro's trademark circling through time to inform the nature of a character's present. The past asserts a strong presence here; the inset piece—the visit to the mysterious

Miss Cronin—is indeed the present confronting the past, in the form of the adolescent narrator being made aware her father has a past that she knew nothing about. But at this point Munro has yet to develop her more elaborate circling through a character's past—which will come to be much longer in page numbers as well as events covered.

The second story in the collection, titled "The Shining Houses," makes effective and even sly use of another major Munro major theme: the social/community outsider. This story, too, offers for useful analysis Munro's employment of a third-person, somewhat omniscient (primarily *not*) point of view—which is not a typical narrative technique for her, at least as indicated in the stories in this first collection. Also, this story, a character study, allows setting a central position on its stage. Setting is organic to character in all of Munro's stories, but in this story setting is a particularly important instrument by which Munro understands character. Thus, character, setting, and plot are tightly coordinated.

Subdivisions in the 1950s were a sociological and demographic phenomenon that spread like wildfire across the landscape in the post–World War II boom. At the edge of towns, new houses encroached on previously rural areas; farming and cocktail parties met, and didn't mix. Such is the milieu Munro explores in this story, essentially through the consciousness of Mary, a suburbanite who, for the story's purposes, functions as a bridge between the "old" world of farms and the "new" world of tract housing. As the story opens, Mary has come to pay her neighbor, Mrs. Fullerton, the money she owes her for eggs. As Mary and Mrs. Fullerton sit and chat, before the former had to go with her little boy to a child's birthday party in her "side" of the world, "Mary found herself exploring her neighbor's life as she had once explored the lives of grandmothers and aunts— by pretending to know less than she did, asking for some story she had heard before; this way, remembered episodes emerged each time with slight differences of content, meaning, colour, yet with a pure reality that usually attaches to things which are at least part legend."[35] What is encapsulated in this long sentence is a cogent (ironically so, given the length of the sentence) statement of Munro's "philosophy" vis-à-vis the impact of the past on the present: more specifically, how her circling back through time, through a character's consciousness and past, as a narrative device is closely patterned after the constant search through memory that a thoughtful, reflective, person goes through, to understand the reality of his or her past.

The topic under discussion between Mary and Mrs. Fullerton is the latter's long-absent husband, about whose nonpresence she is resigned: "Sometimes it seems to me about as reasonable, a man should go as stay."[36] Quick flashes of authorial commentary—insight—fix the old woman's personality and attitude toward her new neighbors: "Mrs. Fullerton did not pay calls herself and she did not invite them, but, once a business pretext was established, she liked to talk."[37] Also this: ". . . she would not show herself to her new neighbours in any sad old-womanish disarray."[38]

When Mary gathers up her son and leaves Mrs. Fullerton's company to go to the birthday party, "when [she] came out of this place, she always felt as if she were passing through barricades. The house and its surroundings were so self-sufficient.... Here was no open or straightforward plan, no order that an outsider could understand; yet what was haphazard time had made final. The place had become fixed, impregnable, all its accumulations necessary . . . "[39] Mary's consciousness defines herself as the outsider; once stepping into Mrs. Fullerton's enclave (which is what her farm is now) that is accurate. But as the action in the story relocates to within the new era, within one of the "new white and shining houses, set side by side in long rows in the wound of the earth,"[40] the opposite case is true.

The small-town atmosphere—its constrictedness—within the subdivision is evoked in this fashion: "Women who saw each other every day met now [at the birthday party] in earrings, nylons and skirts, with their hair fixed and faces applied."[41]

The neighbors, to Mary's discomfort, are discussing the unsightly condition of Mrs. Fullerton's property. Their "conversation, otherwise not troubling, might at any moment snag itself on this subject and eddy menacingly in familiar circle of complaint, causing her to look disparagingly out of windows, or down into her lap, trying to find some wonderful explanatory word to bring it to a stop . . . "[42] They conspire to have the municipality exercise a certain right-of-domain law already on the books, and drive Mrs. Fullerton out. Mary is disconcerted; she feels the pull of a sort of allegiance to the old woman and *her* rights. "'But remember she's been here a long time,' she said. 'She was here before most of us were born.'"[43] Mary, after all, isn't truly the outsider, as she felt when, earlier, she left Mrs. Fullerton's property. A reversal of the social order has taken place; it is Mrs. Fullerton who is the outsider now, an outsider in her own land. The reader's sympathy is drawn to her; Mary is, to a degree, someone to whom the reader's sympathy can be extended, for the *sympathy* she retains for Mrs. Fullerton. But the other people of the subdivision are, collectively, not nice. "'She's been here forty years, now we're here,' one man coldly states.'[44] Munro at this point pulls away from narrating the story from Mary's point of view to assume, for a moment, an omniscient view of these people: ". . . it did not matter much what they said as long as they were full of self-assertion and anger. That was their strength, proof of their adulthood, of themselves and their seriousness . . . they admired each other in this new behavior as property-owners as people admire each other for being drunk."[45]

Group-think is often dangerous, and it certainly is in this situation. Mary refuses to support her neighbors' intended legal efforts to oust Mrs. Fullerton from her property; but, again an indication of her mixed emotions, of her ability, as it were, to see both sides of the issue, she realizes as she leaves the party "that they were right, for themselves, for whatever it was they had to be."[46] On the other hand, Mary observes, as she walks home, "Outside it was quite dark, the white houses were growing dim, the clouds breaking and breaking, and smoke blowing from Mrs. Fullerton's chimney. The pattern of Garden Place [the name of the new subdivision], so assertive in the day time, seemed to shrunk at night into the raw black mountainside."[47] It's as if the place is illusory: the subdivision so insubstantial it fades to nothing when the sun goes down. But Mrs. Fullerton's chimney is like a beacon. Does this signify her ultimate triumph over her encroaching neighbors who have turned *her* into the outsider? Her property may eventually—sooner rather than later, it seems—be torn down and "sewn over" with new homes, but she and it were never so materially and spiritually thin as to disappear with the waning sun.

But Mary is nothing if not judicious, and at story's end, as she walks further from the party toward her own home, she sees her neighbors in balance, as pioneers, really: "But these are people who win, and they are good people; they help each other when there is trouble, they plant a community . . . "[48] The last line of the story poignantly, almost sadly, captures Mary's conflicted feelings: "There is nothing you can do at present but put your hands in your pockets and keep a disaffected heart."[49]

Again, Munro's adept characterization, scene-setting, and plot development are borne on subtle, limpid, but very distinct language. In reference to Mrs. Fullerton: "Her eyes showed it [that she is old], black as plums, with a soft inanimate sheen; things sank into them and they never changed. The life in her face was all in the nose and mouth, which were always twitching, fluttering, drawing tight grimace-lines down her cheek."[50] And this brief but indelible weather comment: "The rent in the clouds had been torn wide open and the sun was shining."[51]

The story is traditional in structure, exhibiting no new exploratory techniques for Munro to bring a character's past into the story frame; in truth, the past, other than the implicit fact that everyone has one, is not a primary conceptual framework. This story is about the present.

Another important theme that Munro can be seen returning to and developing variations upon, one that is sort of a sub-theme of the precocious child learning about the adult world, is an individual's repudiation of small-town life and the impediments that family can impose on personal fulfillment. That theme is given flesh and blood in the story "The Peace of Utrecht," another first-person narrative, this one told through the voice and consciousness of an adult woman—Helen by name. This is a story that entails the brief return to her hometown and family of a woman who left all behind to go on and find her destiny in the bigger world, in a less restrained environment. The issue of breaking free is not a simple proposition; it is muddied in this story by, and the reader's sympathies thus conflicted by, the fact that Helen left her mother in declining health and a sister who thus had to care for their mother by herself. And, because of weather conditions, Helen had not even ventured home for their mother's funeral; now, in the story's present time, Helen has come with her two children on a three-week visit with her sister, who still lives in the family home, "and it [the visit] has not been a success."[52] The atmosphere in the small town of Jubilee (a town name Munro will use regularly in her fiction) is evoked by Munro in swift and indelible description; Helen once again realizes "the rhythm of life in Jubilee is primarily seasonal"[53] and there she faces anew "certain restrictions of life."[54] The true setting of the story, however, is actually a psychological "landscape": within Helen's mind, that is, in which she is back under the family roof, prompting a recollection of the demands placed on herself and her sister by their mother's debilitating disease and dealing with her guilt over having found freedom elsewhere and a marriage and children while her sister stayed behind. "All I can think about that, all I have ever been able to think, to comfort me, is that she may have been able and may even have chosen to live without time and in perfect imaginary freedom as children do, the future untampered with, all choices always possible."[55]

A second, separated section of the story juxtaposes a situation parallel to that of Helen and her sister. Still living, and still residing in town, are their two elderly great-aunts, neither having married and thus forever having lived in their family home: " a polished relationship,"[56] as Helen sees it, which is her way of saying that no one really knows how well or not they get along or what their own true individual natures are. But on one of three visits Helen makes to Aunt Annie and Auntie Lou during her return to town shows the elderly ladies in disagreement—mild, of course—for the first time ever; the point of contention is Helen's mother's clothes. The two aunts kept them all, and one aunt shows, over the other one's objection, Helen what effort they went to to preserve them. Helen is offered a coat of her mother's, which she declines to accept, and in so doing she immediately realizes she's run up against family values: "Things must be used; everything must be used up, saved and mended and made into something else and used again; clothes were to be worn."[57] But what the aunt really wants is to confide in Helen that Helen's sister, in Helen's absence, had forced their ill mother into the hospital because she didn't want her at home anymore, and there she had died—prematurely, perhaps—in two months.

In the story's last scene, Helen admonishes her sister that she, too, needs to go away, to not remain in limbo in life, but seek a new one. The story's last line strikes directly to the heart of not only the sister's situation but also her character: "But why can't I, Helen? *Why can't I?*"[58] The true poignancy of the story arises from the inability of the sister to find freedom for herself; her personality prohibits her from turning her back on what is tried and true, what is predictable. Concomitantly, the reader is released from feeling that Helen ought to feel guilty about having done so herself, even with her mother being so desperately ill. The reader sympathizes with the sister for her "inadequacy" but sympathizes with Helen more for the need she successfully acted on. It was best she saved herself, because the sister could never have done it for *herself*. If she'd stayed, like her sister, they would have ended up deeply routinized together like their two great-aunts, in a "polished relationship" with all their own individual starch gone out of them.

Although *time* is a strong narrative ingredient of this story—specifically, the exertion of their personal pasts on characters' present lives—flashbacks *in* time do occur but are brief, in their brevity imparting only essential background information for a general understanding of each character's present situation. Thus, Munro, in this story, is adhering to traditional story structure: she basically is exercising the form as it has typically been practiced before her, without "revolutionizing" her brand of it into the "Munro" short story. Yet.

Nor, as it turns out, do any of the stories in this, Munro's first collection, break new ground in narrative technique or structure. That is not to say, however, that each story, in addition to the ones already discussed, does not showcase an aspect, or more than one aspect, of Munro as a storywriter that is relevant for analysis in achieving an understanding of her accomplishment. In the story "Images," for instance, the reader realizes that not only are Munro's stories, generally speaking, character studies but also that on certain occasions, with subtlety and, as importantly, quietly, almost with cunning, she sets up her stories as *dual* character studies: of the narrator, of course, or the person through whose consciousness the story is being told (that is, in the rather infrequent instances when first-person is not used) *and* the person who occupies primary space in the story frame along with the narrator.

As seen in this story, the father figure is becoming an important symbol for Munro of fun, freedom, adventure, good health, and physical strength; of the masculine side of the domestic scene, which, ironically, is more comforting to the narrator than the repressed, critical, and discontented female side. On his activities outside the house he wears his boots, itself a symbol; says the narrator, "His boots were to me as unique and familiar, as much an index to himself as his face was.... They had an expression that was dogged and uncompromising, even brutal, and I thought of that as part of my father's look, the counterpoint of his face, with its readiness for jokes and courtesies ... my father came back to us always, to my mother and me, from places *where our judgment could not follow.*" (Italics mine.)[59] (A full-length analysis of the development of Munro's mother-daughter and father-daughter themes is provided in Ildiko de Papp Carrington's "Controlling Memory: Mother and Daughters, Fathers and Daughters," which appeared in *Controlling the Uncontrollable: The Fiction of Alice Munro.*[60])

The motif of death is recurrent in the story, and at the same time Munro never loses touch with attention paid to style, not to draw attention to it but to ensure her limpid, lovely language bears the story along comfortably, for example: "The noise the river made was not loud but deep, and seemed to come away down in the middle of it, some hidden place where the water issued with a roar from underground."[61]

Carol Ann Howells, in her book-length study, *Alice Munro*, sees this story as a "Gothic Tale which figures primitive female fears—nothing less than fears of matricide."[62]

Two stories in the collection exercise Munro's sense of humor: "The Office" and "An Ounce of Cure." In the former, an adult female narrator, a writer, decides she needs office space outside the home—she has developed a room-of-one's-own consciousness and desire. In "An Ounce of Cure," a babysitter has people over— always a formula for trouble.

Munro handles a male narrator well—the atypical gender of a Munro narrator—in "Thanks for the Ride," about two cousins who pick up two girls and take them out into the country. An interesting take on the outsider theme is presented in "The Time of Death." This story works out a variation on that important

Munro theme: here she explores a situation when, on certain occasions, the out-sider in the community is allowed in—but only temporarily, of course.

"Boys and Girls" returns readers to an already familiar Munro place, where the mother's sphere of things is boring and repressive, while what the father represents and presents is freeing and exciting. "It seemed to me that work in the house was endless, dreary and peculiarly depressing; work done out of doors, in my father's service, was ritualistically important."[63]

"Day of the Butterfly," which rests on, in a larger context, the timeless fictional theme of the stranger coming to town and, on a more Munro-specific level, it is a take on her outsider theme. It is a schoolyard tale: how children are simply smaller versions—vessels—of adult prejudice against people who are different.

"Postcard" is a humorous yet poignant story about, again, the restraints of small-town life; in this instance, a woman pays the social price of being considered "loose," a price not exacted from a man in the same situation. A girl in high school narrates "Red Dress—1946," about teenager impatience with parents; and, again, the mother character is boldly set up as representing the traditional feminine side of the household equation, and she is not particularly effective at it. The story is also about teenagers' discomfort in their own skin and, again not uncommon for Munro, social acceptability or *un*acceptability within the school social hierarchy, where popularity determines all. In omniscient third-person, "A Trip to the Coast" relates eleven-year-old May's half-step rebellion against the stagnancy, the deadening routines, of her small-town life. The motif of life's stagnancy in this place is reflected in the heat that makes people simply sit around, as well as in the grandmother's often-spoken philosophy about life: "The old woman had always said that the tourists were fools to think one place was any better than another and that they would have been better off at home."[64] "Sunday Afternoon," the weakest story in the collection, opens with overload: too much information about too many characters. It takes too long to get things sorted out.

The title story can be called a masterpiece. Small-town atmosphere is drawn to a fine point here. Thematically, "Dance of the Happy Shades" concerns collective social consciousness, namely how a certain segment of the community regards an eccentric—someone not like them, that is—in their midst. The mother of the adolescent girl in whose voice the story its told, as Mary functions in "The Shining Houses," is not so much a single character as the consciousness of all other of her ilk. Her response gives airing to the response of all the mothers in the group.

Miss Marsalles is teaching her second generation of piano students, the daugh-ters of her first generation. Today is her annual recital party: the June recital, a small-town social ritual. The mothers don't really want to go; it's boring, and Miss Marsalles is tiresome in her fuddy-duddy ways. Plus, "piano lessons are not so important now as they once were; everybody knows that."[65]

Munro, in her swift, trenchant exploration and estimations of character, often casts important—bright—auxiliary light *off* the narrator and onto the person *about* whom the narrator is chiefly reacting to. Certainly, in this story, the capturing of, the delineation of, the character of Miss Marsalles is paramount;

the youthful narrator takes a back seat to her mother, who as previously indicated, functions as the community consciousness, who herself takes a back seat to the splendidly drawn Miss Marsalles. Munro communicates facets of Miss Marsalles in a series of brief but insightful and indelible descriptions. For instance: "It is one of Miss Marsalles's indestructible beliefs that she can see into children's hearts, and she finds there a treasuring of good intentions and a natural love of all good things. "The deceits which her spinster's sentimentality has practiced on her original good judgment are legendary and colossal; she has this way of speaking of children's fears as if they were something holy; it is hard for a parent to know what to say."[66]

But with that passage a technical problem resurfaces. Isn't the voice assigned to the youthful narrator actually too mature in understanding, too articulate in language usage? The following passage begs the question further: "It will be understood that Miss Marsalles's idealistic view of children, her tender- or simple-mindedness in that regard, made her almost useless as a teacher; she was unable to criticize except in the most delicate and apologetic way and her praises were unforgivably dishonest."[67] The opening line of the story—"Miss Marsalles is having another party"[68]—sets the action in the present, and indicates this is not an event in the past being recalled by an adult who had participated in it years before, a narrative situation that Munro once again finds herself in, which ultimately lets an incongruity into the narrative voice, leaving it with a certain degree of an inauthenticity despite the effectiveness, even beauty, of the actual prose itself. The solution would have been, of course, which Munro has shown herself interested in doing on previous occasions, and she had done on some occasions, to make certain that the story's "real" time is in the future, years after the event being recorded, and the narrator is viewing the episode from an adult—more insightful and articulate, that is—perspective.

Miss Marsalles's sister lives in the same house as she, another Miss Marsalles; and Munro indicates that while this particular small town evidences a certain amount of changing with the times, in the Marsalles' house time has stood still: hence, the discomfort of the mothers—though they are former students—stepping into the house for the June recital. "They [the sisters] appeared sexless, mild and gentle creatures, bizarre yet domestic, living in their house in Rosedale outside the complications of time."[69]

Something unusual takes place at this particular June recital, however. Miss Marsalles has invited a group of special-needs children to whom she has been giving lessons. Now the mothers are even more uncomfortable, "for it is a matter of politeness surely not to look closely at such children, and yet where else can you look during a piano performance but at the performer?"[70] One of the unexpected children, a girl, *unexpectedly* plays well. Miss Marsalles's reaction to this student's performance offers another sheer view of her character: "Her smile is not triumphant, or modest. She does not look like a magician who is watching people's faces to see the effect of a rather original revelation; nothing like that. You would think, now that at the very end of her life she has found someone whom she can teach—whom she must teach—to play the piano, she would light up with the importance of this discovery. But it seems that the girl's playing like this is something she always expected, and she finds it natural and satisfying; people who believe in miracles do not make much fuss when they actually encounter one. Nor does it seem that she regards this girl with any more wonder than the other children from Greenhill School, who love her, or the rest of us, who do not. To her no gift is unexpected, no celebration will come as a surprise."[71]

Coral Ann Howells, in her book-length study, *Alice Munro*, draws parallels between "Dance of the Happy Shade" and Eudora Welty's story "June Recital," finding "distinct affinities" between the two, even going so far as to refer to Munro's story as "her version" of the Welty story. "I believe that Munro learned a great deal from Welty's stories about ways of translating the multidimensional social map of small-town life into fiction."[72]

At the collection's end, a question of redundancy lingers. Are the stories too much alike, too similar in their working out of Munro's basic themes and usual setting? To reiterate what was said at the beginning of this chapter, they are of a piece—a cycle, a suite, in the nature of Sherwood Anderson's *Winesburg, Ohio*, or Eudora Welty's *Golden Apples*. Their effect is cumulative, but without a blurring of their individuality. This is a true *collection*, then.

Munro has yet to take chances with structure; her lengthy explorations of time, of a character's past, which will define a Munro short story, is yet to come. These stories in the first collection are not apprentice pieces, however. They are mature, well-accomplished stories showing Munro's understanding of the traditional form, which of course is the necessary groundwork for her later transcendence of those traditions to make her own mark on the history of the short story.

We look now at her next book, her only novel. One reviewer anticipated it in this fashion: "Munro writes well but hers is not a strong collection. Watch for her next novel."[73]

## Notes

1. W. J. Harding, *Library Journal*, 98(3021) (October 16), p. 93.

2. *The New Yorker*, 49(186) (November 15), p. 73.

3. Rosalie Murphy Baum, "Artist and Women: Young Lives in Laurence and Munro," *North Dakota Quarterly*, 52(3) (1984), pp. 196–211.

4. Alice Munro, *Dance of the Happy Shades*, New York: Random/Vintage, 1998, p. 1.

5. Alice Munro, *Dance of the Happy Shades*, p. 1.

6. Alice Munro, *Dance of the Happy Shades*, p. 1.

7. Alice Munro, *Dance of the Happy Shades*, p. 1.

8. Alice Munro, *Dance of the Happy Shades*, p. 1.

9. Alice Munro, *Dance of the Happy Shades*, p. 2.

10. Alice Munro, *Dance of the Happy Shades*, p. 2.

11. Alice Munro, *Dance of the Happy Shades*, p. 2.

12. Alice Munro, *Dance of the Happy Shades*, p. 2.

13. Alice Munro, *Dance of the Happy Shades*, p. 2.

14. Alice Munro, *Dance of the Happy Shades*, p. 3.

15. Alice Munro, *Dance of the Happy Shades*, p. 4.
16. Alice Munro, *Dance of the Happy Shades*, p. 4.
17. Alice Munro, *Dance of the Happy Shades*, p. 4.
18. Alice Munro, *Dance of the Happy Shades*, p. 5.
19. Alice Munro, *Dance of the Happy Shades*, p. 5.
20. Alice Munro, *Dance of the Happy Shades*, p. 5.
21. Alice Munro, *Dance of the Happy Shades*, p. 6.
22. Alice Munro, *Dance of the Happy Shades*, p. 7.
23. Alice Munro, *Dance of the Happy Shades*, p. 8.
24. Alice Munro, *Dance of the Happy Shades*, p. 10.
25. Alice Munro, *Dance of the Happy Shades*, p. 10.
26. Alice Munro, *Dance of the Happy Shades*, p. 14.
27. Alice Munro, *Dance of the Happy Shades*, p. 15.
28. Alice Munro, *Dance of the Happy Shades*, p. 16.
29. Alice Munro, *Dance of the Happy Shades*, p. 18.
30. Alice Munro, *Dance of the Happy Shades*, p. 18.
31. E. D. Blodgett, *Alice Munro*, Boston, MA: Twayne, 1988, p. 73.
32. Alice Munro, *Dance of the Happy Shades*, p. 1.
33. Alice Munro, *Dance of the Happy Shades*, p. 2.
34. Alice Munro, *Dance of the Happy Shades*, p. 11.
35. Alice Munro, *Dance of the Happy Shades*, p. 19.
36. Alice Munro, *Dance of the Happy Shades*, p. 21.
37. Alice Munro, *Dance of the Happy Shades*, p. 19.
38. Alice Munro, *Dance of the Happy Shades*, p. 20.
39. Alice Munro, *Dance of the Happy Shades*, p. 22.
40. Alice Munro, *Dance of the Happy Shades*, p. 23.
41. Alice Munro, *Dance of the Happy Shades*, p. 25.
42. Alice Munro, *Dance of the Happy Shades*, p. 25.
43. Alice Munro, *Dance of the Happy Shades*, p. 27.
44. Alice Munro, *Dance of the Happy Shades*, p. 27.
45. Alice Munro, *Dance of the Happy Shades*, pp. 27–28.
46. Alice Munro, *Dance of the Happy Shades*, p. 29.
47. Alice Munro, *Dance of the Happy Shades*, p. 29.
48. Alice Munro, *Dance of the Happy Shades*, p. 29.
49. Alice Munro, *Dance of the Happy Shades*, p. 29.
50. Alice Munro, *Dance of the Happy Shades*, p. 20.
51. Alice Munro, *Dance of the Happy Shades*, p. 25.
52. Alice Munro, *Dance of the Happy Shades*, p. 190.
53. Alice Munro, *Dance of the Happy Shades*, p. 194.
54. Alice Munro, *Dance of the Happy Shades*, p. 194.
55. Alice Munro, *Dance of the Happy Shades*, p. 196.
56. Alice Munro, *Dance of the Happy Shades*, p. 203.
57. Alice Munro, *Dance of the Happy Shades*, p. 206.
58. Alice Munro, *Dance of the Happy Shades*, p. 210.
59. Alice Munro, *Dance of the Happy Shades*, p. 36.
60. Ildiko de Papp Carrington, "Controlling Memory: Mothers and Daughters, Fathers and Daughters," *Controlling the Uncontrollable: The Fiction of Alice Munro*, DeKalb, IL: Northern Illinois University Press, 1989, pp. 185–205.
61. Alice Munro, *Dance of the Happy Shades*, p. 37.

62. Coral Ann Howells, *Alice Munro*, New York: St. Martin's Press, 1988, p. 23.
63. Alice Munro, *Dance of the Happy Shades*, p. 117.
64. Alice Munro, *Dance of the Happy Shades*, p. 184.
65. Alice Munro, *Dance of the Happy Shades*, p. 213.
66. Alice Munro, *Dance of the Happy Shades*, p. 213.
67. Alice Munro, *Dance of the Happy Shades*, p. 213.
68. Alice Munro, *Dance of the Happy Shades*, p. 211.
69. Alice Munro, *Dance of the Happy Shades*, p. 214.
70. Alice Munro, *Dance of the Happy Shades*, p. 222.
71. Alice Munro, *Dance of the Happy Shades*, p. 223.
72. Coral Ann Howells, *Alice Munro*, New York: St. Martin's Press, 1988, pp. 28–30.
73. *Choice*, 10(1551) (December 1973), p. 1551.

CHAPTER 2

# SOMETHING DIFFERENT, A NOVEL

*Lives of Girls and Women*, Munro's second book and first novel, was published in Canada in 1971 and in the United States the following year. Munro has indicated on more than one occasion that she is uninterested in writing a second novel. It could be guessed that her publisher has suggested she do so. What can be surmised from reading this single novel of hers that might have been her experience in writing it that has held her back from attempting a second? To discover a possible answer we turn first to Munro herself. In a previously cited article in the *New York Times Magazine*, she posits, "I've tried to write novels.... They turn into strange, hybrid stories." And, furthermore, "I haven't read a novel that I didn't think couldn't have been a better story. I still go into bookstores and look at how few pages you can get away with in a novel. I actually stand there, deducting the white pages in between and adding up the number on my fingers. Do you think you can get away with 110?"[1]

Could the critical response to the novel have been the primary factor contributing to her reluctance to continue working in the novel form? For every positive review statement upon the book's release, such as this one: "The thread of this yarn are common enough stuff. What Alice Munro makes of it is rare"[2]; there were as many if not more negative reactions, such as: "Perhaps the first thing to say about . . . [this book] is that it is not a novel. This is not just carping: it seems to me to be such a good collection of short stories that it would be a mistake to pretend it is anything else."[3] Even the later response of scholars found fault; for instance, this: "It might be described as a novel with built-in fragmentation."[4]

*Lives of Girls and Women* is divided into seven chapters, each chapter given a title, and an epilogue entitled simply that. The narrative never congeals into a true novel. There is not a traditional plot arc to enable it to be seen as a novel: there is no rise—no swell—in the storyline leading to a climactic scene. Each chapter is more or less an individual unit containing within itself a small rise, yet some of the chapters are only minimally active in moving characters from point A to the next point, languorous in contributing to the steady movement of the book's overall storyline. The unavoidable, overall negative conclusion drawn about the book arises *not* from its construction, however. The narrative might indeed suffer a weakness of cumulative effect and still be regarded as, technically speaking, a novel, although not a tightly composed one. By the same token, it could have the same problem of cumulative effect but fall into the category of short-story cycle. The issue, then, is not its construction; in the end, it matters little whether the book is seen as a novel or a cycle of short stories. It is simply a flat, relatively uninteresting book; period. Munro's material in this book—her setting, character types, and themes—are ones she introduced in her previous book. In this book, however, this same material lies flat—not completely inert, for Munro could never *not* breathe life into her fiction. But here she lacks inspiration and thus the illumination of the plights of ordinary individuals, which has come to be universally regarded as her forte, fails in turn to inspire the reader.

As if Munro were supplying a preview of the elements instructive in understanding the novel's strengths and weaknesses, the first chapter, entitled "The Flats Road," offers an introduction to most of the essential traits of the novel as a whole. The opening line, "We spent days along the Wawanash River, helping Uncle Benny fish,"[5] announces that, one, the narrative, at least initially, is in the first person, and second, that Munro, as she practiced in the short stories in the previous book, plunges the reader directly into the action. Farther down on the same page, a brief description of Uncle Benny (who, as it is quickly revealed, is not actually the narrator's uncle, "or anybody's"[6])—"He wore the same clothes every day of his life"[7]—Munro has continued interest in, and fondness for, eccentric individuals, usually male. A later statement about him (an example of Munro's felicitous writing style), is more concrete: "He was not so old as his clothes, his moustache, his habits, would lead you to believe; he was the sort of man who becomes a steadfast eccentric almost before he is out of his teens."[8] The appearance of his house correlates with his own appearance: "tall and silvery, old unpainted boards, bleached dry in the summer, and dark green blinds, cracked and torn, pulled down over all the windows."[9] Obviously, from her short-story writing experience, Munro demonstrates an ability to swiftly identify, even encapsulate, a character, and with quick but careful brushstrokes she lays a solid foundation upon which more depth and sides of that character can be elaborated upon.

With the narrator, out fishing with Uncle Benny, is her brother, Owen, a nonpivotal character but a recurrent one, who nevertheless will play a role in the narrator's growing sense of the world sharply divided into men and their roles and women and their separate ones.

Uncle Benny works for the narrator's father and the time is the early 1940s. The setting is the Flats Road, at the end of which sits the narrator's family house and the acreage upon which her father's foxes are raised (not as pets but for their fur), where town is left behind but open countryside of true farms is not yet encountered. This is the run-down atmosphere—houses looking "more neglected, poor, and eccentric than town houses would ever be"[10]—that, as often occurred in the stories in her first collection, correlates with the fallen-downhill mood within the narrator's household. The character of the mother fits the same construct and shading as encountered in Munro's first story collection: *discontented* would be the most accurate description. She is discontented primarily with the geographical/social location in which she has found herself: "The Flats Road was the last place my mother wanted to live. As soon as her feet touched the town sidewalk and she raised her head, grateful for town shade after the Flats Road sun, a sense of relief, a new sense of consequence flowered from her."[11] But because of her belief of her superiority over her circumstances, she was "not popular on the Flats Road. She spoke to people here in a voice not so friendly as she used in town, with severe courtesy and a somehow noticeable use of good grammar."[12] The mother will become, with the narrator, one of the primary characters.

Another condition and attitude borrowed from the previous book's stories is this: "my father was different."[13] Discontentedness—and this is true in the father characters previously encountered—is not an element of his psychological constitution. He was at home in the Flats Road: "he felt comfortable here,"[14] as opposed to in town, and as opposed to the mother in this regard. However, the influence of the father on the narrator's activities and outlook, strongly in the stories in the previous book, is a lesser force here; it will be not from him but from her mother that the narrator will take her cues—but also set up her revolts against.

And, so, this first chapter, after establishing the comfort or lack thereof of the father and mother within their present life, returns to where it began: with the eccentric character, Uncle Benny. He is one element of the Flats Road and her discontented existence there that the mother has accepted; he not only works on the fox farm for the father but he also eats at the family table. Benny is currently in the market—finally—for a wife, and to that end he answers a want ad in the newspaper, using the narrator's fourth-grade compositional abilities to aid him. He gets a response, borrows the narrator's father's car, and goes to the neighboring town where she lives to more or less pick up what he has ordered; and he returns having done more than that: he's married her.

The new wife keeps to herself, avoiding contact even with the narrator's mother; and the narrator's parents learn that she has brought a child with her. But she doesn't hang around very long before running off with not only her little girl, but also some of Uncle Benny's household items.

One day shortly thereafter, Uncle Benny receives a letter from her asking that a few of her possessions be mailed to her; she includes an address in Toronto to which they may be sent. Benny decides to go there himself and retrieve the little girl; he is more open now with the narrator's parents about Madeleine's mistreatment of the child. But, daunted by the confusion of the big city, he simply retreats after having gotten thoroughly lost. In a beautiful passage, Uncle

Benny's existence is encapsulated, but also the narrator's family's appreciation of its differences from most other peoples' lives:

> So lying alongside our world was Uncle Benny's world like a troubling distorted reflection, the same but never at all the same. In that world people could go down in quicksand, be vanquished by ghosts or terrible ordinary cities; luck and wickedness were gigantic and unpredictable; nothing was deserved, anything might happen; defeats were met with crazy satisfaction. It was his triumph, that he couldn't know about, to make us see.[15]

Uncle Benny's experience also compels the narrator to draw a higher conclusion, one more relevant to her own life. As they listened to Uncle Benny relate his aborted mission, "my mother sat in her canvas chair and my father in a wooden one; they did not look at each other. But they were connected, and this connection was plain as a fence, it was between us and Uncle Benny, us and the Flats Road, it would stay between us and anything."[16] And Uncle Benny's wife fades into family history. "We remembered her like a story . . . "[17]

This is the end of the novel's first chapter, wrapped up with a tidiness often found and usually expected in a short story. There is no implied ellipsis at the chapter's conclusion, nothing left hanging that compels the reader to automatically turn to the next chapter.

Other features of this first chapter—features that are technical, or thematic, or stylistic—call for attention; and these features, too, set patterns for the entire narrative to come. The most prominent of these overarching features is Munro's use of the first-person narrator, which, as we have seen, was frequently a structural technique in the stories in her first collection. Emphatically, this is *not* an incidental aspect of the novel; it not only shapes this chapter and all the ones that follow but also supplies the mood. Further, it does not simply shade all the characters but also forges them. Munro's most interesting handling of a first-person narrator in her stories was, as has been pointed out previously, the "observing" narrator positioning herself at the center of all activity but generally serving as stage manager, directing *other* characters than herself to step forward, thus she having in effect decided which characters are given most or lesser prominence. Munro's control of this technique, her adeptness at executing it, unfolds what becomes a dual analysis of these characters. How the narrator sees them is how the reader initially sees them, but the first impression is not necessarily the lasting one. The narrator is in effect setting these characters up according to her vision, based on her absolutely subjective experience with them, and Munro leaves *us* to determine the bias that is informing the narrator's portrayals. Readers may come away with a view not in contradiction to the narrator's, but with a somewhat different interpretation of these characters.

The question hovering over this important feature of the novel is: Will the narrator remain relatively invisible, remain the "hostess" to readers as they meet and get to know the interesting characters populating her life, or will she come to occupy center stage and thus make the novel first and foremost about herself, sharing these characters with the reader but lending further development of them through her eyes solely as impactors on *her* development.

The second of the novel's chapters is titled, "Heirs of the Living Body." Several pages of slow reading come before narrative steam is built up. Again, the point of view is from the adolescent female narrator. Death is a recurrent motif in this chapter: possibly the most difficult aspect of adult life for a young person to comprehend and find relevance to their young life. The prominence of the mother and father in the previous chapter is substituted by the narrator's great-uncle and two great-aunts, who live in a town apparently not too far from the one in which the narrator and her family live. The two great aunts, sisters, step to the fore to become, in their eccentric but meaningful ways, the vehicles by which the narrator gathers an increasing awareness of traditional male and female roles and how she will respond to those roles as she grows older and wants her own choices to make about the forthcoming nature of her own adult life. Munro has used the great-aunt motif previously, in the story, "The Peace of Utrecht," in *Dance of the Happy Shades.* The two unmarried elderly sisters living together who appear in this chapter of the novel—never to feature again in the rest of the book (again, a factor contributing to the perception of it as a collection of stories over a true novel)—are vague symbols to the narrator of a unique situation in an otherwise distinctly defined world in which the female sphere is neatly divided from the male one.

Initially, Aunt Elspeth and Auntie Grace seem to be a heightened, concentrated form of the femaleness that strikes the narrator as a kind of über-domesticity, to which she had never been, so far, seen to gravitate toward. They reinforce in the narrator that the world is cloven into male world and female spheres, and never the twain shall meet. They keep busy with traditional female chores, which basically outline the map of domesticity in those days: "marathons of floor scrubbing, cucumber hoeing, potato digging, bean and tomato picking, canning, pickling, washing, starching, sprinkling, ironing, waxing, baking."[18]

Their old-fashionedness in terms of female place and personality clash with the narrator's mother's sense of the same issues (which is ironic, since the narrator, in the stories of her first collection and now so far in the novel, finds the mother as a polestar for female ways that is *not* the direction in which she is drawn). When the aunts visited the narrator's house, they "turned sulky, shy, elderly, eager to take offense."[19] They were not pleased by the housekeeping of the narrator's mother. "They would bend over the pans, scraping, scraping off every last bit of black that had accumulated since the last time they visited here."[20] Nor pleased were they with the mother herself, especially "her directness, her outrageousness"[21]—in their eyes, from the perspective of being too long hidden away in their hermetically sealed world, that is. And, in turn, the narrator's mother was dismissive of the aunts as relics, ineffectual and inconsequential—but inevitable and unavoidable. "My mother went along straight lines. Aunt Elspeth and Auntie Grace move in and out around her, retreating and disappearing and coming back, slippery and soft-voiced and indestructible. She pushed them out of her way as if they were cobwebs: I knew better than that."[22]

But the narrator was stimulated by the aunts, appreciative of their household—their world—"of work and gaiety, comfort and order, intricate formality."[23] Yet another clash in the way the aunts viewed the world and the narrator's mother's worldview comes in the form of differing attitudes toward personal advancement. The aunts "liked people turning down things that were offered: marriage, position, opportunities, money."[24] The mother interprets this behavior as simply being too afraid to assert oneself.

The narrator is aware of duplicity underlying her great aunts' genialness. "There was a whole new language to learn in their house. Conversations there had many levels. Nothing could be stated directly, every joke might be a twist turned inside out. My mother's disapproval was open and unmistakable, like heavy weather; theirs came like tiny razor cuts, bewilderingly, in the middle of kindness. They had the Irish gift for rampaging mockery, embroidered with deference."[25]

The second half of the story/chapter is the place where the action, such as it is, gathers itself and proceeds with a degree of momentum lacking in the first half. The turning point is the death of Uncle Craig, the brother of the two maiden great aunts. The narrator, whom we finally know as Del, is taken aback, not so much by the loss of Uncle Craig but by facing the mystery of death and its associated rituals. "I wanted death pinned down and isolated behind a wall of particular facts and circumstances, not floating around loose, ignored but powerful, waiting to get in anywhere."[26]

Many pages are devoted to the assembly of family and friends for Uncle Craig's funeral. Del's stake in the event is to avoid having to attend the event and see Uncle Craig dead. She acts out, biting the arm of her annoying cousin. "When I bit Mary Agnes I thought I was biting myself off from everything. I thought I was putting myself outside, where no punishment would ever be enough, where nobody would dare ask me to look at a dead man, or anything else, again. I thought they would all hate me, and hate seemed to me so much to be coveted, then, like a gift of wings."[27] But Del quickly realizes that freedom, which is what Munro's characters, her adolescents at least, are generally seeking, "is not so easily come by."[28] The family, appropriately, reacts with horror over Del's action. Her act will live on in family history. "They would remember that I was highly strung, erratic, or badly brought up, or a *borderline case*. But they would not put me outside. No. I would be the highly strung, erratic, badly brought up *member of the family*, which is a different thing altogether."[29]

After Uncle Craig's death, his unmarried sisters, Aunt Elspeth and Auntie Grace, relocate to the same town where Del and her family live; as Del proceeds through her high-school years, she visits them less often, and their environment becomes even more a place that time left behind. "Their house became like a tiny sealed-off country, with its own ornate customs and elegantly, ridiculously complicated language, where the news of the outside world was not exactly forbidden, but became more and more impossible to deliver."[30] One day the aunts drag out the manuscript on local history Uncle Craig had been writing and give it to Del, with the hope that she will finish writing it some day; but later the manuscript is completely ruined in a basement flood. This chapter/story ends with a harsh statement about the responsibility the aunts had tried to shove onto Del: "I felt remorse, that kind of tender remorse which has on its other side a brutal, unblemished satisfaction."[31]

As sharply drawn as the two aunts are, and as lean and crisp as Munro's prose style is here, this chapter is easily forgotten; in other words, events do not resonate much past the reading of them. Munro seeks primarily to establish character here, as in the previous chapter of this "novel" and in all the stories of her first book; despite that, for their viability, depth, and identifying uniqueness as individuals, there is lack of movement on the characters' part, not movement as in growth of personality and experience but in action. The context into which the characters are fit in this chapter is too static, and thus by their relative inaction the characters cannot truly reveal their three dimensions.

Small-town and rural Canada is well evoked, down to the last blade of grass in the two aunts' front yard, as well as the social hypocrisy found there, a natural element even in such a less complicated environment as a 1940s farm town—and it is explained with a humor that neither mocks nor savages the locals.

Munro's primary thematic concern in this chapter is a career-abiding one for her: the impress of family on individual expression and on the formation of an individual's worldview carried through life. The earlier pages of an analysis of this chapter, the question was posed of whether the great aunts would "hold up" as they were originally presented, as Del, despite her precocity, sees them through her limited experience in the world: as heightened versions of femininity and domesticity. The reader comes to realize, in peering around Del for a first-hand observation of the aunts, that actually they are a bridge between the separate worlds of male and female interests and occupations. Fussy perhaps they are, and within their household only their vision of the outside world reigns, but the fact remains that they have established a household without husbands; and after the death of their brother Craig, they operate a household completely free of male influence and attachment.

In the third chapter, titled "Princess Ida," the actual point of the novel begins to take shape: establishing Munro's real objective and the book's significance, which is the mother growing and firming up as a fully dimensional character and exerting the most important—both in positive and negatives senses—on Del as she grows into young womanhood. The chapter begins directly: "Now my mother was selling encyclopedias."[32] Not until the sixth page is it revealed that the mother now rents a house in town, and Del lives with her; Del's parents are not separated, it is simply economics that seem to be the reason for the division of households (just for September to June, though, and Del's father drove in most nights for the evening meal and stayed overnight). Del is now a town girl, not a farm girl, and quite conscious of the change: "It was a house that belonged to a town; things about it suggested leisure and formality, of a sort that were not possible out on the Flats Road."[33] And this as well: "I missed the nearness of the river and the swamp, also the real anarchy of winter, blizzards that shut us up tight in our own house as if it were the Ark. But I loved the order, the wholeness, the intricate arrangement of town life, that only an outsider could see. Going home from school, winter afternoons, I had a sense of the whole town around me . . ."[34]

The mother, then, regardless of her previous role as symbol of the domestic side of the marital equation has now stepped across the line of separation and is, at least in town, the breadwinning head of the household, getting out and experiencing people and places like a man. "She drove our thirty-seven Chevy over all of the highways and back roads of Wawanash County . . ."[35] In the mother's selling of encyclopedias, she and Del have a bond: Del loves the feel and look of the volumes as physical objects as well as the knowledge contained within their pages. In fact, Del begins to partner her mother in her sales jaunts, rattling off to potential customers some of the facts she has learned. But Del achieves a quiet revolution against her mother by simply stopping her cooperation in the dog-and-pony show. Her mother, not pleased, comments, "You want to hide your brains under a bushel out of pure perversity but that's not my lookout. You just do as you please."[36]

The setting is typical Munro country: "We drove through country we did not know we loved—not rolling or flat, but broken, no recognizable rhythm to it; low hills, hollows full of brush, swamp and brush and fields. Tall elm trees, separate, each plainly showing its shape, doomed but we did not know that either. They were shaped like slightly opened fans, sometimes like harps."[37] And this lovely line about Del's new place of residence: " . . . all these things, rituals and diversions, frail and bright, woven together—town!"[38]

At this point in the chapter, nearly twenty pages in, an event occurs that finally gives the narrative a degree of dramatic tension; this event is based on the hoary storytelling devise of "a stranger comes to town," which is exactly what happens—a stranger to Del, at least. Del's mother's American brother comes to visit, with his wife. Del immediately views her surroundings from her uncle's rich-American perspective. Riding in his "big cream-and-chocolate, clean-smelling car . . . from that car I saw . . . the whole street, differently. Jubilee seemed not unique and permanent as I had thought, but almost makeshift, and shabby; it would barely do."[39] The uncle's wife is symbolic to Del. "She reached some extreme of feminine decorativeness, perfect artificiality, that I had not even known existed; seeing her, I understood that I would never be beautiful."[40]

The following chapter, titled "Age of Faith," is about Del's obsession with searching for religious assurances. Faith in God is not sufficient, for she wants concrete evidence. The chapter is tiresome, however, suggesting an authorial overextension of material to fill up required pages for a novel. Del's precocity has worn thin. Munro superimposes the issue of faith onto the characters, which has the effect of draining them of other qualities and they emerge—especially Del—unconvincing. (E. D. Blodgett, in the full-length study of Alice Munro, in a discussion about the religiosity of this chapter, concludes: "The thematic link between the sections of the chapter is the limits of prayer."[41]) This chapter evidences Munro's struggle with the novel form: a slackness in narrative tension but also an inability to simultaneously handle more than one aspect of a character.

This chapter strongly suggests Munro's vision is strongest when focused on a single aspect of a character, which is in keeping with the traditional temperament of a short-story writer. The only significant contribution this chapter makes to the narrative is that for the first time Del is not only the narrator but also the chief character, having stepped out from the background of her own narrative to take center stage. She is emerging as an increasingly strong character.

"Changes and Ceremonies" is the tale of a schoolgirl crush, and here Munro regains strength. The first paragraph points once again to Del's preference for and admiration of the traditional male personality and character traits over female ones. "Boys' hate was dangerous, it was keen and bright, a miraculous birthright.... Girl's hate, in comparison, seemed muddled and tearful, sourly defensive."[42] Her sentiments toward the male are mixed at this young age, with fear of their power. "The things they said stripped away freedom to be what you wanted, reduced you to what it was they saw, and that, plainly, was enough to make them gag."[43] This chapter introduces (late, nearly halfway into the book) Del's best friend, Naomi. Del had been a loner when she lived out on the farm, but now that she and her mother and brother live in town, things have changed. "I had not had a friend before. It interfered with freedom and made me deceitful in some ways, but it also extended and gave resonance to life,"[44]

Munro continues to establish the novel's setting with quiet but telling brush strokes. "This was the normal thing in Jubilee, reading books was something like chewing gum, a habit to be abandoned when the seriousness and satisfactions of adult life took over. It persisted mostly in unmarried ladies, would have been shameful in a man."[45] During the long and socially important process of putting on the annual school operetta, Del develops a crush on Frank Wales; it ultimately goes nowhere, as Frank leaves school to get a job. Munro wraps the chapter up neatly; once again, by structure and effect, this is a short story.

By the next chapter, titled "Lives of Girls and Women" (a chapter in a novel and the novel itself sharing a title: another indication of a more appropriate view of this novel viewed as a short-story collection), scenes are drawn out to thinness, as if—it is difficult to resist the conclusion—to simply occupy space and fill out the required pages for a novel. On the other hand, and ironically so, the chapter has strong points that contribute strength to the novel as a whole. One, the dimensions of the mother character continue to be filled out, by which she gains an increasing depth and additional sides to her personality. Two, a female character previously but only briefly introduced, Fern Dogherty, who is the boarder Del's mother keeps in their rented house in town, is one of the Munro's few sympathetically drawn female characters encountered so far in her oeuvre (just as a new male character introduced in this chapter, Fern's gentleman caller, Mr. Chamberlain, is the first male character so far who is developed by Munro with *no* empathy for his faults), and Del takes an important step in maturation as her sexuality burgeons, moving beyond the puppy-love level.

Del's mother is replacing her father as the dominant figure in her life, the most influential, and the one she most directs her attention toward, since she and her mother's move from the farm to the rented house in town. Lending realism to the situation, the mother's dominance does not automatically mean a new support and understanding of her for Del. Now that Del is becoming a young woman and with a growing sense of important things waiting for her somewhere far away, even more distance is developing between Del and her mother. "It was glory I was after, walking the streets of Jubilee like an exile or a spy, not sure from which direction fame would strike, or when, only convinced from my bones out that it had to. In this conviction my mother had shared, she had been my ally, but now I would no longer discuss it with her; she was indiscreet, and her expectations took too blatant a form."[46]

Fern, Del's mother's boarder, on the other hand, represents an almost alternative type of personality. "All these qualities my mother had developed for her assault on life—sharpness, smartness, determination, selectiveness—seemed to have their opposites in Fern, with her diffuse complaints, lazy movements, indifferent agreeableness."[47] Fern's boyfriend is a significant though certainly not heroic catalyst for Del's catapult into adult sexuality. He makes inappropriate and secretive sexual advances, to which Del responds positively; he is a predator and manipulator. On the other hand, Del is exploiting him as well, for her new sexual exploration; she is using the "material" available to her, as it were. "His moral character was of no importance to me there; perhaps it was even necessary that it should be black."[48] Mr. Chamberlain leaves town abruptly. But Fern must deal with his departure. In her commentary on this situation, Del's mother reveals herself to be rather a protofeminist, despite earlier depictions of her as mired in domestic chores and, as unhappy as we have witnessed her stuck in that condition, not following or even seeing paths out of it until she, with Del and Del's brother, moved into town and began her own male-type job of door-to-door selling. In that way, she blurred Del's sense of the world definitely divided into male and female arenas; and now Del hears her mother espousing what will later become identified as "feminist" ideas: "There is a change coming I think in the lives of girls and women,"[49] her mother believes. She is an advocate of birth control; but, more, she advocates just plain self-respect for women.

Del, of course, is bound to reject anything her mother stands for, and this chapter ends with Del recalling—reflecting on the fact—that her mother's advice about women's plights was based on "being female made you damageable, that a certain amount of carefulness and solemn faces and self-protection were called for . . ."[50] Whereas, "men were supposed to be able to shrug off what they didn't want and come back proud. Without even thinking about it, I had decided to do the same."[51]

"Baptizing" is the last chapter of the novel, and at seventy pages, the longest. It deals in both literal and figurative senses with what the title suggests: baptism of a religious nature, but also baptism into the adult and confusing world of sex (of a more conventional sort, that is, as opposed to the undercover-of-darkness, inappropriate, even abrasive kind that Del experienced in the previous chapter). The most important aspect of this chapter is that it brings to the fore a realization that there indeed has been a connective thread throughout the narrative, from the beginning to this point drawing itself to a conclusion. There has indeed been a slow, deliberate building of Del, the main character: which is, ultimately, the connection, the *continuation*, from one chapter to the next. This ultimate chapter is the turning point in the novel, the arc of its plot line, what all chapters before it have been leading up to. Ironically, then, but perhaps too late, the book finally identifies itself more as a novel than a cycle of short stories.

Del is in high school now, and she is still aware of her outsiderness in fitting into traditionally feminine activities, attitudes, and even personal hygiene: "Well-groomed girls frightened me to death. I didn't like to even go near them, for fear I would be smelly. I felt there was a radical difference, between them and me, as if we were made of different substances."[52] That is not to say Del didn't appreciate that she *should* pay more attention to grooming than she did; after all, "Love is not for the undepilated."[53] Del turns her attention and energy to her studies. "I got A's at school. I never had enough of them. No sooner had I hauled one lot of them home with me than I had to start thinking of the next. They did seem to be tangible, and heavy as iron. I had them stacked around me like barricades, and if I missed one I could feel a dangerous gap."[54] This masculine assertiveness and competitiveness brings her into contact with the brightest student in school, Jerry Storey; the romance that he and Del begin has its basis in intellectualism not sensuality. Their sexual expressions with one another are clumsy. He is patronizing toward her, proving what Del's mother had warned her was the prevailing male attitude in general society: that women have no brains.

Del is still of her gender and her time; she adheres to time-sustained notions that women need to dissemble to get along with men. "I felt in him what women feel in men, something so tender, swollen, tyrannical, absurd; I would never take the consequences of interfering with it: I had an indifference, a contempt almost, that I concealed from him."[55]

Del attends a revival meeting in town, there encountering a young man, different from Jerry: a "bad boy" who has done time in jail. There is immediate sexual interest on her part. Like her previous history even as a girl with her father, Del is led by a man into new places: church-going on a frequent basis, and to baseball games. And into a new sexual life. Now, "sex seemed to me all surrender—not the woman's to the man but the person's to the body, an act of pure faith, freed in humility."[56] In exploring true, raw emotion, Munro reaches great heights of language: "That very word, *pleasure*, had changed for me; I used to think it a mild sort of word, indicating a rather low-key self-indulgence; now it seemed explosive, the two vowels in the first syllable spurting up like fireworks, ending on the plateau of the last syllable, its dreamy purr."[57]

Del's mother's reaction to Del's new boyfriend displays the realistic dichotomy in her character that Munro has been developing in this novel. She lectures Del about losing herself over a boy who represents a contrast to Del's intelligence and with whom marriage would mean staying in their town for the rest of her life and being, basically, a nobody. The mother has been advocating—*pushing*—Del into understanding the need for a woman's independence and freedom but she is, ironically, attempting to restrict Del in this new exploration; ultimately, however, this inconsistency makes sense: she is seeing through this flirtation with a new kind of boy to what it could become, which is a tied-down, routine, domestic life for Del—the kind of situation we have witnessed, in this novel and in the short stories in the previous book, the mother character was not only frustrated over but also angry with.

Interesting, too, is Del's father's reaction to her news that she is a sexually mature female, which is usually an uncomfortable if not difficult transition point for a father. "He approved of me and he was in some way offended by me."[58] Del, meanwhile, is obsessed with the physicality of her boyfriend. "I had to think, instead, of the dark, not very heavy hairs on Garnet's forearms."[59] Meanwhile, Del's best friend gets pregnant and gets married, and Del must face the potential consequence of her own intimate relations with her own boyfriend. Her reactions to the pregnancy and impending marriage of her girlfriend is certainly antidomestic; Del may be quite taken with Garnet but she has not done an about-face on how she feels about domestic life and women's traditional place and chores within it.

Del takes college entrance examinations and, although passing, fails to win a scholarship. Her boyfriend proposes they have a baby. From somewhere—and Del herself isn't sure where—comes the answer "Yes." He insists she be baptized first. But Del stands her ground; this is not something she wants to do, and she finds within herself a determination to resist even him. Her precocious individualism has blossomed into a mature, adult strength of character. "I felt amazement . . . that anybody could have made such a mistake, to think he had real power over me. . . . I was too amazed to be angry, I forgot to be frightened, it seemed to me impossible that he should not understand that all the powers I granted him were in play, that he himself was—in play, that I meant to keep him sewed up in his golden lover's skin forever."[60]

Her boyfriend consequently steps out of her life, and Del, maturely, recovers from the blow and, in the novel's appropriate ending, is ready to get on with her life, the novel having reached a natural dénouement. The building up of Del as a mature individual and not simply a precocious child reaches its apex.

However, this last chapter is not actually the conclusion of the novel. An "epilogue" is tacked on, and unfortunately it leaves the ending less firm. It is a tail (and tale) that is unnecessary. The last actual chapter drew the storyline to an effective conclusion; this epilogue serves to add what amounts to an ellipsis—in effect, unwrapping again what the last chapter had sufficiently wrapped up. Specifically, the epilogue is about Del's desire to be a novelist and how the town of Jubilee and its inhabitants would be her materiel.

To estimate the novel as a whole, as we need to consider how smoothly, effectively, seamlessly Munro moves Del, the narrator, out from being more or less a witness to events to occupy not only the center of the stage but also *about* whom all events revolve, the story becomes *her* story and how she relates to the other characters, rather than how other characters relate to each other and to the world and Del simply observing them doing so. This progress to center stage correlates realistically with an adolescent not so much moving away from being the center of their universe but stepping onto the adult stage on which they play a mature role and their actions truly have a consequence on their future lives.

Another interesting, well-handled, and convincing progression is the transition of the mother character from a figure who represents domesticity and the repressiveness of female roles on individualism to being the person insisting Del have a better life by letting a man and marriage trap her into the same routine-bound and essentially featureless existence as has been the mother's plight. The character of the mother broadens and deepens as Del not so much gains respect for and confides and trusts her, as not being unable to avoid her, since she and her mother and little brother relocated to a house in town.

The development of the mother character, as well as Munro's depiction of all of her female characters prior to this, leads to a provocative question: Does Munro *not* care for women, despite her preference for them as fictional characters. Her male characters, while usually drawn as eccentrics, with the exception of Del's father, are generally wrought more sympathetically than her female characters. Munro "likes" Del, her alter ego; she ensures at every turn that the reader understands and sympathizes with her. But it is through Del's eyes we see women generally unfavorably and men the opposite way (the exception being, as pointed out previously, the sexually predatory Mr. Chamberlain, the boyfriend of the boarder in their house in town). This question bears future investigation in her short-story collections to come.

Another aspect of the novel that Munro renders wholly convincing is the setting. With the least number of brush strokes, with the subtle evocativeness of a watercolor, Munro paints small-town life with indelible hues. As has previously been pointed out, her language usage—*style* in other words—remains poised and powerful, and even gains strength in this novel. On the opposite side of the coin, the narrative suffers from a technical flaw that adds itself to the list of factors contributing to a decision that this book is less a novel than a cycle of short stories; it is a technical flaw *only* in terms of effective novel structure. Supporting characters appear and disappear, most of them, after they arrive onto the scene late in the novel, are simply dropped from sight. This is particularly obvious when it comes to Del's brother, who is so far on the shallow side of being developed into viability that his existence in the novel often fades from the reader's memory until his name is incidentally brought up by Del in passing.

The ultimate impression left by Munro's novel is that brilliant, insightful moments are too few and far between; generally, then, it is simply too easy to forget what happens. Aside from these too-few moments, this overlong narrative does not remain in the reader's consciousness very long.

## Notes

1. Daphne Merkin, "Northern Exposures," *The New York Times Magazine* (October 24, 2004), p. 62.

2. Geoffrey Wolff, *Time*, 101(79) (January 15), p. 73.

3. Heather Jackson, *Canadian Forum*, 51(76) (January/February 1972), p. 12.

4.  Coral Ann Howells, *Alice Munro*, New York: St. Martin's Press, 1988, p. 33.

5.  Alice Munro, *Lives of Girls and Women*, New York: Random/Vintage, p. 3.

6.  Alice Munro, *Lives of Girls and Women*, p. 3.

7.  Alice Munro, *Lives of Girls and Women*, p. 3.

8.  Alice Munro, *Lives of Girls and Women*, p. 4.

9.  Alice Munro, *Lives of Girls and Women*, p. 5

10. Alice Munro, *Lives of Girls and Women*, p. 10.

11. Alice Munro, *Lives of Girls and Women*, p. 10.

12. Alice Munro, *Lives of Girls and Women*, p. 11.

13. Alice Munro, *Lives of Girls and Women*, p. 11.

14. Alice Munro, *Lives of Girls and Women*, p. 11.

15. Alice Munro, *Lives of Girls and Women*, pp. 30–31.

16. Alice Munro, *Lives of Girls and Women*, p. 31.

17. Alice Munro, *Lives of Girls and Women*, p. 32.

18. Alice Munro, *Lives of Girls and Women*, p. 38.

19. Alice Munro, *Lives of Girls and Women*, p. 42.

20. Alice Munro, *Lives of Girls and Women*, p. 42.

21. Alice Munro, *Lives of Girls and Women*, p. 42.

22. Alice Munro, *Lives of Girls and Women*, pp. 42–43.

23. Alice Munro, *Lives of Girls and Women*, p. 43.

24. Alice Munro, *Lives of Girls and Women*, p. 44.

25. Alice Munro, *Lives of Girls and Women*, p. 43.

26. Alice Munro, *Lives of Girls and Women*, p. 53.

27. Alice Munro, *Lives of Girls and Women*, p. 63.

28. Alice Munro, *Lives of Girls and Women*, p. 63.

29. Alice Munro, *Lives of Girls and Women*, p. 65.

30. Alice Munro, *Lives of Girls and Women*, p. 67.

31. Alice Munro, *Lives of Girls and Women*, p. 71.

32. Alice Munro, *Lives of Girls and Women*, p. 72.

33. Alice Munro, *Lives of Girls and Women*, p. 78.

34. Alice Munro, *Lives of Girls and Women*, p. 79.

35. Alice Munro, *Lives of Girls and Women*, p. 73.

36. Alice Munro, *Lives of Girls and Women*, p. 76.

37. Alice Munro, *Lives of Girls and Women*, p. 77.

38. Alice Munro, *Lives of Girls and Women*, p. 79.

39. Alice Munro, *Lives of Girls and Women*, p. 94.

40. Alice Munro, *Lives of Girls and Women*, p. 97.

41. E. D. Blodgett, *Alice Munro*, Boston, MA: Twayne, 1988, p. 47.

42. Alice Munro, *Lives of Girls and Women*, p. 129.

43. Alice Munro, *Lives of Girls and Women*, p. 129.

44. Alice Munro, *Lives of Girls and Women*, p. 133.

45. Alice Munro, *Lives of Girls and Women*, p. 131.

46. Alice Munro, *Lives of Girls and Women*, p. 158.

47. Alice Munro, *Lives of Girls and Women*, p. 158.

48. Alice Munro, *Lives of Girls and Women*, p. 184.

49. Alice Munro, *Lives of Girls and Women*, p. 193.

50. Alice Munro, *Lives of Girls and Women*, p. 194.

51. Alice Munro, *Lives of Girls and Women*, p. 194.

52. Alice Munro, *Lives of Girls and Women*, p. 196.

53. Alice Munro, *Lives of Girls and Women*, p. 197.
54. Alice Munro, *Lives of Girls and Women*, p. 214.
55. Alice Munro, *Lives of Girls and Women*, p. 215.
56. Alice Munro, *Lives of Girls and Women*, p. 239.
57. Alice Munro, *Lives of Girls and Women*, p. 239.
58. Alice Munro, *Lives of Girls and Women*, p. 252.
59. Alice Munro, *Lives of Girls and Women*, p. 253.
60. Alice Munro, *Lives of Girls and Women*, p. 260.

# CHAPTER 3

# HER FIRST MASTERPIECES

Munro advanced technically in her third book, which was her second collection of short stories, titled, *Something I've Been Meaning to Tell You*, published in the United States in 1974. Of the thirteen stories gathered here, at least four are worthy of being classified as "masterpieces." The thematic linkage between all of them actually finds expression in this statement by one certain character: "People carried their stories around with them."[1] By "stories" Munro means, of course, events in ordinary people's lives that while they have specific details unique to their personal biographies are nevertheless universal in their appeal, resonance, relevance, and comprehensibility to *all* our lives, the isolation and examination of which has been the purpose and procedure of her fiction from the outset.

The four best stories, the ones worthy of being designated as "masterpieces," are the title story, "Something I've Been Meaning to Tell You," "Material," "How I Met My Husband," and "Tell Me Yes or No." The title story is a third-person narrative, with alternating points of view, including omniscient views. It is the story of a conventional woman, who is unmarried, a busybody, and who possesses jealous and even vengeful tendencies. Char and Et are sisters, now older women, but from the first paragraph it is apparent that Char's looks have always been an issue for her sister, Et. "She [Char] was like a ghost now, with her hair gone white. But still beautiful, she couldn't lose it."[2] A man by the name of Blaikie Nobel has come back to their little resort town on a lake. Char and Et knew him in their younger days, and his family used to own the hotel; he now runs a bus tour of the local sights—modest as they are. Et, as the story opens, has gone on one of his tours; and the sense that Blaikie has always been, and continues to be, a ladies' man is apparent from the story's first line, when Et says to her sister, about her experience on the tour with Blaikie, "Anyway he knows how to fascinate the women."[3] He talks to them "in a voice like cream, scornful and loving."[4] In two brief, parallel characterizations, Munro speaks volumes about Blaikie's experience with the opposite sex and Et's lack of it: "He bent to each woman he talked to—it didn't matter how fat or scrawny or silly she was—as if there was one thing in her he would like to find"[5]; and, about Et, in her response to Blaikie's smoothness with women: "was that the look men finally had when they made love, that Et would never see?"[6]

But obviously there is a history here: in referencing Blaikie—his return to town, specifically—this is said about the sisters: "A name [Blaikie's] that had not been mentioned between them for thirty years."[7] When Et first encountered Blaikie once he'd returned to town, running into him on the street, his instincts about females informed him of this: "He never asked was she married, taking for granted she wasn't."[8] Munro emphasizes that Et is nearly obsessed with her sister Char's beauty; in fact, this circumstance of Et's life is given a two-page digression set off from the flow of the narrative by white spaces. This fact of Et's life and psychology is driven home by such lines as: "Et remembered the first time she understood that Char was beautiful."[9] "Her beauty was not of the fleshy timid sort most often featured on calendars and cigar boxes of the period, but was sharp and delicate, intolerant, challenging."[10] "She [Et] had almost thought beautiful women were a fictional invention."[11]

In delineating something else about Et, Munro takes the omniscient point of view: "At school she was respected for her self-possession and her sharp tongue."[12] "Et was a person who didn't like contradictions, didn't like things out of place, didn't like mysteries or extremes."[13]

In a flashback section, again one set off by white spaces, Blaikie Noble's past in this small resort town is described. He was, as it turns out, the hotel manager's son, and in keeping with Et's obsession with her sister's looks, Et is everconscious of Blaikie's good looks as well: "His good looks [back in his younger days, during his prime residency in town] were almost as notable as Char's but his were corrupted by charm, as hers were not."[14] Char had only one boyfriend back in school, Blaikie: "Char's looks and style did not attract men, perhaps intimidated them."[15] Blaikie's exuberance back then was not characteristic of local boys. "None of this, the bounding or jumping, was done the way some boy from Mock Hill High School might have done it, awkwardly yet naturally. Blaikie Noble behaved like a man imitating a boy; he mocked himself but was graceful, like an actor."[16] Munro endows Blaikie with exoticism in addition to his handsomeness, rendering him an inevitable match with the specialness of Char's beauty. Back then, Et decided she didn't like Blaikie, but she actually is obsessed with him as much as she is with her sister's beauty, both of these fixations arising from her own resentment. Blaikie, on the other hand, apparently the bigger person, "had taken the position that he liked Et."[17] One evening Et caught Char and Blaikie in a compromising position; Et found it a moment of superiority over her beautiful sister, for Et "was left knowing what Char looked like when she lost her powers, abdicated."[18]

But Blaikie ran off and married a much older woman, and Char swallowed laundry bluing, which, of course, didn't kill her—which, of course, was not her real intention, but just another instance of her life always possessing more drama than Et's. More of Et and Char's past now is filled in: Munro, employing her increasing fondness for and aptitude with the technique, making excursions through the past as the best method for developing a character from the inside out. Char married a much older man, Arthur, a teacher at the high school. Et saw, beneath Char's agreement to marry Arthur, actual contempt for him, as Char "[tried] to clutch onto his goodness."[19] For his part, as it was so obvious to Et, "Just the way he said her name indicated that Char was above, outside, all ordinary considerations—a marvel, a mystery. No one could hope to solve her, they were lucky just being allowed to contemplate her."[20] This, of course, represents another point of jealousy and resentment toward her sister.

Et went into the dressmaking business, and she made a success of it. As has been Munro's tendency in viewing unmarried women, in her previous story collection and in her novel, she sees Et and her enterprise as a crossing of the gender divide, a subtle, nonconfrontational one, operating, at least to a degree, within the traditional male universe, in this instance running her own business, dressmaking though it be (a domestic pursuit, yes, but taken by Et out of the house and— Et maintains a shop on the town square—into the business world, a traditional male domain.) Her abilities were so superior that no other dressmaker in town could compete, and Et is like a better-antlered male driving the other bucks away. "They had been meek, unimportant creatures anyway."[21] One customer with whom Et took special pains was her own sister. Is it an altruistic motivation that compels Et to dress Char so well? Although apparently unrecognized by Et, her behavior is obviously a way of co-owning Char's beauty: showcasing it with her own dressmaking talent. And Et had one more thing she could hold over Char: the latter had a tendency for weight gain, a many-years-long struggle for her, and she demonstrated binge-purge habits that now would be recognized as an eating disorder. But Et, on the other hand, was free of such worry and behavior. In fact, during Char's purge periods, when she wouldn't look at food for two or three days in a row, Et would step in and make meals for Arthur, Char's husband—another way, by acting as fill-in wife, of exacting some more revenge on Char for her everlasting beauty.

Et's busybody nature, even a streak of cruelty in how she treats her sister, surfaces when Blaikie—the story has now returned to its "present" time, when Blaikie has returned to town now in middle age and is conducting bus tours of the local sights—once again leaves in a hurry in the company of a woman: as he had run out on Char many years ago. Et brings the news up to Char "only to throw things into confusion"[22] between Char and Blaikie, to disrupt their "relationship," such as it is, even these many years after they actually had one.

The end of the story brings a shock, but the reader has been prepared for it: Char kills herself by taking poison, a rehearsal having been done many years previously, upon Blaikie's first departure. The last paragraph offers a beautifully conceived conclusion. It is a view into the future, with Et more-or-less functioning as Arthur's wife; in fact, she moves into the house again (she had moved out of when she went into business for herself). And even though she intended to reveal to Arthur that Char and Blaikie had a past—"There's something I've been meaning to tell you"[23]—this remnant of her jealousy of her beautiful sister and her abiding need to seek revenge in her own subtle but meaningful way fades as "Et let it go, day to day,"[24] because: "If they had been married, people would have said they were very happy."[25] (Judith Maclean Miller views many of Munro's stories, especially this one, as murder mysteries.[26])

The second story in the collection, also of masterpiece quality, is "Material," in which Munro returns to her comfortable first-person narration, although the narrator here is an adult woman rather than the typical adolescent. This is a story of a woman still obsessed with her first husband; the story consequently is in essence a history of her first marriage. Technique is a strong element of this story's success, but does not call attention to itself as technique for technique's sake. Munro moves the so-called back story—the slice of a character's history that pertains to and provides a meaningful context to what is transpiring in the story's present—into such a prominent place in the narrative that it becomes more than simply a referencing of this said past, gaining for the reader a more secure grounding and thus deeper understanding. The past, then, becomes a full partner to the story's present time, even to the point of occupying an equal number, if not more than an equal number, of pages. It maintains, thus, an equal prominence. Of course, a trap hides in waiting for the less skilled writer using such a technique: that the prominence accorded the backstory will serve only to create blind alleys and distractions for the reader and will unravel the narrative.

In the first line, the first husband's name and his line of work are disclosed: "I don't keep up with Hugo's writing."[27] A bitterness soon reveals itself, about literary men and women's traditional reactions to them. "Bloated, opinionated, untidy men, that is how I see them, cosseted by the academic life, the literary life, by women."[28] Here as elsewhere in this story as in previous ones, Munro rests her fiction on an abiding consciousness of, even sensitivity to, the female role as traditionally assigned to and practiced by women who are unused to or even uninterested in knocking over such traces. In her narrator's view here of the male literary figure, Munro expresses it in this fashion: "Girls, and women too, fall in love with such men, they imagine there is power in them."[29] Further: "their husbands are such brilliant, such talented incapable men, who must be looked at for the sake of the words that will come from them."[30] The narrator's self-denigration/bitterness extends even to believing the women in the audience listening to literary male figures "absorb the contempt of the men on the platform as if they deserved it; they believe they do deserve it, because of their houses and expensive shoes, and their husbands who read Arthur Hailey."[31] (The citation of that particular popular writer's name dates the story, for better or worse.)

All that editorializing off her chest, the narrator now explains her marital situation as of the present moment: married to an engineer, Gabe, who is Rumanian-born but has lost his fluency in his native language. The narrator's edginess toward men and the women who coddle them extends even to this man, who is her second husband; she doesn't believe him that his experiences back in Romania during World War II were not horrible for him. "I required him to be an ambassador from bad times as well as distant countries."[32] (Disclosed at this point, too, is that Hugo and the narrator had a daughter together and that he has since had two more wives and several children by them.) Gabe is serene, uncurious, unself-conscious, yet underneath his calm he has a mysterious past the narrator does not know much about. But the physical impression her first husband, Hugo, made on her lasted beyond her marriage to him and into her marriage to Gabe. With Hugo there was passion and even besottedness, all of which, of course, is missing from her feelings for and reactions to Gabe—"he does not disturb me, any more than he is disturbed himself."[33]

Now, on the fourth page of the story, the actual "story" itself is briefly unfolded, as if just a hint, for this story's "real" time is actually kept at a minimum. Gabe has discovered in a bookstore a new anthology of short stories containing one by Hugo and shows it to the narrator, who cannot seem to refrain from putting a slightly negative spin—her bitterness seeping out—on everyone, in this case about the obviously devoted Gabe: "I wondered if he sometimes went and looked for things by Hugo. He is interested in Hugo's career as he would be interested in the career of a magician or popular singer or politician with whom he had, through me, a plausible connection, a proof of reality."[34] Gabe believes she should buy it for her daughter, which she does; the daughter turns out to be interested only in Hugo's photograph on the jacket and what his current appearance says about *her* future appearance.

For several pages—what amounts to the heart of the story, the meat of it—the narrator recalls the house in which she and Hugo lived when she was pregnant with her daughter; specifically, it is a fellow tenant, Dorothy, who monopolizes the narrator's recollection, Dorothy being "the kind of colorless puzzled woman you see carrying a shopping bag, waiting for the bus."[35] However, the narrator had recommended to Hugo that he use Dorothy as material for his fiction; and, in fact, he does at a later point—the story Gabe found in the bookstore based on her. "There is Dorothy lifted out of life and held in light, suspended in the marvelous clear jelly that Hugo has spent all his life learning how to make . . . she [Dorothy] was lucky to live in that basement for a few months and eventually to have this done to her, though she doesn't know what has been done and wouldn't care for it, probably, if she did know. She has passed into Art. It doesn't happen to everybody."[36] This sensitive observation of the artist's practices is, at the same time, on Munro's part, a refulgent example of Munro's writing style that has crystallized into pristine unfussiness but at the same time remaining supple and unself-consciously metaphoric. But the narrator realizes, too, that her issues with Hugo, the problems between them that necessitated the marriage eroding, have not been laid to rest; but at story's end, she is also realizing Gabe's compassion, tenderness, and understanding when he carefully learns how to sort through her feelings about Hugo after having read his story.

"How I Met My Husband" is the third story in the collection and the third to qualify as a masterpiece. The narrative voice—that of, once again, an adolescent female—is truly the calling card here; Munro's use of first-person reminiscence is flawless in correlating the character she has chosen to narrate the story, and the authentic way this particular character speaks: in diction, vocabulary, language usage, tone, and sophistication level. She is called Edie.

Both the time period in which the story is set and its basic premise, as well as the first taste of the narrator's hospitable voice, are all quietly evoked in the story's opening line: "We heard the plane come over at noon, roaring through the radio news, and we were sure it was going to hit the house, so we all ran into the yard."[37] The "radio news" suggests the time period, before the widespread advent of television into small-town and rural areas. The next line gives away the narrator's relative lack of experience in life: "We saw it come in over the tree tops, all red and silver, the first close-up plane I ever saw."[38] Edie draws back from her reaction to the plane to interject facts establishing the setting. She works as a housekeeper for a veterinarian—"animal doctor," in his language—and his wife, who have moved out from town to live on a farm, not to actually farm, which according to Edie, is simply the local trend: town-to-country relocation, to live rurally without being and acting as farmers. But the doctor's wife reveals her true feelings about her new rural surroundings—with the reader given to assume her sentiments are in line with those of the other town people who have moved to the country—when, after the plane has landed in the old fairgrounds just across the road from where the doctor and his wife live, she says to Edie and the children, "Let's not stand here gawking like a set of farmers."[39]

Still on this information-packed first page—but Munro never allowing a claustrophobic sense of overcrowdedness in imparting all this information—a well-drawn secondary character appears at the screen door, and will make repeated reappearances. Loretta Bird is her name and she is a local, living on the "next place" over. However, indigenous character that she is, the differentiation in types of employment, by which small-town people are everconscious, and any individual's reputations for any kind of behavior that—deliciously—crosses the line of acceptability, is encapsulated in Edie's statement about Loretta Bird's husband. He "didn't farm, he worked on the roads and had a bad name for drinking."[40] Personally irritating to Edie and to the family with whom she lives, Loretta Bird represents to the reader an ironically compelling, even amusing, type of character owning the low-level vision and modest world-experience of the people the veterinarian and his wife have moved away from, and for whom the wife feels distanced from if not disdain for. This particular milieu, the post–World War II small-town sprawl into the countryside and the relocation of town dwellers to farms, which they treat as suburban villas, is a successful, almost ideal, Petri dish for Munro to cultivate her abiding interest in the female adolescent's struggle to overcome gender and social proscriptions in the small-town element.

Loretta Bird has narrative purpose in making her first appearance in the story: to bring news of the airplane landing, the pilot on a tour to give people rides (for a price, of course). The next day, the vet's wife takes the children to get their hair cut, and Edie uses the opportunity of being alone in the house to try on one of the wife's nice dresses—and is observed through the screen door by the pilot, who introduces himself, requests the use of the pump out back, and jokes, "Were you going to a dance?...Or is that the way ladies around here generally get dressed up in the afternoon?"[41]

Her youth is a detriment to verbal reciprocity. "I didn't know how to joke back then. I was too embarrassed."[42] (This line falls into place as one of the indications that the narrative is actually being narrated from the perspective of adulthood—a remembrance tale, then, which we will see is to become almost the standard Munro kind of story.) Edie admits to him she is simply the hired girl, and although "some people changed when they find that out,"[43] his demeanor toward her did not alter. In fact, he compliments her on how she looks: "so nice and beautiful."[44]

The flirtation arising between them—she the naïve, small-town girl, and he the older, heroic pilot who had been in the war—makes happen some life-altering consequences for Edie. Loretta Bird rears her silly head in the narrative again, this time as the (*important*) vehicle by which another stranger is brought out to the farm. "I heard her inquire in the hotel coffee shop where I was having a Coke,"[45] says Loretta; "her" in reference to the pilot's self-proclaimed fiancée, who is trying to find him. But the pilot confides in Edie that he plans to skip out on this supposed fiancée, and in an honestly tender scene, he kisses her more than once. Then, like a phantom (which is exactly how he entered the story), he packs up and is gone. The woman for whom Edie works asks Edie if she knew where he is off to, and demonstrating her precociousness, Edie "lied for him, and also, I have to admit, for me."[46] She let her employer and the pilot's "fiancée" believe he was heading for another town not too far distant, obviously hoping the woman would chase him there and thus he would have more time to escape her, wherever he was intending to escape to. The narrator's actual adult age emerges once again with the comment: "Women should stick together and not do things like that. I see that now, but didn't then."[47]

Further inquiry by the woman she works for leads Edie to admit she and the pilot were intimate; and, of course, the fiancée throws a fit, calling Edie a "loose little bitch."[48] The nosey neighbor, the less than gracious and graceful Loretta Bird, is present during the interview—the inquisition—and "she was swollen up with pleasure at being in on this scene."[49] Apparently not so much spurred by an urge to be compassionate as by a need to seek clarity in the midst of this domestic chaos—Edie is crying hysterically now—but, on the other hand, arising from a desire to protect anything that is "hers" from the unappealing fiancée, Edie's employer elicits from Edie how she defines "intimate" and thus realizes no true intimacy had taken place. Consequently, she refuses to allow the fiancée, who is a nurse, to physically examine Edie to determine the status of her virginity.

The effect of this episode is not a drawing closer of Edie and her employer, despite her employer having closed ranks with her against the fiancée. The scene ends with the employer insisting, "I have a headache. As soon as you can, go and wash your face in cold water and get at the dishes and we will not say any more about this."[50]

Edie interjects once again, a view coming from her adult perspective, obviously years in the future, saying that a long time after this incident with the pilot, his fiancée, and her employer, she realized how much trouble she had *not* gotten into; her employer was never very polite to Edie and continued being that way, but at least she'd been fair to Edie.

Edie awaits a letter from the pilot, but one never comes. After a while, she realizes it is best to quit waiting, and that no letter is forthcoming. "I thought, I was never made to go on like that," she relates in her consummate plainspokenness, "So I stopped meeting the mail. If there were women all through life waiting, and women busy and not waiting, I knew which I had to be."[51]

In a surprising but not concocted ending, one that is not without a believable foundation and actually wraps the story in a concluding charm, Edie is asked out by the mailman, whom she eventually marries. "He always tells the children [thus we are brought up to the story's "real" time, which is the present] the story of how I went after him by sitting by the mailbox every day, and naturally I laugh and let him, because I like for people to think what pleases them and makes them happy."[52] The narrator's genial voice, on which is borne her eternal life-wisdom, is a consistently important factor in this story, to the end.

Brian Sutton, in his essay "Munro's 'How I Met My Husband,'" explores the theme of secret-keeping in this story.[53] For our purposes here, the story re-poses a question asked earlier, one that concerns the nature of Munro's female characters as a response to—a reflection of—her own personal attitude toward her own gender in general. A strong impression has been imparted so far that Munro "likes" her adolescent female characters, sympathizes with their yearnings for more excitement, more freedom of expression, than can be found—obtained—in the small-town environment in which she finds herself growing up. It is, however, through her narrator's eyes that the Munro "gender world" is organized. Munro is ever-conscious that in the setting she most often uses, at the particular place and time in which she usually sets her stories, the world is rather neatly divided into male and female spheres, into their own traditionally defined arenas of activity. Also through the narrator's eyes, it is a fact that men and their traditional roles are *viewed* more favorably: more useful, more interesting, more exciting, more likely to make a difference in the world or at least in some other peoples' lives. The men themselves, often created as eccentrics, nevertheless *themselves* show more compassion and sympathy than the female characters; they are simply nicer people than the female characters, as simple as that.

So, the question is: Does this story follow that pattern? The answer is: Absolutely. Munro demonstrates sympathy for the young narrator's naiveté, her eagerness not to be young and naïve, and the small degree of victimization forced on her by the pilot (which, of course, was not serious and was, in the end, a further spur for her to grow up and see the adult world—of broken hearts and hearts that actually quickly heal from breakage). For the three other female characters, Munro exhibits disdain: the woman who employs the narrator is cold, distant, and supercilious, and comes to Edie's defense vis-à-vis the pilot's disappearance only because something of "hers" was being attacked by the pilot's so-called fiancée; and she, the fiancée, enters the scene as a touch of glamour and remains in the story as a touch of evil; and the neighbor lady is a complete fool—providing comic relief to the narrative but as the worse kind of busybody, a stupid one. Oppositely, *quite* oppositely, the pilot has an exciting occupation, he is romantic and gentle, and despite his kissing session with Edie, he is respectful of her—*sees her* as a real person, recognizes her for herself, rather than simply *discusses* her as if she were a background object, like an article of furniture, as do the women in the story.

The fourth story in the collection deserving the label "masterpiece" is the sixth story in order of appearance, titled, "Tell Me Yes or No." This first-person narrative assumes the monologue by an adult female addressing herself to another individual, as if this were a long letter: a man with whom she had had an affair, who, in truth, has recently died. Also in truth, who the addressee is and on what occasion this monologue is being delivered remains unclear for a few pages into the story, and the exact chronology of the events the narrator is recalling requires an even longer amount of reading time to comprehend. Ultimately, the reader must let the chronology stay inexact and work, mentally, with a very general time line. Despite some confusion in this regard, the story is an astoundingly deep and sensitive understanding of character. Munro's stories being fundamentally character studies from the very beginning, of course, Munro nevertheless reaches, in this story, her greatest heights so far in her pursuit of character fathoming and delineation. Munro demonstrates here an early exercise of what will be her signature technique by which to accomplish such deep character exploration: that is, her excursions through time, her backtrack through a character's past.

The narrator begins by flashing back to her early motherhood, drawing an evocative contrast between young women at the time in which the story's "real" time is set, "growing their hair to their waists, traveling through Afghanistan, moving—it seems to me—as smoothly as eels among their varied and innocent and transitory loves."[54] At that age, the narrator was taking care of babies and feeling so tired she fell asleep on the couch in the evening. But then the narrator turns around and refutes herself with: "We are pitied from this bygone drudgery, women of my own age are, we pity ourselves, but to tell the truth it was not always bad, it was sometimes comfortable—the ritual labors, small rewards of coffee and cigarettes, the desperate, humorous, formalized exchanges with other women, the luxurious dreams of sleep."[55]

Upon the story's opening, she and her husband lived in married housing on a college campus. The time period at that point is set, is evoked thus: "You know, everybody knows, the catalogue of delusions we subscribed to in the fifties; it is too easy to mock them, to announce that maturity was indicated by possession of automatic washers and a muting of political discontent, by addiction to childbearing and station wagons. Too easy and not the whole truth, because it leaves out something that was appealing, I think, in our heaviness and docility, our love of limits."[56] The 1950s, then, emerges as the story's initial level of time, when both she and he were married and going to school and barely knew each other; a second time level is offered as two years prior to the "present," when the narrator and the man to whom this monologue is addressed come across each other in a city where neither one lived and begin a long-distance affair, their correspondence vastly important in her life. Consequently, she refers to her mailbox as "that the box [that] has been the central object of my life."[57]

On the story's sixth page emerges what perhaps can be considered the story's plot, if a true plot exists, for this story is the quintessence of character study, in which the "events," the steps by which the story progresses from page one to the end, are more internal, more about how a character reacts to crises, than external. That is, less about detailed reconstruction of the outside forces that are causing the character to react in the first place. This plot establishes (thin though it is, the plot does indeed have a clarifying value) the story's actual "real" time: the narrator, having recently learned of her lover's death (just happens to see his death notice in a week-old edition of a newspaper she ordinarily does not look at), goes to the city where he lived and died, where she has never been before. "I see myself searching these streets for some memory of you as I once looked for clues in the articles you wrote for newspapers and magazines, in the books you wrote so efficiently to serve other's purposes, never your own."[58]

She repeatedly goes to the bookstore owned by his wife, till one day the wife confronts her, handing her a bag and indicating she is aware who the narrator is—no, *what* the narrator was in her husband's life—and telling her to leave the store. The narrator knew the bag would contain her letters to him, but back in her rented apartment she is faced with the fact the while these are letters alright, they are not *her* letters, but ones written to him by another woman. As the cliché goes, the plot has thickened. Munro draws all the levels of time, as well as and the exploration of the narrator's mind during these various periods of time, into a devastating final *external* event: the narrator takes the letters back to her dead lover's wife and pretends that her assuming the bag of letters to be hers, and pushing them into her hands, was all some sort of misunderstanding in the first place.

The depressing mood the narrator creates, which is sustained—unrelieved—throughout the story is not to be listed as a fault. In the first place, the mood does not detract from the story's power, it does not lessen the point of it, which is, of course, to understand this woman's need for closure in her relationship with this man to whom she was not married; in the second place, for the author to have to create a mood other than the one she did create would be invalid and thus would indeed detract from the story's power and point.

The remaining nine stories in the collection are only marginally lesser efforts than the four I have deemed masterpieces. "Walking on Water" has its differences from previous Munro stories. It is a third-person narrative told from the point of view of an older man, and is set in what is apparently a city or at least a large town. It is a story about a generation gap; but this time, Munro has the older person regarding with derision the habits of young people—rather than vice versa, which is customary for Munro. The old man lives in the same building as the elusive, enigmatic, arresting Eugene, who seems neither old nor young; the old people in the neighborhood, in fact, "saw him as gentle ambassador from the terrible land of youth."[59] The chronology of events is perfectly straightforward; this story is not an example of Munro's soon-to-be-standard circling through time to achieve maximum character exploration. The story's irresolution at the end is appropriate to Eugene's New Age-type nonacknowledgement of having to stay within the lines of cultural traditions.

E. D. Blodgett, in the book-length study, *Alice Munro*, finds this story "striking" because of the connections between the old man's real world and a dream he has. "The design of the story makes it appear that Mr. Logheed dwells in two worlds simultaneously."[60]

A grown woman narrates "Forgiveness in Families." This woman has a husband and children, and her personal, conversational voice is perfectly correlative to the homely, unpretentious, and unsophisticated character she unfolds to be. This story is about how a sister views her brother based on how often and how much their mother has excused his slacker ways, ending with this no-nonsense, concise, even maxim-worthy line: "Forgiveness in families is a mystery to me, how it comes or how it lasts."[61] The story is a provocative, to say nothing of unusual, take on the mother figure for Munro; here, the mother dominates the story, but instead of being a negative, discontented mother, this one is— this element most surprisingly—aggravating to the narrator, but because of the mother's false, "rose-colored glasses" attitude. The most useful view of this story for our purposes here is as a further demonstration of Munro's ability to create, to understand the fundamentals of, the traditionally told short story: with no elaborate excursions through time, that is, which will of course be her future practice. Upon the framework of the traditional short story, Munro will fashion her own brand of the form.

"The Found Boat" returns us to "Munro country": the Wawanash River area, where many of the stories in her first collection took place, as did her novel. It is a slight piece about boys and girls and burgeoning sexuality; its slightness appears to stem from Munro actually needing more-than-traditional short-story length to summon and properly exercise her writing powers (the story runs into only thirteen pages). But "Executioners" does achieve power by virtue of both its style and the technique employed. This is a story of revenge and social punishments. The first-person narrator is an adolescent girl, an outsider—this emerging as one of Munro's most emphatic expressions of the outsider theme. Munro's language is faultless, from the first paragraph, when we encountered this lovely passage about someone who would never look someone else in the eye: "I became familiar with sidewalks, and the ground under trees, neutral things that I would look down at, meaning no offense."[62] And this, in reference to children's voices that are soon to develop into harsh adult ones: "Sweet voices they had, just on the edge of sincerity, deadly innocence."[63] This is a remembrance piece, narrated not as it is actually taking place but from the perspective of many years after the fact—a device which, as we have witnessed, is a common and comfortable one for Munro. In this one case, though, the reader is not left to assemble evidence leading to the conclusion that this indeed is the situation but, instead, is offered concrete proof at the story's end: "I am a widow, a civil servant, I live on the eighteenth floor of an apartment building . . . thinking uselessly and helplessly, almost comfortably, about things like this that I had forgotten . . ."[64] At this point, Munro has yet to fully develop her more elaborate, detailed, page-consuming swings through time and past events in her exploration of character, but these narrated-as-an-adult pieces looking back on a childhood or adolescent event was her method of handling the impress-of-the-past-on-the-present conditions, which has been of abiding interest to her since the beginning. Simply put, this technique was the major evolutionary step she took in at what would come to be defined as the Munro short story. Despite all this, despite the strength and beauty of her prose style in this story and its value in charting her technical development, this is not an especially interesting story as a story per se: plot-wise, it does not grip readily and tightly.

"Marrakesh" is another generation-gap story; specifically, it tells a story of two sisters, the title referring to worldliness in travel experiences, an example of the "new" things tried by the younger generation. The two sisters are older women, now living together as widows; two sisters in advanced age, now cohabiting, is of course, a scenario Munro has previously explored. (The small-town milieu in which they reside, particularly the typical small-town mindset, is well caught in this passage: "From the time she was widowed until the time of her retirement Dorothy had taught Grade Seven in the public school, and because of this people were apt to forget that she had any life that might be called private . . . they never look at her for anything beyond that."[65]) One of the sisters is being visited by her grown granddaughter, who has earned a Ph.D. and teaches in college. It is she who is not "understood"—by her own grandmother, that is. She is now in her thirties and still dresses like, and retains the figure of (in her grandmother's opinion, that is), a child. The grandmother attempts to introduce her granddaughter to a local man—a set-up, in other words—but what she sets into motion only aggravates her sense of the differences in generations. The story bases its charms on that predicament.

"The Spanish Lady" is Munro's take on a venerable theme in literature: adultery, which Munro connects with another theme, this one of particular interest to her, the outsider. In this instance, the outsider is the woman narrator, who is conscious of being "teamed up" against by her husband and her friend, who is her husband's mistress. Munro dexterously probes the woman's psychology. Ultimately, the story lacks a final finish of "real life"—a sense of real vitality coursing through its veins—for it to rise to individuality above its ordinary theme. It is simply a cold story, the characters passionless.

The main character in "Winter Wind" has been encountered many times before in previous stories: perhaps not the *same* character, but ones just like her, an adolescent in high school, living in a small town in the area of the Wawanash River. Here, she lives on a farm outside town, but a winter storm necessitates her spending the night at her grandmother's house in town. Thus is the crux of the story; and once again Munro visits the environment of two women living together, two sisters (typically)—the narrator's grandmother and the grandmother's sister, both widows. The atmosphere within this house is indeed grandmotherly: "The hallway of this house was all wood, polished, fragrant, smooth, cozy as the inside of a nutshell."[66] That which reigns in her own house is an atmosphere quite different, and the mother character, caught incisively in this thumbnail sketch, is characteristic of the mother character encountered in previous stories: "Dirt and chaos threatened all the time. My mother often had to lie down on the couch, and tell her grievances."[67] The storm lasts more than one day, and the narrator stays more than one night, but the pull of her own house draws her away from this clean, well-ordered environment: "And comfort palls. The ironed sheets, the lovely eiderdown, the jasmine soap. I would give it all up for the moment in order to be able to drop my coat where I chose, leave the room without having to say where I was going, read with my feet in the oven, if I liked."[68] The story's ending is beautiful. The grandmother, understanding her granddaughter is eager to leave and return to her own home, regardless of its lack of cleanliness and orderliness, "had become another old woman whom people deceived and placated and were anxious to get away from."[69]

Two adult sisters are also the chief characters in "Memorial," this time not living together but temporarily under the same roof, a premise borrowed from "The Peace of Utrecht," in Munro's first collection of stories, *Dance of the Happy Shades.* This story, told from a third-person omniscient point of view, is purely a character study. Munro uses a particular circumstance to bring out the differences in the sisters' natures; thematically, the story is about social pretense. One sister has just lost one of her children in a car accident, and the other sister, who is divorced and lives in another town, is staying for a while with her grieving sister and her family. But it is a kind of household she is not used to, "the world of objects, their serious demands.... There was a morality here of buying and use, a morality of consumerism."[70] The extreme efficiency of this household and her sister's family hits the woman squarely in the face during this short stay with them: "this orthodoxy,"[71] as she thinks of it. "Here was a system of digestion [her sister's household, that is] which found everything to its purposes. It stuck at nothing. Japanese gardens, pornographic movies, accidental death. All of them accepted, chewed and altered, assimilated, destroyed."[72]

The last story in the collection is titled "The Ottawa Valley," which is, again, a remembrance piece by a female adult, who recalls an episode from childhood: not unusual for Munro, how an event is remembered for what it informed the narrator about her mother. The latter character, as drawn here in keeping with the typical Munro mother type, is priggish and beset by a sense of being better than the circumstances in which she lives. ("My mother had not led me to believe we were related to people who dressed like that or who used the word bugger. 'I will not tolerate filth,' my mother always said."[73]) This story, for want of thematic clarification, falls into the category of an adolescent learning life's experiences. Munro immerses the reader into a "familiar" Munro situation, but within a fresh context and with fresh results.

In conclusion, at least four stories in this collection represent a leap forward for Munro, as if she were rebounding from the mixed experience of writing a novel to reassume command of the short-story form with even more understanding of its workings, flexibility, and vigor in the pursuit of her objectives in studying character. Steps taken by her as reflected by the collection as a whole include a broadening out, an expansion, of her range, to include more types of narrator than simply the precocious female adolescent living on a farm at the edge of town. The collection demonstrates Munro's increasing awareness, comfort with, and even flair for correlating voice to character: the tone of voice, the expressions used, and the level of language facility all inferring age, socioeconomic background, and gender. It is an effective use of the hoary old practice of showing rather than telling. Concomitant to that, the collection as a whole reveals an increased understanding of the characters Munro is placing before the reader and the ability to recognize the telling nuances of their personalities. Her plotting stands well-balanced between internal events and external ones; she neither packs her narrative with such a quantity of twists and turns that the narrative rides too low in the water for the fast, quick, effect a short story should give, nor does she spend too much time in a character's head that the reader screams for release.

As considerably high as Munro's reputation had grown by this point, review opinion was still divided upon the release of this, her second, short-story collection. "Munro achieves new control and shows herself to be an artist of real accomplishment. Only in a story by V. S. Pritchett, among contemporaries, have I come across such a successful evocation of childhood intimations of sexuality as Munro has given us..."[74]

On the other hand, this opinion: "They [the stories in this collection] are journeyman's work. But they are not more than that.... And much of the writing seems to be designated to win our love rather than stir us with character or prose."[75]

## Notes

1. Alice Munro, *Something I've Been Meaning to Tell You*, New York: Random/Vintage, 2004, p. 201.

2. Alice Munro, *Something I've Been Meaning to Tell You*, p. 1.

3. Alice Munro, *Something I've Been Meaning to Tell You*, p. 1.

4. Alice Munro, *Something I've Been Meaning to Tell You*, p. 2.

5. Alice Munro, *Something I've Been Meaning to Tell You*, p. 2.

6. Alice Munro, *Something I've Been Meaning to Tell You*, p. 3.

7. Alice Munro, *Something I've Been Meaning to Tell You*, p. 4.

8. Alice Munro, *Something I've Been Meaning to Tell You*, p. 5

9. Alice Munro, *Something I've Been Meaning to Tell You*, p. 5.

10. Alice Munro, *Something I've Been Meaning to Tell You*, p. 6.

11. Alice Munro, *Something I've Been Meaning to Tell You*, p. 6.

12. Alice Munro, *Something I've Been Meaning to Tell You*, p. 7.

13. Alice Munro, *Something I've Been Meaning to Tell You*, p. 7.

14. Alice Munro, *Something I've Been Meaning to Tell You*, p. 8.

15. Alice Munro, *Something I've Been Meaning to Tell You*, p. 8.

16. Alice Munro, *Something I've Been Meaning to Tell You*, p. 9.

17. Alice Munro, *Something I've Been Meaning to Tell You*, p. 9.

18. Alice Munro, *Something I've Been Meaning to Tell You*, p. 11.

19. Alice Munro, *Something I've Been Meaning to Tell You*, p. 16.

20. Alice Munro, *Something I've Been Meaning to Tell You*, p. 17.

21. Alice Munro, *Something I've Been Meaning to Tell You*, p. 18.

22. Alice Munro, *Something I've Been Meaning to Tell You*, p. 22.

23. Alice Munro, *Something I've Been Meaning to Tell You*, p. 23.

24. Alice Munro, *Something I've Been Meaning to Tell You*, p. 23.

25. Alice Munro, *Something I've Been Meaning to Tell You*, p. 23.

26. Judith Maclean Miller, "Deconstructing Silence: The Mystery of Alice Munro," *Antigonish Review*, 129(2002), pp. 43–52.

27. Alice Munro, *Something I've Been Meaning to Tell You*, p. 24.

28. Alice Munro, *Something I've Been Meaning to Tell You*, p. 24.

29. Alice Munro, *Something I've Been Meaning to Tell You*, p. 24.

30. Alice Munro, *Something I've Been Meaning to Tell You*, p. 25.

31. Alice Munro, *Something I've Been Meaning to Tell You*, p. 25.

32. Alice Munro, *Something I've Been Meaning to Tell You*, p. 25.

33. Alice Munro, *Something I've Been Meaning to Tell You*, p. 27.

34. Alice Munro, *Something I've Been Meaning to Tell You*, p. 27.

35. Alice Munro, *Something I've Been Meaning to Tell You*, p. 32.

36. Alice Munro, *Something I've Been Meaning to Tell You*, p. 43.

37. Alice Munro, *Something I've Been Meaning to Tell You*, p. 45.

38. Alice Munro, *Something I've Been Meaning to Tell You*, p. 45.

39. Alice Munro, *Something I've Been Meaning to Tell You*, p. 45.

40. Alice Munro, *Something I've Been Meaning to Tell You*, p. 46.

41. Alice Munro, *Something I've Been Meaning to Tell You*, p. 50.

42. Alice Munro, *Something I've Been Meaning to Tell You*, p. 50.

43. Alice Munro, *Something I've Been Meaning to Tell You*, p. 50.

44. Alice Munro, *Something I've Been Meaning to Tell You*, p. 51.

45. Alice Munro, *Something I've Been Meaning to Tell You*, p. 55.

46. Alice Munro, *Something I've Been Meaning to Tell You*, p. 61.

47. Alice Munro, *Something I've Been Meaning to Tell You*, p. 61.

48. Alice Munro, *Something I've Been Meaning to Tell You*, p. 62.

49. Alice Munro, *Something I've Been Meaning to Tell You*, p. 63.

50. Alice Munro, *Something I've Been Meaning to Tell You*, p. 64.

51. Alice Munro, *Something I've Been Meaning to Tell You*, p. 65.

52. Alice Munro, *Something I've Been Meaning to Tell You*, p. 66.

53. Brian Sutten, "Munro's 'How I Met My Husband,'" *Explicator*, 63(2) (Winter 2005), pp. 107–110.

54. Alice Munro, *Something I've Been Meaning to Tell You*, p. 106.

55. Alice Munro, *Something I've Been Meaning to Tell You*, p. 106.

56. Alice Munro, *Something I've Been Meaning to Tell You*, p. 107.

57. Alice Munro, *Something I've Been Meaning to Tell You*, p. 110.

58. Alice Munro, *Something I've Been Meaning to Tell You*, p. 116.

59. Alice Munro, *Something I've Been Meaning to Tell You*, p. 77.

60. E. D. Blodgett, *Alice Munro*, Boston, MA: Twayne, 1988, p. 65.

61. Alice Munro, *Something I've Been Meaning to Tell You*, p. 105.

62. Alice Munro, *Something I've Been Meaning to Tell You*, p. 138.

63. Alice Munro, *Something I've Been Meaning to Tell You*, p. 138.

64. Alice Munro, *Something I've Been Meaning to Tell You*, p. 154–155.

65. Alice Munro, *Something I've Been Meaning to Tell You*, p. 158.

66. Alice Munro, *Something I've Been Meaning to Tell You*, p. 193.

67. Alice Munro, *Something I've Been Meaning to Tell You*, p. 193.
68. Alice Munro, *Something I've Been Meaning to Tell You*, p. 202.
69. Alice Munro, *Something I've Been Meaning to Tell You*, p. 206.
70. Alice Munro, *Something I've Been Meaning to Tell You*, p. 210.
71. Alice Munro, *Something I've Been Meaning to Tell You*, p. 217.
72. Alice Munro, *Something I've Been Meaning to Tell You*, p. 216.
73. Alice Munro, *Something I've Been Meaning to Tell You*, p. 229.
74. Hilda Kirkwood, *Canadian Forum*, 55(42), 75.
75. Frederick Busch, *New York Times Book Review*, 74(October 27) p. 53.

# CHAPTER 4

# HER FIRST SIGNATURE BOOK

Munro's next book of fiction, her fourth, was her third collection of short stories. It was published in Canada in 1978 as *Who Do You Think You Are?* and in the United States in 1979 titled *The Beggar Maid: Stories of Flo and Rose.* The collection, comprising ten stories, remains one of her most recognizable titles with the general reading public. The subtitle intimates the book's format: a cycle of stories obviously featuring as recurrent characters, the eponymous Flo and Rose. The most apparent question, then, is how different in structure is this story cycle from her novel, which, as we observed, is more accurately called a short-story cycle.

Coral Ann Howells diplomatically addresses the issue in her book-length study, *Alice Munro*, by saying, "*The Beggar Maid* has a similar structural organization as of *Lives of Girls and Women* [Munro's novel] although one is called a collection of short stories and the other a novel. Both belong to the genre of the 'whole book story sequence' where disparate stories are linked through a single narrator's perspective...."[1]

Rose is Flo's stepdaughter. The setting—initially, anyway—is a small Ontario town, called Hanratty, which is essentially identical to all the small Ontario towns in Munro's fiction thus far. Flo retreats offstage about halfway through the cycle (to reappear later), Rose thus assuming center stage and character primacy from that point on. Clearly from the start, the book's central storyline is Rose's struggle to find herself: a precocious teenager bound for horizons wider than available in her limited hometown, yet at the same time always conscious of her outsiderness. The cycle rises and falls not via a narrative arc followed by the collection as a whole but within, and thus repeatedly and sporadically, the individual stories. From the opening stories, a sense of repetitiveness arises, a pall of redundancy hanging over them. The early Rose too closely resembles her precocious adolescent predecessors in previous stories. A couple of stories in the middle of the cycle, however, are masterpieces, some of the finest fiction Munro has written. Unfortunately, the collection's stamina, highly reached by the masterpiece stories, is not sustained throughout; the final two stories in particular have little strength, and seem only to serve to bring the story of Rose to a conclusion.

In this collection, Munro takes steps that advance her storytelling technique and in developing her acumen in psychological fathoming of characters. At the same time, other aspects of her ability, certain patterns of hers, in other words, while not retreating, do indeed simply remain in stasis.

"Royal Beatings" sets the stage for the flowering of Rose; it introduces her and her stepmother, Flo, and Rose's father and stepbrother, Brian. Also, the town of Hanratty is introduced—or, more specifically, West Hanratty, the poor part of town, with the store run by Flo located "on the struggling end of the main street."[2] This story also introduces the tenor of the relationship between Flo and Rose, which, as it is introduced, will remain the nature of the atmosphere between them, which essentially arises from Flo's side of the equation: she being crude, loud, and suspicious of Rose's moods and intelligence and envious of her being younger in years and facing future possibilities far more expansive than Flo would have ever realized. Despite her irritation with Rose, to the point of flinging constant criticism, Flo also has a streak of almost motherly protectiveness toward her stepdaughter, which has the effect of broadening, deepening, and lengthening Flo as a character, into a more sympathetically realistic figure. Flo's mixed attitude toward Rose is established in this first story, by an act after which the story gets its title: Flo loses patience with Rose, calls in her husband to discipline his daughter, who beats her to a degree that in contemporary times would be considered child abuse. Flo is mortified at his overreaction and in effect rescues Rose by admonishing her to go to her room, and to the best of Flo's stubborn ability, tends to Rose afterward in her humiliation. Of course, Rose has strength of her own, and in her own way can give as good as she gets; she is not above manipulating her father and stepmother, wringing every advantage out of what has just happened to her. She'll show them, either by killing herself or running away from home—revealing an adolescent nature despite her precocity. Rose realizes that she and Flo will once again reach an uneasy peace, yet the war between them will always continue.

One technical feature of this story represents a significant step in Munro's mastery of the short-story form and in making the form suit her own storytelling needs; a second technical feature is a practice that actually detracts from the strength of the narrative. The former, the "royal beating" incident, fixes in the reader's mind the antagonistic, competitive nature of the relationship between Rose and Flo, which will continue throughout their lives and in this collection of stories. What needs emphasis is that this is presented as hypothetical: perhaps not happening exactly this way, but representative and paradigmatic of incidents like it. "The royal beatings. What got these started? 'Suppose a Saturday, in spring.[3] Munro unfolds this particular incident, then shoves the story ahead in time: "One night after a scene like this they were all in the kitchen. It must have been summer."[4] Again, the suggestion of its hypothetical, here's-an-example quality is made. Rose, her father, and Flo are having an amusing conversation that, its purpose to show up Flo's ignorance, nevertheless imparts "a feeling of permission, relaxation, even a current of happiness, in the room."[5] This is a rare moment of peace in the household, in the on-going struggle of wills between Rose and Flo. The realization is now there to behold that this is the *actual* story: these two pages, this brief scene of peacefulness, is the story's "real" time—in time frame, the ground floor of the story. All that came before simply pointed to the rarity and temporariness of the genial atmosphere within this household on this one occasion. This practice will come to be an important component of the generally recognized Munro-type story: the ground floor its real time, occupying relatively small space, as Munro circles back through time to explore the antecedents—previous incidents and characters' experiences that define the ground floor—of the particular event/incident at hand. This casting back through time is very effective here in its it-could-have-happened-this-way, here's an example, hypothetical property.

Now, the aforementioned second technical feature of the story—cited as a negative one—is an example of a bad habit Munro has fallen into, adding a "coda" into the story's end, for some sort of wrapping up of what's gone on before, sealing things up with some kind of hindsight that apparently—apparently Munro's intention—seeks to add a final clarification to the story's meaning. In actual effect, however, this device leaves the story to sputter out rather than end cleanly.

This story, when viewed in conjunction with the three stories following it, "Privilege," "Half a Grapefruit," and "Wild Swans," creates a problematic issue: redundancy. The character of Rose in this quartet of stories, in which she appears as an adolescent, and as a carefully and sensitively drawn adolescent character as she is, emerges not quite distinct from the female adolescent characters that have appeared in Munro's previous stories and in her one novel. "Privilege" is a rather static picture of the place and the characters important to Rose at the time: the remembrance of a teacher and fellow students back in school days. It is plotless; it features a schoolgirl crush, but is in fact an inert depiction of that often tempestuous time (at least so within the adolescent schoolgirl's heart and mind). Flo remains the hard, cynical, even mean person as she was presented in the collection's first story, but in this story she is drawn incompletely, in two dimensions. This is not a stand-alone story; its walking legs, such as they are, are supplied by its inclusion in this collection featuring the same characters. Its collection mates, then, are a crutch. In "Half a Grapefruit," Rose passes her entrance examination to go to the high school across the bridge in the good part of Hanratty; this story, then, is about her new desire for acceptance by the students who live on that side of town, at a time in life—to which all readers can relate—that is "hazardous" because "disgrace is the easiest thing to come by."[6] The story is also about Rose and Flo reversing roles within their household. "Rose was the one bringing stories home . . . Flo . . . waiting to hear."[7] But, again, this story imparts a sense of place-keeping in the Rose-Flo chronicles rather than an independent, viable, interesting-in-its-own-right story. It is too diffuse; what is it really about, for all its sixteen pages? Like the previous story, this one is plotless. The question is left in the reader's mind that if Munro isn't moving through levels of time as a narrative device, can these remembrance pieces avoid tiredness?

"Wild Swans," however, while presenting a Rose not especially distinct from other protagonists of the same age and social situation found in previous stories as well as in the one Munro novel, elevates itself above "Privilege" and "Half a Grapefruit" in one regard: it is an adventure story, in which Rose expands her horizons, learning about vulnerabilities in the outside world, particularly of a sexual nature and particularly for young women. It is a short narrative, ten pages. The title, referring to something so universally symbolic of purity, dignity, even majesty, is in ironic contrast to the motif of sexual *im*purity that Munro works out in the narrative. Rose takes a train trip to Toronto by herself, and will stay the night with her father's cousin; as it happens, Rose has won a prize for an essay she wrote and is financing this trip herself. It is the dawn of a new era for her, which Rose doesn't fully realize, which is not to say that she is ignorant of the likely consequences of this particular transforming experience. On the train out of town, "she felt Flo receding, West Hanratty flying away from her, her own wearying self discarded as easily as everything else."[8] She enters a whole new physical setting as well: "They were traveling south, out of the snow belt, into an earlier spring, a tenderer sort of landscape. People could grow peach trees in their backyards."[9]

Rose's step in the direction of increased worldliness does not go in the direction of cultural refinement but as an increased awareness of the sordidness of real life. A man soon sits beside her on the train, claiming to be a minister, and quickly he is relating to her a moving scene involving wild swans that he recently witnessed, attempting to, it would seem, release between himself and Rose a tone, a mood, of beauty and serenity, which shows itself to be an ironic and misleading preamble to the action he now takes: making a pathetic sexual gesture—a hand placed inappropriately—that Rose goes along with. "Victor and accomplice"[10] so she sees herself; her ambivalence toward this disgusting, degrading act arises from contrasting moods of "disgrace" and "greedy assent."[11] Her maturation process, her steps taken in seeing the world, is concomitant to a burgeoning sexuality; and her sexual curiosity compels her to be not so much a willing as unresisting victim in this sordid predicament, which could even be taken as child abuse. "What recommended him? She could never understand it. His simplicity, his arrogance, his perversely appealing lack of handsomeness, even of errantry grown-up masculinity?"[12] But, at story's end, Rose still looks forward to being someone new.

The crown jewel of the collection is the title story, one of Munro's masterpieces. "The Beggar Maid" finds Rose in college, and the story opens with an unambiguous declaration of what the forthcoming narrative will be about: "Patrick Blatchford was in love with Rose."[13] And this concrete image of how his feelings led to specific actions is expressed in this fashion: "He waited for her after classes, moved in and walked beside her, so that anybody she was talking to would have to reckon with his presence."[14] Patrick's presence is one of the features making this story not only arresting in its own right—he is a well-drawn, well-rounded character—but significant in Munro's oeuvre *because* of his presence and well-roundedness: that is, a male character that plays a prominent and not simply supportive role in the story, and not simply set up as a symbol of the excitement of traditional male activities and the relative freedom of personal experience society grants that gender. Munro's creation of him reaches far beyond symbolic levels for him to become, within the pages of this electric story, a man of great nobility, worthy of sharing center stage with Rose herself—which, considering what his role in her life is to be, is to be seen the correct degree of emphasis. Simply stated, Munro has created and presented him wisely, for Patrick not only opens major doors in Rose's path to worldliness but also becomes her husband.

Up to this point, with Rose as well as with most of Munro's "heroines" in her stories so far and in her novel, the world is seen to be bifurcated by male roles and female roles and by town life and country life. Rose now comes face to face with additional bifurcation, which she had previously been aware of but not so acutely: smart people and those who aren't, and rich people (*very* rich) and those who aren't.

A third major character in "The Beggar Maid" reigns over the story's activities and sets the tone of these activities. This character provides not only a plot wrinkle but also prompts us to further reflect on the issue of Munro's general attitude toward women. Dr. Henshawe is on the faculty of the college Rose attends and also takes in coed boarders, Rose being one. "You are a scholar, Rose," Dr. Henshawe would say. The point of that comment is to admonish Rose to leave boys alone. In fact, Dr. Henshawe will be a force on Rose, pulling her in the direction of *not* getting serious with Patrick; he, in turn, senses her animosity and sees it as animosity toward men in general. Dr. Henshawe is drawn as a disagreeable character, as if she has been created for the express purpose of representing the sentiment that a woman who has lived her life emphasizing her intellect loses not only femininity but also sexuality. But Dr. Henshawe, by example, specially the example of her home into which Rose has taken temporary domicile ("sitting in the dining room with a linen napkin on her knee, eating from fine white plates on blue placemats"[15]), and Patrick by direct comment ("What would Patrick have to say about [her family]? What would someone who was offended by a mispronunciation of Metternich think of Bill Pope's stories?"[16]); Rose, while growing in sophistication and knowledge of the world, from academic topics to tasteful interior decoration, experiences as part of her sophistication a growing awareness of the poverty and ignorance of her family.

In keeping with her character, and in parallel with previous young female protagonists of Munro's, Rose is an outsider even in college, in that she'd rather not be part of the cheering crowd at football games but, instead, "the buildings and the books in the Library were what pleased Rose most about the place."[17]

Patrick is a new kind of man for Rose, not only because he is very smart but also because even he admits there is nothing rugged or even outwardly strong about himself. "I suppose I don't seem very manly,"[18] he says to Rose, who thinks the opposite. "He did seem masculine to her. Because he took . . . chances. Only a man could be so careless and demanding."[19] This is certainly a broadening and deepening of Rose's concept of what constitutes—or, what *can* constitute and still qualify—a "real" man. And having no previous experience around rich people, she had no sense in that direction. "Rose had no idea at the beginning, how rich Patrick was. Nobody believed that. Everybody believed she had been calculating and clever . . ."[20] He is older than she, he patronizes her, but nevertheless he adores her; and her attraction to him was based on "her own appetite, which was not for wealth but for worship."[21] And the levels of sexual experience—orgasms, in other words—she reaches with him are unprecedented for her.

E. D. Blodgett, in his full-length study, *Alice Munro*, sees that "The Beggar Maid" story "forms the central section of the book. Rose is at once a beggar, because of her modest origins, and a maid, because of her being so perceived by her future husband as a damsel in distress."[22]

So, this masterful story is about how and why she came to marry Patrick, their courtship including a visit to his parents in their wealthy business-owner situation in Vancouver and one to Rose's considerably more modest family situation in Hanratty, both of which, coming one right after the other, provided a twist and turn in Rose's sentiments about her upbringing: "Nevertheless her loyalty was starting. Now that she was sure of getting away, a layer of loyalty and protectiveness was hardening around every memory she had, around the store and the town, the flat, somewhat scrubby, unremarkable countryside"[23]—in contrast to beautiful, dramatic British Columbia, from where Patrick hails. The story's only false note—and out-and-out clank of discordance—is the result of Munro's habit of ending a story with a codicil, by which she moves the story ahead in time to bring it to a head, as it were, to set the story in a time context that—in Munro's mind apparently—will "wrap it up" and answer any questions about what might happen next and what all *has* happened has "meant." In this case, in this otherwise perfect story, it is a tacked-on scene, set a few years subsequent to Rose and Patrick's divorce. Couldn't—*shouldn't*—it have been left at surmising their marriage would be rocky and might not last? The tacked-on ending, which we have indicated earlier is a tactic Munro should avoid, gives an unpleasant sense that Munro attempts to stand with one foot in each genre, the short story and the novel, as if she were responding to subverting a still-nascent tendency to *want* to write a novel.

(Munro's "play" with time in the stories in this collection is given support in a piece that appeared in *The New Republic*: " . . . with sudden shifts in time that would stop the narrative flow of a novel but which this less linear hybrid happily accommodates."[24]).

"Mischief" is a close companion to "The Beggar Maid," dealing with Rose's marriage to Patrick and her leaving him. It thus is seen as an almost necessary filling in of that backstory: the ending of "The Beggar Maid" almost demanding it.

On the other hand, "Mischief," read soon after the previous story, is too repetitive; there is simply too much going over old ground. Another problem exists because Munro is overly analytical, resides too internally (within character) that both narrative flow and reader interest suffer.

Thematically, it is the story of an affair. (Munro is as good as John Updike in chronicling the hesitations and sidesteps of adultery, said Ted Morgan in a review of *The Beggar Maid* for *Saturday Review*[25]) The chronicling begins with the opening line: "Rose fell in love with Clifford at a party which Clifford and Jocelyn gave and Patrick and Rose attended."[26] The next sentence conveys the information that this event took place only three years into their marriage. The next paragraph begins "She would often afterward look back...,"[27] thus identifying this as a remembrance piece, related in the third person, as have been all the Rose stories up to this point (and will continue to be throughout this collection), but taking the ultimate form of a glance backward in time from the perspective of a point much later in time.

Munro's character, everconscious of the world divided into halves, into various polar-opposite, black-and-white hemispheres, from gender to economic standing to "smarts," play to form when it comes to Rose; Rose recalls this particular episode in her life as, "In those days the barriers between people were still strong and reliable; between arty people and business people; between men and women."[28] Rose and a woman by the name of Jocelyn meet in the maternity ward in a Vancouver hospital; and Rose, from the wealthy, business-owning side of things, though she is aware of her lack of education, and Jocelyn, from the artistic side, cross the second divide in place back in those days and become friends. At a party Rose meets Clifford, Jocelyn's husband, "and their eyes met, a few times, without expression, sending a perfectly clear message that rocked her on her feet."[29] Rose now found herself "transformed, invulnerable."[30] They plan a rendezvous—not simply a couple of hours at a local hotel, but a much more elaborate tryst that includes Rose leaving town by airplane. Plans go awry and the consummation Rose had planned for does not happen; Clifford has cold feet, calling what they are up to—this rendezvous—"mischief."[31] But "the sane and decent thing Clifford has said cut no ice with Rose at all. She saw that he had betrayed her."[32]

Following a white space, the story sails abruptly into the future, with Jocelyn and Clifford living in Toronto, he quite successful in his music career. Rose had remained friends with both of them: as a couple, that is, not in any way separately. She is back in Ontario, teaching. Patrick, so we learn, has married a second time. An incident is related concerning one time when Rose was visiting Clifford and Jocelyn; she witnesses an argument between them and their self-analysis of why they stayed married, and Rose's detachment—not still interested in Clifford—is obvious, and certainly strikes a chord of authenticity in attitude.

A white space again separates the narrative; now the scene is actually a brief backstory that fills in, in most basic detail, what transpired after Rose and Clifford's unsuccessful rendezvous: Clifford and his wife left Vancouver shortly thereafter, and Rose left Patrick not long after as well. The story's ending is well wrought, with none of the overdwelling on wrapping up that Munro has exhibited in her tendency to tack on a codicil. This ending brings the Rose-Clifford relationship to a firm, resonant, nonsputtering-out conclusion. Rose is over again, visiting him and his wife in Toronto, and in postparty languidness, Clifford makes love—finally—to Rose, with his wife's approval and with her in attendance. After sorting through her various reactions, Rose concludes she would "go on being friends with Clifford and Jocelyn, because she needed such friends occasionally, at that stage of her life."[33] A practicality has enclosed her vulnerability, and Rose is all the stronger for it, without any of Flo's closed-minded, unworldly cynicism impeding her movement toward new horizons.

As evidence of Munro's evolving technique, this story is significant. The past as an impress on the present, but even more meaningful to Munro, the past as *explanation* of the present, especially in terms of how to understand a character, has ranked as a major theme—no, the primary theme—of hers since the beginning of her career. The direction she is taking to that objective is, as we have witnessed, to eschew a strictly linear time line, instead, adopting a narrative flow that moves back and forth through time, to illuminate telling episodes in a characters' past—and also, as she habitually does, a character's future—and thus lend illumination to the character's *character*. The movements through time in this story are at once graceful and informative; the reader clearly attends Munro in her time shifts, eagerly and easily accompanies her, with comfort and edification.

"Providence" is a story about Rose and Patrick's daughter, Anna, who up to this point in the collection has hardly been mentioned; but it is also a story about Rose's attempts to connect with another man in whom she is interested. The story opens with Patrick still in the picture; thus the demise of their marriage continues to cast its gloomy shadow over another story in the sequence, remaining a "presence" to be illuminated for its damaging qualities from different perspectives. Munro is reluctant to set it aside, an attitude correlative to the nature of the marriage's end itself: not a clean and surgically precise severing. Pretty much in one fell swoop, Rose announced to Patrick her intention of leaving the marriage, but the after-effects linger: as is the usual case when children are involved.

Rose is now living in a relatively small mountain town, working at the local radio station; she is interested in a man she had met in this town but who actually lives in another place. Anna had stayed with Patrick when Rose left, but now Rose had Anna come to live with her. Unlike Rose at school-age, and unlike other adolescent girls in Munro's previous stories, Anna "did not shrink or suffer as an outsider,"[34] but gets on easily at school and immediately has a set of friends. But, as the cliché goes, and goes with truth and meaning, apples don't fall from the tree, and exactly *like* Rose and previous adolescent girls in Munro's stories, Anna "was beginning to sound more competent, and seemed to be looking forward to getting the better of her mother."[35] Rose is quickly resensitized to having a child not only in her care but also occupying space with her; Rose is aware of, and proud of, making her own way and Anna's as well. On the other hand, Rose's independence isn't complete, at least her mental independence is not; she still feels the need for a man. "Without this connection to a man, she might have seen herself as an uncertain and pathetic person; that connection held her new life in place."[36]

As in the previous story, Rose plans a rendezvous with the man she is interested in, and again as in the previous story involving elaborate plans of going to another town; and several pages of the story are given over to these plans—and, as in the previous story, her plans go awry. This romantic disaster sours Rose on the town in which she is living, and she realizes she isn't providing Anna with an appropriate environment here. (The setting, this mountain town in which Rose has found herself, is evoked with a small degree of telling brushstrokes, but not as resonantly and convincingly as Munro calls up the physical and emotional setting of rural Ontario). "Poor, picturesque, gypsying childhoods are not much favored by children..."[37] In a tight, perfect, nonflickering-out ending, Anna goes back to living with Patrick and his new wife, and Rose is made aware that Anna now has all that Rose could not provide her.

Although Rose's career as a radio personality and an actress has not been much of a focus in the adult-Rose's stories, it apparently has been happening behind the scenes, a fact learned in the next story in the collection, "Simon's Luck." This story could be subtitled "Rose the Rambler." Rose, as found here, is still trying to find herself, still attempting a connection with a man. (Readers impatient with this particular aspect of Rose's life-direction should remind themselves of the social mind-set of the post–World War II years, during which Rose was raised, as in a small-town, nonprogressive environment, before women could comfortably discover and establish themselves through no help, either social or financial, or of a man.)

Again evidencing her by now undoubtedly unconscious awareness of the benefit in short fiction of the attention-grabbing opening line, Munro begins "Rose gets lonely in new places; she wishes she had invitations."[38] She no longer lives in the mountain town and working at the local radio station; she is back in Ontario, teaching drama at a community college. The central situation in the story is a party to which Rose was invited. There she encounters a former student of hers, who is drunk and quite rude to her, which of course unsettles her. What had she done to that young man to so provoke him: done back when he was her student, that is? (Tangentially, but an important piece of information for the reader in understanding where this story is in time, it is revealed that Anna, her daughter, is now in her late teens.) Rose overhears a group of young faculty members talking: "They were giving her quick, despising looks."[39] And they make references to "the establishment," which, apparently, they believe Rose to be a part of. The outsider motif is exercised here; Rose has become part of the establishment in the young faculty's eyes but it is to their group to which she wants to belong.

Anyway, Rose meets a man, Simon, at the party and she takes him home with her. But further rendezvous prove complicated by what has become standard for Rose: miscalculations in scheduling. "This was a situation she had created, she had done it all herself, it seemed she never learned any lessons at all. She had turned Simon into the peg on which her hopes were hung and she could never manage now to turn him back into himself."[40] This honest self-evaluative statement of Rose, then, actually stands as the crux of the story, the premise around which the storyline revolves. A further self-realization is this: "How many crazy letters she had written, how many overblown excuses she had found, having to leave a place, or being afraid to leave a place, on account of some man."[41] Rose abruptly relocates to Vancouver, and in a particularly graceful as well as poignant way of bringing the story to a conclusion, Munro quickly draws the narrative ahead in time—but on this occasion it is not to tack on one of her unnecessary and even harmful codicils. Rather, this is an almost necessary flash-forward, to a point in time—a year later than the story's "real" time—when, in Vancouver, Rose, now acting in a television series, encounters a person whom she had met at the party, who informs her Simon had died of cancer and apparently had been suffering from it for a quite a while. From this, Rose sees the probable cause of their scheduling problems in getting together.

This is not a strong story but stronger than the succeeding one, "Spelling." This is in fact a slight story without much meaning on its own outside the collection, separate from the events in Rose's life preceding it. It seems to feature in the collection only as a place filler, or rather a time-filler, to bridge any chronological gap in Rose's life story. On a positive note, it is—delightfully, for she has gone missing and been missed—a Flo story. Rose's stepmother resurfaces, as does Brian, Rose's half-brother, who has been a rather illusory character all along, one of Munro's male characters who, once they've been introduced, never emerge from the shadows to assume anything close to well-roundedness. Flo is old now, indicated by her having to walk with double canes, and she is no longer very mentally alert. When Rose comes home to visit Flo these days, the latter often doesn't even recognize her stepdaughter. Another aspect of the past remains to jar the present: the run-down condition of Flo's house: "The change from Hanratty to West Hanratty [going from the good part of town to the not so good, that is] was hardly noticeable. West Hanratty had got itself spruced up with paint and aluminum siding; Flo's place was about the only eyesore left."[42] And it is up to Rose and her half-brother, Brian, and Brian's wife to take care of Flo, now in her dotage; they make arrangements to place her in a home. Rose, by the way, at this point is still involved in acting, and being around her brother, a successful engineer in Toronto but still, so Rose intuits, disapproving of her, as well as being back in her small hometown—both of these forces exert their reductive pull on her. "If you stay in Hanratty and do not get rich it is all right because you are living out your life as was intended, but if you go away and do not get rich, or, like Rose, do no remain rich, then what was the point?"[43]

"Who Do You Think You Are?" concludes the collection and is a sort of nostalgia piece concerning people in her hometown whom Rose remembers; its purpose, and its accomplishment, is as a closure to the Rose cycle, specifically bringing her back to clear out and shut down Flo's house. Brian again features as a primary character, but the two stories together, this one and the previous one, do little to broaden and deepen him; he remains if not a shadow at least an opaque individual into whom Munro offers little observation, imparting little insight into him. In this tying-up-loose-ends story, Rose and Brian together recall a town character, Milton Homer, and their shared and combined memoirs of this town eccentric draw them into a relative closeness. They resist, together, Brian's wife's labeling Milton Homer, basing her conviction on what Rose and Brian are saying, as the village idiot. In the first place, Rose cannot envision her hometown as a village, which, to her, is more "a cluster of picturesque houses around a steepled church on a Christmas card."[44]

Do the characters of Rose and Flo hold up, grow as characters as they grow older; but at the same time, do they remain faithful to their underlying character traits as established in the first stories in the collection, remaining consistent to themselves while their experiences and reactions to those experiences expand as more years are lived? Do Rose and Flo learn from these experiences? The difference in that happening makes the difference between a true short-story cycle and merely a collection of stories written with little or no pre-planning of the collection as a whole. Unequivocally, this book stands up to its label of short-story cycle. Rose enters the stage stubborn, willful, always the outsider, and never in complete synchronization with anyone else—and her adult life comes to be a riff on these very traits. Flo is equally stubborn and willful, she, for her part afraid of circumstances that show up her inadequacies of education and limitations of experience, both intimidated by and living vicariously through Rose. On the other hand, this book is not a novel, and unlike *Lives of Girls and Women*, has not been wrongly called that.

This collection exhibits Munro's increased ability to fathom character. She continues to go deeper into her characterizations without overlaboring them and wringing then out to dry. Concomitant to that, Munro's style here has intensified—metaphors lovelier yet remaining crystal clear in meaning, carrying resonance even further than before, like a bell with a pitch even closer to perfection. (For example, this: "She felt that planes, on the other hand, might at any moment be appalled by what they were doing, and sink through the air without a whisper of protest."[45])

In this collection, Munro's male characters tend to melt away, don't really signify; the exception is, of course, Patrick, the man Rose married. He is a dominant character in more than one story, and he is drawn with depth. Although unlikable, he is an understandable character, and the latter is what counts. Like other male characters in previous collections, Patrick is a polestar indicating a path in life, a place in the universe, different from that which is traditionally offered to females; their way held the allure of adventure and freedom, far afield from boring domestic activities. Patrick, however, turns out to hold only superficial allure—wealth—and Rose quickly comes to see what is worth possessing wealth and what is not worth it. The example of Patrick would seem to indicate that the male-as-hero, or male-activities-and-occupations-as-heroic concept, can be sustained by Munro only with the quick glimpse, which in a more thorough exploration of a male character, such as with Patrick, she is bound to see more negative, less heroic, qualities. That would stand to reason. Munro is a consummate character builder, and moving a male character—that is, Patrick—to the fore, she would be incapable of *not* filling in all his dimensions and consequently see him in an unidealized light.

That issue leads to a renewed discussion of the important topic of Munro's attitudes toward women. We have posed the question before: Although of course her fiction is primarily devoted to female lives, does she actually *like* women? *The Beggar Maid*, in that regard, is a transition. Prior evidence, in previous books, indicated a negative answer to the question. Now, in this book, Munro launches Rose and Flo in buoyant well-roundedness and lets them be likable or not, depending on the reader's personal interpretation, and releases them of any symbolism, paradigmatic value, or as personal statements issued forth by the author herself. In Rose and Flo, Munro takes a more centrist, more balanced, stance toward her own gender, by simply removing herself from weighing in on the female gender as a whole. In this book, she looks at women as individuals first.

## Notes

1. Coral Ann Howells, *Alice Munro*, New York: St. Martin's Press, 1988, p. 55.
2. Alice Munro, *The Beggar Maid*, New York: Random/Vintage, 1991, p. 6.
3. Alice Munro, *The Beggar Maid*, p. 12.
4. Alice Munro, *The Beggar Maid*, p. 21.
5. Alice Munro, *The Beggar Maid*, p. 22.
6. Alice Munro, *The Beggar Maid*, p. 41.
7. Alice Munro, *The Beggar Maid*, p. 42.
8. Alice Munro, *The Beggar Maid*, p. 60.
9. Alice Munro, *The Beggar Maid*, p. 60.
10. Alice Munro, *The Beggar Maid*, p. 65.
11. Alice Munro, *The Beggar Maid*, p. 65.
12. Alice Munro, *The Beggar Maid*, p. 66.
13. Alice Munro, *The Beggar Maid*, p. 68.
14. Alice Munro, *The Beggar Maid*, p. 68.
15. Alice Munro, *The Beggar Maid*, p. 70.
16. Alice Munro, *The Beggar Maid*, p. 71.
17. Alice Munro, *The Beggar Maid*, p. 75.
18. Alice Munro, *The Beggar Maid*, p. 78.
19. Alice Munro, *The Beggar Maid*, p. 78.
20. Alice Munro, *The Beggar Maid*, p. 79.
21. Alice Munro, *The Beggar Maid*, p. 80.
22. E. D. Blodgett, *Alice Munro*, Boston, MA: Twayne, 1988, p. 94.
23. Alice Munro, *The Beggar Maid*, p. 91.
24. Jack Beatty, *New Republic*, 181(40) (October 13 1979), p. 40.
25. Ted Morgan, *Saturday Review*, 6(76) (October 13, 1979), pp. 76–78.
26. Alice Munro, *The Beggar Maid*, p. 101.
27. Alice Munro, *The Beggar Maid*, p. 101.
28. Alice Munro, *The Beggar Maid*, p. 102.
29. Alice Munro, *The Beggar Maid*, p. 113.
30. Alice Munro, *The Beggar Maid*, p. 112.

31. Alice Munro, *The Beggar Maid*, p. 125.
32. Alice Munro, *The Beggar Maid*, p. 128.
33. Alice Munro, *The Beggar Maid*, p. 136.
34. Alice Munro, *The Beggar Maid*, p. 142.
35. Alice Munro, *The Beggar Maid*, p. 144.
36. Alice Munro, *The Beggar Maid*, p. 147.
37. Alice Munro, *The Beggar Maid*, p. 155.
38. Alice Munro, *The Beggar Maid*, p. 156.
39. Alice Munro, *The Beggar Maid*, p. 162.
40. Alice Munro, *The Beggar Maid*, p. 171.
41. Alice Munro, *The Beggar Maid*, p. 173.
42. Alice Munro, *The Beggar Maid*, p. 180.
43. Alice Munro, *The Beggar Maid*, p. 184.
44. Alice Munro, *The Beggar Maid*, p. 197.
45. Alice Munro, *The Beggar Maid*, p. 142.

# CHAPTER 5

# ANOTHER UNEVEN COLLECTION

Munro's fifth book and fourth collection of short stories, *The Moons of Jupiter*, was published in 1983 in Canada and in the United States. Nearly half of the dozen stories were previously published in the *New Yorker*, by this point in her career obviously a place she found ready acceptance. *The Moons of Jupiter* is inconsistent, in keeping with previous collections. Several stories are eminently successful and other stories are among the flattest she's written.

Her language usage, and not simply in the four masterpiece level stories, has by the time of the appearance of this collection, become consummately effective: limpid, supple, and yet capable of breathtaking metaphors and, as she builds lovely sentence upon lovely sentence, stunningly rich and meaningful verbal pictures of characters and places. What is obvious, too, in this collection is Munro's second nature in shaping a story: the narrative as a whole as well as scenes within a story. This near-intuition of hers in giving a story the shape it needs for maximum effectiveness is found in her keen understanding of the need, in a short story, to eliminate detail, in order to *affect* the effect: that is, what to leave out for narrative "cleanliness" but also what to leave in to avoid thinness and a watery taste.

Her control of technique, characterization, setting, and style is manifest in the first story in the collection, "Chaddeleys and Flemings: Connection" (which is actually the first part of a two-part story, both of which bear the same primary title but different subtitles; each part of the story stands as a whole, each one was previously published as a separate story on its own, and thus will be regarded for our purposes as such). The subtitle suggests the story's theme: the connection of the individual to family history. The second level of connection this story is concerned with is how people from outside an individual's narrow milieu bring connection of that individual to the larger world outside. The story is a first-person narrative told in the voice of a never-named female character; it is itself presented in two parts, but not so cleanly as to need Roman numeral headings, only a white space separating them. The narrator is an adolescent in the first part, and in the second part a married woman with children. The setting, initially, is the small-town Ontario to which Munro has anchored so many of her stories before, and then the setting shifts to a nice neighborhood in Vancouver (a city that is not an uncommon location for her stories). Both sections, both settings, and both time periods involve a visit by relatives and the narrator's experiences with and reactions to them. The first visit by relatives is like a wave: one summer four of the narrator's mother's cousins come for a lengthy stay. All four represent a character type Munro has investigated before: the unmarried woman of a certain age. "Maiden ladies," the narrator calls them. "Old maids was too thin a term, it would not cover them. Their bosoms were heavy and intimidating—a single, armored bundle—and their stomachs and behinds full and corseted as those of any married woman."[1] Munro has used unmarried women, or the old sisters living together in widowhood, as "laboratories" before, to experiment with how they either straddle the traditional gender roles of the time period upon which Munro focuses—the 1940s and 1950s—or do they stand for repressed traditional female roles that have been distilled, refined, and defined to a highly concentrated degree? In this story, the four cousins of the narrator's mother fall into the former category: "girded into shapes whose firm curves and proud slopes had nothing to do with sex, everything to do with rights and power."[2]

Munro's physical descriptions of the cousins are at once graphic and lovely, at once realistic and subtlety metaphoric. For example, they wore "stockings that hissed and rasped when they crossed their legs."[3] Her language speaks volumes by actually saying very little; but what is said evokes sights and sounds completely and easily understood. The second part of the story is occupied by a visit by one of the old unmarried cousins, one from the first section of the story, not to rural and small-town Ontario but to Vancouver, and this cousin's advent into the narrator's household, where her marriage has obvious tensions, taps into the narrator's selfish need to be relieved of insecurities: specifically, for her cousin *not* to embarrass the narrator in the eyes of a husband who already looks down, from the vantage point of family money, on the narrator's "background" ("... he had put himself in a chancy position, marrying me. He wanted me amputated from that past which seemed to him such shabby baggage; he was on the lookout for signs that the amputation was not complete; and of course it wasn't,"[4]) and in turn to impress her cousin with her husband's money and house.

The two events—the two family member visits—with their two individual time periods and two quite different settings are smoothly integrated: linked plausibly and meaningfully, their juxtaposition not setting up a sense of two *separate* stories trying—artificially—to be told as one. Munro's method here is not to circle through a character's past, which has, of course, become a favored technique, but instead, circling through the narrator's *family* history. Thus in the second part of the story, her family history collides with her husband's.

The unmarried cousins, four of them, when they came for a summer visit in the narrator's adolescence, bring an attitude of "taking charge of yourself," and with that temporarily introduce a certain cosmopolitanism into the household. "They all smoked, too, except for Flora, the Winnipeg school-teacher. A sign of worldliness then; in Dalgleish, a sign of possible loose morals. They made it a respectable luxury."[5] The mother character, speaking in "a festive but cautioning tone,"[6] is in that way typical for a Munro mother character. These women bring a different version of womanhood into the place. "Audience and performers, the cousins were for each other."[7] Their sense of fun influences the narrator's mother, who at one point, amazingly to the narrator, "put on a pair of my father's trousers and stood on her head."[8]

In a smoothly handled, certainly relevant digression from the direct narration of events, the narrator steps aside from the cousin's visit back in her adolescence, and in what amounts to an aside to the audience, she at first gazes at the milieu in which she lives, the setting described thus: "We lived at the end of a road running west in Dalgleish over some scrubby land where there were small wooden houses and flocks of chicken and children. The land rose to a decent height where we were and then sloped in wide fields and pastures, decorated with elm trees, down to the curve of the river."[9] Predictably, the narrator's mother looks down on the town; as we have witnessed on numerous occasions Munro's mother characters tend to find themselves better than their surroundings, in which they married into. This mother much prefers the town in which she was raised, the town her and her cousins' grandfather had come to from England. This is the connection of the story's title. "That is what it was all about. The cousins were a show in themselves, but they also provided a connection. A connection with the real, and prodigal, and dangerous, world. They knew how to get in on it, they made it take notice. They could command a classroom, a maternity ward, the public; they knew how to deal with taxi drivers and train conductors. The other connection they provide, and my mother permitted as well, was to England and history."[10] Several pages are devoted to a narration of family history, into which Munro places colorful detail but not to such a degree as to drag the story down.

One of the cousins, Iris, the most interesting and amusing of them in the story's first section, subsequently pays the narrator a visit in her married and motherly state in Vancouver. The narrator, as previously cited, wants to impress her cousin with her success in marriage and simultaneously impress her overly critical husband with someone in her family not quite the yokel he believes them all to be. Consequently, the visit is fraught with personal issues for the narrator. Cousin Iris doesn't exactly put on airs, but nevertheless "when she spoke of Dalgleish and my parents [her tone] was condescending. I don't think she wanted to remind me of home, and put me in my place; I think she wanted to establish herself, to let me know that she belonged here, more than there."[11] This insight into character, conveyed in minimal but effective words, is followed by the three pages given to painting Iris more in depth: the opposite pole to a married women, who is fun and free to let loose, go places, be herself, and dress as she pleases.

The narrator's reaction to Iris is ambivalence. She tires of Iris' company but is uncertain why. Her husband, though, reacts more specifically; upon Iris' departure, he harshly refers to her as "a pathetic old tart."[12] In a surprising but credible move, the narrator throws a plate at him. Nothing comes of it in terms of further events; the story is nearly over; the actual ending wraps up the story not in artificial tidiness but in a truly conclusive fashion: a brief flashback to the narrator's adolescence and the visit of the four cousins, she remembering "their high sprits and grand esteem, for themselves and each other."[13] Thus, the past is best kept there.

This story adds emphasis to an unavoidable idea growing story by story: that in Munro's estimation, marriage means trouble for women, and that husbands are critical and repressive, and that without a husband women blossom in their own particular fashion. Concomitant to this is Munro's apparent conviction that despite the precocity with which she imbues her adolescent female characters, and the strength of her adult ones, they are at heart insecure, in need of continuous validation, and that too, usually from a man. This can be viewed as a sub theme of Munro's abiding interest in the outsider: that without a man, a woman has no place to fit in. But here is the intriguing corollary to that "maxim": if the women are of a certain age, either widowed or never married, then Munro sees them as free to be themselves and in possession of quite a functioning self-esteem.

The next story in the collection is, as we have indicated, a companion to the first one; it bears the same primary title, "Chaddeleys and Fleming," and has as its subtitle: "The Stone in the Field." It is a good story, but not nearly on the same level of success as the first one. The opening line connects the second story to the first: "My mother was not a person who spent all her time frosting the rim of glasses and fancying herself descended from the aristocracy."[14] (The first story was about, of course, social pretension and the way people interpret and present their family history to others.) Apparently, from this first line the primary character—or, rather, the primary character the narrator will be focusing on, is her mother. That early prediction is quickly verified by the next few lines, which create a vibrant, telling verbal picture of the woman, her enterprise, and her household, worthy of quoting in full:

> She was a businesswoman really, a trader and dealer. Our house was full of things that had not been paid for with money, but taken in some complicated trade, and that might not be ours to keep. For a while we could play a piano, consult an *Encyclopedia Britannica*, eat off an oak table. But one day I would come home from school and find that each of these things had moved on. A mirror off the wall could go as easily, a cruet stand, a horsehair love seat that had replaced a sofa that had replaced a daybed. We were living in a warehouse.[15]

The next paragraph clarifies the situation: that the narrator's mother works for an antiques dealer, who also works out of his house. As explained, the era of antiquing had yet to arrive, and rather than living on the crest of a wave, the mother and her boss peaked too early and didn't do well in the business. Poppy, the boss, is a colorfully drawn character, not enviable by any means but also not despicable despite his previous internment for lewd behavior toward two other men on a train. Even before that event, Poppy was such a strange person the narrator—yes, an adolescent female—was embarrassed by her mother's association with him: as parents and their goings-on will inevitably embarrass a teenager. Does the mother really understand Poppy's proclivities? The narrator isn't certain her mother's acceptance of him is liberal and open-minded or simply based in naivety.

But the story broadens into more than just about her mother's antique sales and her affiliation with Poppy, and into a story about—and this is the connective theme to the previous story, its companion—family and family history. The mother holds a sentiment about her husband's family that is by its negative nature in common with most of Munro's mother characters: in essence, she finds them odd. The father character is drawn typically for Munro, too: quieter than his wife, more content with life and less judgmental of others, consequently more psychologically free to see beyond the four walls of domesticity the mother characters often resist or, as usually happens, go along with but with lots of accompanying murmuring and even out-loud complaining. The narrator introduces a whole bevy of characters—en masse, really, rather than as distinct individuals—that also are examples of a type Munro is fond of exploring: unmarried women, particularly those who are sisters and who remain, as adults, living under the same roof. These are the narrator's father's six sisters—he the only son in the family. They had spent their lives removed from the outside world: "... these six sisters were very odd in themselves, at least in the view of many people, in the time they lived in. They were leftovers, really; my mother said so; they belonged in another generation."[16]

These women are introduced upon a specific occasion: the narrator and her parents drive out in the country to pay them a visit. The atmosphere of the setting is specified, just as Munro's precise style and graceful, unshowy way, with metaphor given witness to, in this passage: "These high, thick bushes, dense and thorny, with leaves of a shiny green that seemed almost black, reminded me of the waves of the sea that were pushed back for Moses."[17]

The story's ending draws a further, concluding connection between this story and the previous one, drawing a swift and poignant comparison between the two groups of relatives featured in the story's two parts: the narrator's mother's cousins and the narrator's father's sisters. "However they behaved they are all dead."[18]

"Dulse" is not a perfect story but still a very successful one. It is more of an "intellectual" story than thus far encountered; the characters discuss "ideas" more than usual in a Munro story. (Specifically, the writing career of famous American novelist Willa Cather and later the nature of love.) But, fortunately, the story is given no airs of pretension; the narrative flow is never impeded by "ideas."

Lydia is on a short trip away from her life and job in Toronto. The story is told in third person, from Lydia's point of view, and the shape of the story quickly becomes recognized as its most salient quality. In other words, the story's construction is impeccable, with graceful intrusions of the past into the story's "real" time, these "interruptions" not perceived by the reader as such at all, but are easily recognized as edifying supports to a broader understanding of the characters. Munro's bringing in relevant events from a character's past, not simply referencing them rather in passing, to perform the function in character building she desires, is achieved here not simply with proficiency but also with naturalness: nothing contrived or awkward in the time shifts.

Lydia is forty-five years old and thus has reached the age when she's ceased attracting attention. She has secured a room in a guesthouse for her overnight visit on an island off the southern coast of New Brunswick. Two sentences imply volumes about the setting: "The Atlantic coast, which she had never seen before, was just as she had expected it to be. The bending grass; the bare houses; the sea light."[19]

In the dining room, Lydia meets a man who is also staying at the guesthouse; it is with him she engages in a discussion about American writer Willa Cather: this island being where Cather had a summer cottage and is buried. (An in-depth discussion of this feature of the story is to be found in "The Cather Connection in Alice Munro's 'Dulse,'" in which the author points out connections between Cather's traditionalism and Munro's "return to her roots in conservative Southwestern Ontario."[20]) A series of flashbacks imparts the facts and tone of Lydia's backhome life; obviously, this island trip is a brief idyll in contrast to her regular life. In subsequent conversations with people in the guest house— the woman of the couple who run it, as well as some telephone crew members temporarily on assignment on the island—she fills them in on the man with whom she recently broke up. "And hadn't she told this simply to establish that she had know Duncan—that she had recently had a man, and an interesting man, an amusing and adventurous man? She wanted to assure them that she was not always alone, going on her aimless travels."[21] Lydia responds in a sexual fashion to the crew men; even these secondary characters spring boldly to life as Munro ably evokes and conjures, getting to their essence in brief time and space: "Lawrence wore a carefully good-natured expression, but he looked as if something hard and heavy had settled inside him—a load of self-esteem that weighed him down instead of buoying him up. . . . He was sharp and sly but not insistent; he would always be able to say the most pessimistic things and not sound unhappy."[22]

Munro temporarily abandons her refraction of events through Lydia's consciousness to enter, for the time being, into the consciousness of Vincent, another man on the phone crew. It is a brief digression, and serves to broaden and strengthen him as a character. "Graceful" is this move into another character's perspective.

A flashback reveals details about the man with whom she has just broken up, specifically about her first encounter with him. It was, in her words, a "collision," not in a sexual way but as a clash of strength of character and personality, a quick struggle she immediately lost. "She asks herself what gave him his power. She knows who did. But she asks what, and when—when did the transfer take place, when was the abdication of all pride and sense."[23] Reader impatience with Lydia now sets in: for this very "abdication" of herself to a man. What emerges in the reader's awareness is that this kind of situation is actually a common theme of Munro's: the strong woman who nevertheless surrenders too much control over her fate and her peace of mind to a man who does not appreciate it and who usually exploits it to the woman's detriment, and this situation is obvious to *her*. As a theme, as a path by which to explore female-male relationships, which is valid, realistic, and interesting. What causes a problem in this particular fleshing out of that theme is the difference in mood between the past and present levels of the story. The present time level is more attractive; here the mood is hopeful. The flashbacks evoke a less alluring mood of depression, dejection, and lack of self-esteem. ("She believed that Duncan's love—love for her—was somewhere inside him, and that by gigantic efforts to please, or fits of distress which obliterated all those efforts, or tricks of indifference, she could claw or lure it out."[24])

"The Turkey Season" is a remembrance piece narrated in first person from adulthood, concerning an episode in a woman's adolescence. She is fourteen years old at the time in which the remembered events occur, and the story's time frame is narrow and specific: her Christmas-season experience working at a peculiar place doing a peculiar job. For that brief but "colorful" (meaning "strange") time, she was employed as a turkey gutter, in a small processing plant. Interestingly, Munro, who excels at setting-evocation, employs an equally narrow setting here, the action never extending beyond the walls of the Turkey Barn, but Munro uses that specific setting as a stage set, and the story emerges as a dramatic work intended for the stage—but not stilted and stagy. If the purpose of a well-drawn setting is to create a palpable atmosphere as well as anchor the events to a specific reality, the Turkey Barn functions extremely well in doing so. It behaves as a microcosm of human nature with an elegant sharpness.

The narrator sets the tone of the story; the Turkey Barn is awash in sexual tension, between certain individuals working there and what it stirs up in herself. The voice is subtly yet securely correlated to the character, an appealing mix of adult perspective and youthful expression, epitomized in this one sentence: "There are different ways women have of talking about their looks."[25] Even more so in this longer, beautifully written line: "It is impossible for me to tell with women like her whether they are as thick and deadly as they seem, not wanting anything much but opportunities for irritation and contempt, or if they are all choked up with gloomy fires and useless passions."[26] The story has definite reader-resonance, for everyone remembers their first job as a teenager, encountering all sorts of adults and their individual lives and philosophies that have never been experienced before. This coming face to face with newness is a motif threaded through the storyline. As the narrator expresses it (and, again, refracted through the lens of adulthood, which adds both clarification and eloquence), "It seems unlikely that on my way to the Turkey Barn, for an hour of gutting turkeys, I should have experienced such a sense of promise and at the same time of perfect, impenetrable mystery in the universe, but I did."[27] That in this small Ontario town in the 1940s an adolescent's awakening to the adult world takes place in such a mundane setting and not accomplished by, say, a year abroad, is in true keeping with the character, milieu, and time.

Another common theme of Munro's is also given riff on: that of the outsider. The narrator is indeed an outsider when she joins the crew, but soon she becomes a part of them: "So it was a surprise and then a triumph for me not to get fired, and to be able to turn out clean turkeys at a rate that was not disgraceful."[28]

But an important aspect of the narrator's awakening to the adult world during her brief tenure at the Turkey Barn is her own sexual awakening, especially when a teenage boy hires on; and in describing him Munro offers a stunning picture of male beauty: "He had amazing good looks: taffy hair, bright-blue eyes, ruddy skin, well-shaped body—the sort of gook looks nobody disagrees about for a moment. But a single, relentless notion that got such a hold on him that he could not keep from turning all his assets into parody."[29]

This story brings to unequivocal notice how effectively Munro handles the technique of first-person narration from the perspective of many years later subsequent to the event(s) being recalled. This technique *does not*, at least as Munro practices it, reduce the freshness and originality of the adolescent' point of view, but rather adds clarity to the perspective. The prism of maturity through which past events are refracted ironically renders the adolescent perceptions of them not only more focused but also more meaningful in long-term significance.

"Accident" brings the total number of outstanding stories in this collection to four; these four can be called masterpieces. The time in "Accident" is made explicit in the story's second line: 1943. Where it is set is established in the first line: the small Ontario town of Hanratty, where also the Rose and Flo cycle of stories was set. The story is told in third person, related though the consciousness of an adult female, Frances, the high school music teacher. She is well described in the first paragraph (which also indicates Munro's consciousness of the accouterments of the time period):

> Frances' outfit is fashionable for that year: a dark plaid skirt and fringed, trian-
> gular shawl of the same material, worn over the shoulders with the ends tucked
> in at the waist; a creamy satin blouse—real satin, a material soon to disappear—
> with many little pearl buttons down the front and up the sleeves. She never used
> to wear such clothes when she came to teach music at the high school; any old
> sweater and skirt was good enough. This change had not gone unnoticed.[30]

The mentioned change in Frances' wardrobe is an alert to perhaps more to her "story," perhaps a situation needing prompt explanation: which comes soon, for Frances is having an affair with another high school teacher, who is married. Ah, yes, the story of an affair, not unfamiliar terrain for Munro. The title of the story references what will become the pivotal event in the affair and thus in the story itself. During the height of Frances's relationship with this man, his son is killed; and a friend of Frances, to whom Frances has confided her secret, reflects the consciousness of the time and place in her declaration that the boy's death is the price the man paid for his indiscretion. Frances's reaction to the boy's accidental death is simply one of selfishness, regardless of when and where the story is set. "She felt fury at that child, at his stupidity, his stupid risk, his showing off, his breaking through into other people's lives, into her life."[31] Through a system of flashbacks and forward time movements, the history of the affair as well as its future (Frances and the man do indeed marry, leave town, and have children) are the two side panels in a triptych (the story's "real" time, the accident and its immediate aftermath, the central panel) that is at once delicately beautiful in its detail and of remarkably sturdy construction.

(Its one flaw, minor as it turns out to be, is the occasional—perhaps on only four occasions—instance when a point of view problem rears its problematic head. In those four instances, the point of view abruptly shifts from third person to om-niscient, to allow either authorial commentary on Frances or momentarily enter the consciousness of another—and minor—character. To cite this as more than a *minor* flow would exaggerate damage done to the narrative's immaculateness.)

At thirty-two pages, "Accident" prognosticates the traditional Munro short story: her brand, that is, which is *long*. "Accident" is the first true, actual occasion in which the long Munro short story as it is recognized today begins to define itself: not just long for long's sake, as in a certain number of pages to be filled up, but a novel's worth of material finely honed to its essence and—this the keystone element—without an aftertaste that no character or plot situation was *under* developed. Munro's understanding of character in "Accident" is complete; Frances is richly and deeply drawn, and her affair, contrary to affairs Munro has tracked in previous stories, leaves her not empty and ego-damaged but on a path to accomplishment and with a sense that through it all, into marriage and motherhood, she has always lived true to herself. In addition, the fellow school teacher with whom she had the affair is a viably rendered male character, more fully than the two dimensions by which she usually wrought her male characters, especially those men involved in an affair with her "lead" female character. Another property of this story that heralds a technique to come—or, rather, the technique, which has been introduced in previous stories, is perfected in this one. It will be a staple technique of what will become the universally recognized "Munro" short story. That is, she adjusts chronology, telling the story—relating events—out of strict order in which they happen, not to confuse the reader or add gimmickry to the narrative but to at once fill in necessary background as well as heighten the effect of the drama transpiring in the story's present, "real" time. Thus "Accident" is *the* Munro story in full dress, its first appearance in its "adult" stage after having emerged from the chrysalis stage.

"Bardon Bus," a first-person narrative, is also a story of an affair, but one that is an obsession. It is much less successful a story than the previous one; the dis-jointed chronology is jarring, with little redeeming value. (A contrary opinion is offered in Coral Ann Howells's full-length study, *Alice Munro*, in which the author avers: "A remarkable feature of this story is its shifts in focus as the narrator remembers seemingly disparate episodes and anecdotes which did not seem sig-nificant at the time but which through hindsight seem to shape themselves into patterns of inevitability."[32]) The mood established by the narrator is one of "feel sorry for me," which leads to a nearly fatal reader impatience with her; she is so much on the underside of the relationship with the man in question that she is begging for scraps from him. The story's point takes too long to get established; it is far too talky, too slow in movement. At the same time, Munro's style is at its best of gorgeous simplicity, some examples worth citing: "I come of straightened people, madly secretive, tenacious, economical."[33] "She takes up a man and his story wholeheartedly. She learns his language, figuratively and literally."[34] "I was twenty-one, a simple-looking girl, a nursing mother. Fat and pink on the outside; dark judgments and strenuous ambitions within. Sex had not begun for me, at all."[35]

Although Munro has proven to be adept at the thumbnail sketch comfortably embedded in a story narrative, by the five-page "Prue" she does not prove herself capable of the story-as-thumbnail sketch. "Labor Day Dinner" is a reminder that domestic situations and crises remain an overarching theme of Munro's, but in that regard it serves double notice: as well, the typical Munro drama within that context is an affair, and she does not always handle the story of an affair with the compellingness of, say, "Accident." As in "Bardon Boy," her prose style is immaculate, and differently from some previous stories she is adroit here at alternating the point of view; it is third person and moves smoothly from the consciousness of one character to another. But the plot is flat, as are the characters; the main one, a woman, remains unconvincing. She is a type, and Munro doesn't move her beyond that.

"Mrs. Cross and Mrs. Kidd" is a simple tale, with no deep psychology or complications of plot. Like "The Turkey Season," it takes place on a very colorful stage, and like that previous story is almost like a play in that regard. The two characters cited in the title reside in an establishment for senior citizens; their friendship survives a threat by the intrusion of a man coming between them. It is a charming, delightful, almost fable-like story that avoids patronizing the characters or their milieu; in fact, Munro creates the setting with great verisimilitude. The lesson is that life is always like high school, with alliances and crushes, no matter how old one gets.

"Hard-Luck Stories" takes too much time at the beginning to get the characters sorted out; reader boredom sets in early. According to the book's credits page, this story was not previously published before inclusion in this collection.

"Visitors" ushers readers into the middle of yet another domestic scenario: adult members of a family who are no longer accustomed to each other's company. The story's theme, then, can be called the uneasiness of family visits: more specifically, the tensions compounded by the family members not knowing each other well. As is the case here, "This is the first time Wilfred had seen his brother in more than thirty years."[36] These are relatively simple and uneducated people, without sophistication; and Munro, with no raised eyebrows, steps into their lives and milieu demonstrating grace and understanding. The narrative is rendered in the third person, related through the eyes and consciousness of one of the sisters-in-law, which, technically, proves a sound authorial decision, since it is this woman's house in which the visit is taking place and she is the "official" hostess. Also, not being a blood relative but only married into the family, she is a natural observer and commentator, from her the reader gaining the most out of all the characters. The story's ending strikes a resonant note: family ties survive even under the strain of living in too close company for a time.

The title story appears last in the collection. Told in first person by a grown woman, who quickly establishes a wistful tone that permeates the rest of her recollection; the story it is about the woman's visit to her dying father in the hospital. But this is an "acceptance" story as well: of the inexorableness of the cycles of life, children going off to pursue what they will persist in doing, one generation following the next. (The narrator, now a well-known writer, has indeed done so.) The narrator relates, "Once, when my children were little, my father said to me, 'You know those years you were growing up—well, that's all just a kind of blur to me. I can't sort out one year from another.' I was offended . . . But the years when Judith and Nichola [her daughters] were little, when I lived with their father—yes, blur is the word for it."[37]

Predictably, review reception to this collection varied greatly upon its publication, from "*The Moons of Jupiter* is more uneven than any of its predecessors"[38] to "her strongest collection to date . . . there isn't a single disappointing story in this collection."[39] But a more final word was this: "[A]rguably the most significant turning point in Munro's fiction-writing career."[40]

## Notes

1. Alice Munro, *The Moons of Jupiter*, New York: Random/Vintage, 1996, p. 1.
2. Alice Munro, *The Moons of Jupiter*, p. 1.
3. Alice Munro, *The Moons of Jupiter*, p. 1.
4. Alice Munro, *The Moons of Jupiter*, p. 13.
5. Alice Munro, *The Moons of Jupiter*, p. 3.
6. Alice Munro, *The Moons of Jupiter*, p. 3.
7. Alice Munro, *The Moons of Jupiter*, p. 4.
8. Alice Munro, *The Moons of Jupiter*, p. 4.
9. Alice Munro, *The Moons of Jupiter*, p. 6.
10. Alice Munro, *The Moons of Jupiter*, p. 7.
11. Alice Munro, *The Moons of Jupiter*, p. 15.
12. Alice Munro, *The Moons of Jupiter*, p. 17.
13. Alice Munro, *The Moons of Jupiter*, p. 18.
14. Alice Munro, *The Moons of Jupiter*, p. 19.
15. Alice Munro, *The Moons of Jupiter*, p. 19.
16. Alice Munro, *The Moons of Jupiter*, p. 22.
17. Alice Munro, *The Moons of Jupiter*, p. 23.
18. Alice Munro, *The Moons of Jupiter*, p. 35.
19. Alice Munro, *The Moons of Jupiter*, p. 37.
20. Klaus P. Stich, "The Cather Connection in Alice Munro's 'Dulse,'" *Modern Language Studies*, 19(4) (Autumn 1989), pp. 102–111.
21. Alice Munro, *The Beggar Maid*, p. 44.
22. Alice Munro, *The Beggar Maid*, p. 45.
23. Alice Munro, *The Beggar Maid*, p. 50.

24. Alice Munro, *The Beggar Maid*, p. 53.

25. Alice Munro, *The Beggar Maid*, p. 63.

26. Alice Munro, *The Beggar Maid*, p. 66.

27. Alice Munro, *The Beggar Maid*, p. 68.

28. Alice Munro, *The Beggar Maid*, p. 66.

29. Alice Munro, *The Beggar Maid*, p. 69.

30. Alice Munro, *The Beggar Maid*, p. 77.

31. Alice Munro, *The Beggar Maid*, p. 94.

32. Coral Ann Howells, *Alice Munro*, New York: St. Martin's Press, 1998, p. 79.

33. Alice Munro, *The Beggar Maid*, p. 110.

34. Alice Munro, *The Beggar Maid*, p. 116.

35. Alice Munro, *The Beggar Maid*, p. 118.

36. Alice Munro, *The Beggar Maid*, p. 199.

37. Alice Munro, *The Beggar Maid*, p. 222.

38. Sam Solecki, *Canadian Forum*, 62(20) (October 1982), pp. 24–25.

39. Bharati Mukherjee, *Quill & Quire*, 48(57) (September 1982), p. 57.

40. Coral Ann Howells, *Alice Munro*, p. 67.

CHAPTER 6

# ANOTHER SOLID COLLECTION

Munro's sixth book, her fifth collection of short stories, was published in Canada and in the United States in 1986, appearing in both countries under the title, *The Progress of Love*. Three of the eleven stories are outstanding, two prove ultimately not successful, and the remaining stories are solid, perhaps not advancing an appreciation of Munro's ability but certainly sustaining it.

Critical opinion of the collection seemed to focus on what by now, certainly by the appearance of this collection, was emerging as the single most defining trait of Munro's short stories, her rather elaborate excursion through time, through a character's past, in order to deeply contextualize the character's present. Upon the book's publication, this was said about her habitual "passages through time" that this collection "is marked by a deepening of this aspect of her art."[1] But that reviewer went on to say, in a full-length study of Munro, this more qualifying statement: "Everyone is in a certain measure diminished by nostalgia and the sense that the past is irrevocable. But it is also possible for the past to so encroach upon the present that the latter has little significance by comparison."[2] Another full-length study was less equivocal. "It is this emergence of story via digressions which generate new meanings and resonances that is the distinguishing mark of *The Progress of Love*."[3]

The title story appears first in the collection and ranks as one of the best. It is told in first person by an adult woman: a remembrance piece. A considerable amount of space in the story is given over to the primary character's past, at various points in time. These past events, however, do not represent literal shifts back and forth in time but are refractions of the past through the prism of adult memory, of adult selection, emphasis, and interpretation. Thus, the story's real time is actually the time in which the narrator exists as she recalls and narrates, which, however, is never explicitly identified. "The Progress of Love" emerges, in fact, as a prime example of Munro's creative "use" of time—her adroit assemblage of time periods—to not only tell a story but also, fundamental to Munro's interest in illuminating the dimensions of a character; this story in particular manifests Munro's adept selection and arrangement process in deciding which segments of the central character's past to bring to the table and in what order; and importantly, as well, how far in depth to explore each of these featured segments to illustrate (to the point of reader comprehension but not saturation) how the character in question arrived at the present situation in which Munro has established as the particular narrative's "real" time. However, the story is not just about simple recollection of the past; it broadens to encompass a sub-theme, a subcategory, of the major theme of "I remember when." That sub-theme is how family stories differ in substance and significance among family members: each one remembering the same events, conditions, and conversations differently, to the point of every family member wondering if the others were actually present and paying attention.

Additionally, this story is an advancement of another common Munro theme: an adolescent, most commonly a girl growing up in socioeconomic conditions relatively limited in not only material resources but also in customs, practices, habits, and attitudes that would generally be regarded as indication of sophistication, now faces exposure to a degree of sophistication.

This story begins in what initially seems like the story's real time—the narrative's grounding in time—but that will prove simply to be the first level of time Munro visits. The first paragraph introduces the narrator as a divorced mother of school-age boys, employed in a real-estate office and, as the initial frame upon which the plot will be hung, we come into the story as she had just received a call at work from her father. The point of the call is to deliver serious news: the narrator's mother has just died. Munro is not content to let facts lie on the page but, instead, uses them to contribute to her ultimate goal, the exploration of a character; to that end, she proffers this about the narrator's father's phone call—specifically, his demeanor in the face of an awful event: "My father was so polite, even in the family. He took time to ask me how I was. Country manners. Even if somebody phones up to tell you your house is burning down, they ask first how you are."[4]

In a page-and-half insertion/digression set off by white spaces, Munro shows the mother in her religiosity: born again at age fourteen, down on her knees praying three times a day. "Every day opened up to her to have God's will done in it."[5] (This is new "territory" for Munro; up to this point her characters have not been religious—have often been quite the opposite.) We read that while the narrator's father wasn't as religious, at least in the practice of religion, as her mother; but he was a serious, hardworking man, several years older than this wife, and he was faithful and devoted to her. A brief section, again separated off by itself by white space at front and back, flashes forward to a point when her father was very old and now a widower, living in a retirement home, makes a quick comment to the narrator indicating a deep-seated, probably unspoken impatience with his wife's religious bent, especially her need to pray so often.

The story now gets down to actual business; most of the story's business, given that it is a remembrance piece, will be told in flashbacks. The first of these flashbacks is in the year 1947, when the narrator was twelve and her mother's sister, Beryl, is coming for a visit. Elaborate preparations are being made, since the two sisters have not seen each other in several years; in fact, her mother "and Beryl had met only once or twice since they were grown up. Beryl lived in California."[6] Their mother had died when they were young and the narrator's mother stayed in their hometown with a neighbor couple while Beryl went away with their father and his new wife.

The farm on which the narrator's family lives is simply but trenchantly evoked in this brief passage: "The country we could see through the mesh of screens and the wavery old window glass was all hot and flowering—milkweed and wild carrot in the pastures, mustard rampaging in the clover, some fields creamery with the buckwheat people grew then."[7] The narrator anticipates with eagerness her aunt's advent into the household. Her assertion that "I was excited because Beryl was coming, a visitor, all the way from California" is a version of the hoary old storytelling device of the stranger coming to town. But the narrator is doubly excited: besides her unknown aunt due to arrive, so is the news of how she had done on the exams that would permit, or not, her going on to high school. Her parents' attitude was predictably narrow for that time and milieu; they would have to let her board in town, since there were no buses back then, and they had no spare money for that. Additionally, they saw no purpose in it; she would stay at home and work around the house with her mother, until she got married. Further, the mother's religiosity stood in the way of the narrator's educational advancement. "God isn't interested in what kind of job or what kind of education anybody has, she told me. He doesn't care two hoots about that, and it's what He cares about that matters."[8]

A white space now separates off a narration that takes the reader further back into the narrator's family history, and it is startling to read, quite a dramatic set of events; to integrate it into what has come before it in this story initially requires the reader's faith in its relevance to Beryl's impending visit. This disturbing flashback ventures all the way back to the narrator's mother's childhood. (Importantly, in keeping characters and matters straight, the narrator's mother's name is cited as Marietta.)

The house in which she lived was a duplex, the other half occupied by the Sutcliffes. Startlingly, to say the least, comes this line: "Mrs. Sutcliffe was the one who talked Marietta's mother out of hanging herself."[9] The rest of this insertion, this flashback as far back in time as the story will go, is taken up with this shocking episode. Marietta came upon her mother standing on a chair, a noose around her neck, and the other end of the rope around a roof beam. Marietta ran to find her father, but Mrs. Sutcliffe had intervened before Marietta returned. In and of itself, this is a strange and confusing interlude. What was the psychological provenance of such a dramatic gesture that apparently Marietta's mother had no intention of actually carrying through? Nor is it made quite clear what impact the horrible experience had on Marietta. Why is it even part of the story? It is only to be hoped that with the visit of the narrator's aunt Beryl, the suicide attempt will be made to make sense.

When Beryl arrives, she has brought her current boyfriend, a Mr. Florence; and, with Mr. Florence, Munro shows herself in her element in citing physical traits and peculiarities of behavior as subtle but trenchant keys to character: "He was a tall, thin man with a long, tanned face, very light-colored eyes, and way of twitching the corner of his mouth that might have been a smile.... His favorite place to be was in his car. His car was a royal-blue Chrysler, from the first batch turned out after the war. Inside it, the upholstery and floor covering and roof and door padding were all pearl gray. Mr. Florence kept the names of those colors in mind and corrected you if you said just 'blue' or 'gray.'"[10]

In the narrator's eyes, Beryl possesses an exotic side: "Instead of staying in the house and talking to my mother, as a lady visitor usually did, she demanded to be shown everything there was to see on a farm. She said that I was to take her around and explain things, and see that she didn't fall into any manure piles."[11] Arising from the narrator's entertainment of her aunt is a vivid imparting of the time and place in which the story is set. "I took Beryl to the icehouse, where chunks of ice the size of dress drawers, or bigger, lay buried in sawdust. Every few days, my father would chop off a piece of ice and carry it to the kitchen, where it melted in a tin-lined box and cooled the milk and butter."[12] On the other hand, the narrator admits to a disappointment in her aunt. "She seemed intent on finding things strange, or horrible, or funny."[13] This is simply an indication of the narrator's narrowness of experience: that a curious person, especially a woman wanting to see how things work outside her own familiar environment, is perceived by the narrator as condescending, and further, being unable to discern that Beryl is simply being a good guest, a good interactor with things she's being shown.

But Beryl remains exotic, vivid, in the narrator's eyes. In two beautiful lines, how she comes across to the narrator is summarized: "She was so noisy and shiny, so glamorously got up, that it was hard to tell whether she was good-looking, or happy, or anything ... Beryl slept in a peach-colored rayon nightgown trimmed with ecru lace. She had a robe to match. She was just as careful about the word 'écru' as Mr. Florence was about his royal blue and pearl gray."[14] From Beryl the narrator is exposed to ways of presenting herself better. "'Always do your hair wet, else it's no good doing it up at all,' Beryl said. 'And always roll it under even if you want it to flip up. See?' When I was doing my hair up—as I did for years—I sometimes thought of this, and thought that of all pieces of advice people had given me, this was the one I had followed most carefully."[15]

In another instance of the awakening that Beryl's visit induces within the consciousness of the narrator, a broadening and expansion of her experiences, Beryl and her boyfriend take the family on a Sunday drive, proceeding through countryside the narrator has never seen before, even though they travel less than twenty miles from their house! This particular increase of sophistication level continues when Beryl, taking the initiative, deposits the narrator's two brothers off at the neighbor's house to play: Catholic kids and girls not boys, and they go play while still dressed in their good Sunday clothes! All such new things! Further—another layer of this day's rich offering, like a delicious, delicate cake of a type never eaten before—Beryl takes then all to the Wildwood Inn for dinner. Eating out! But, of course, the path to sophistication can be uncomfortable, confusing, and self-conscious; indeed, the narrator's remembrance is thus: "Nevertheless this was a huge event. Not exactly a pleasure—Beryl must have meant it to be—but a huge, unsettling event. Eating a meal in public, only a few miles from home, eating in a big room full of people you didn't know, the food served by a stranger, a snippy-looking girl who was probably a college student working at a summer job."[16]

Dinner conversation turns to Beryl recalling her mother's sense of humor— her propensity for joking; and she specifically cites the attempted suicide as illustration of it—as an example of her mother carrying a joke too far, explained by Beryl over Sunday dinner as "she wanted to give Daddy a scare."[17] Beryl's recollection and interpretation of that event illustrates Munro's theme here, how a family event is remembered differently by each family member, not only in terms of what actually happened but also in terms of its provenance and significance. Every interpretation comes down basically to "me": what it had to with, or to, *me*.

Of course, the narrator's mother insists (as she apparently has insisted over the years) that her mother was serious in her attempt at suicide, and Beryl acknowledges to the gathered family over dinner that that is the narrator's mother's view, and while it differs from her own, she does not dispute it. In an exquisitely positioned flash forward, only a paragraph in length, the reader is swept from this scene to Beryl as an old woman, "all knobby and twisted up with arthritis."[18] The narrator is paying what the reader understands is her only visit to her aunt, and Beryl, the exotic, fancy Beryl, admits that she felt no real closeness to her sister—the narrator's mother, that is—but had always recognized and was intimidated by her superior physical attractiveness. This brief jump forward in time swiftly but significantly adds a meaningful layer to an understanding of the family dynamics at play in this story, which is another instance in which Munro uses the adolescent girl narrator as the central consciousness. But, typically, the narrator's focus, which directs the reader's line of vision as well, is on the character who is, at this time, her primary teacher in life, *about* life. In this story, that character shifts from being the narrator's mother to her aunt Beryl, which has as it purposes the working out of the story's theme: how the same event in family history is remembered differently by different family members.

This brief flash forward gives way to another white-spaced section of three short paragraphs, which presents the actual crux of the story: the narrator, obviously an adult now, reflects on how she absorbed both her mother's and her aunt Beryl's version of their mother's attempted suicide, concluding, "Why shouldn't Beryl's version of the same event be different from my mother's?"[19] Subsequent to that, the narrative moves to another time period, one previously unvisited, which is apparently after the narrator's father's death, for this segment is about the sale of the farm. For several years it was a commune; and the narrator, as a real-estate agent, has access to the house when it goes on the market following the disestablishment of the commune, and takes her current boyfriend out there for a look around. For him she recalls a peculiar incident in her childhood in this house: her mother burning $3,000 in cash, her inheritance from her detested father. The narrator's take on the incident, as she explains it to her boyfriend, "My father letting her do it is the point. To me it is. My father stood and watched and he never protested. If anybody had tried to stop her, he would have protected her. I consider that love."[20] The boyfriend calls it "lunacy."[21] The narrator remembers that was the word Beryl had used as well: again, an instance of the different interpretation of family events, this time the difference being between the narrator and Aunt Beryl.

The story now draws to its artful, even beautiful, conclusion, in two final, separate sections. The first of these concluding sections finds its setting in the narrator's family, returned home by car after the fancy Sunday dinner Beryl had treated them to. Here is where, when Beryl asked what her sister had done with her share of their father's inheritance—Beryl reveals she invested hers in real estate—that Beryl learned of her sister's burning her portion up in the stove. Beryl is aghast; and what is revealed is that the narrator's father actually was not present when her mother committed what Beryl labels a crime.

To draw the story to an end, Munro selected, from the various time periods she visited in the course of developing the narrative one that is initially a surprising choice but actually not the least surprising once its effectiveness is realized, which happens quickly. This selected time period is when the narrator's father is gone and the narrator, as a real-estate agent, is walking around inside her old farm house with her current boyfriend; it is then (as it will be remembered from a previous section of the story) that the narrator shares the story about her mother burning the money she inherited from her father. In the previous section it was revealed that, despite the narrator's version of the story, which is how she chooses to "remember" it despite her not being present on the occasion, the narrator's father was not present either and thus not giving his tacit approval to the act. As the narrator must acknowledge despite her preference for "remembering" it differently, her father did not know about the inherited money and its burning until that Sunday when Beryl took them all out to dinner and the subject came up during the drive home. The story's major theme of conflicting family versions of past events makes its final reiteration in the narrator's conclusion that, "How hard it is for me to believe that I made that up. It seems so much the truth it is the truth; it's what I believe about them."[22]

"Lichen" is about a middle-aged Lothario who dyes his hair and pursues increasingly younger women, a story told in third-person, omniscient voice. It further indicates a new direction Munro is traveling in creating male characters; her male characters in her earlier stories, as strongly witnessed, were, like the typical narrator's typical father figure, quiet, rather noble characters given to pursuits that—although typically male activities from the rural and small-town environments in which most of these stories are set—nevertheless allowed them personal freedom not found by mother figures bound to domestic chores and narrowness of experience. Then Munro began creating male characters neither like a father figure nor as, as she had occasionally done, an eccentric male with strange but not harmful ways and viewed by Munro with not only interest but also compassion. She began creating psychologically and morally unattractive male characters. This is certainly the case here. The man, named David, is bringing his new girlfriend to meet his wife of many years, Stella, from whom however he is separated, at her family summer cottage on the shore of Lake Huron, where Stella now lives year-round. David and Stella have remained friends, and David visits every summer on the occasion of the birthday of Stella's father, who now lives in a near-by nursing home.

Munro's elimination of detail is faultlessly executed. Her understanding of "just enough" in the description of setting and in relating necessary back story to reveal what this marriage had been like, why it ended, and the nature of the couple's current relationship, is unerring.

As it turns out, the girlfriend whom David brought with him, he's now tired of, and he confides in Stella—actually he's showing off, rubbing her nose in the fact he has a girlfriend—that a new one is already in the wings, and he maintains that surely the one he brought must sense the situation, because "there's a smell women get.... It's when they know you don't want them anymore. Stale."[23]

Stella recognizes the mean streak in him. "His voice when he talks about this girl seems to Stella peculiarly artificial. But who is she to say, with David, what is artificial and what is not? This special voice of his is rather high-pitched, monotonous, insistent, with a deliberate, cruel sweetness ... Stella gives a sigh that is noisier and more exasperated than she meant it to be and puts down an apple, half peeled. She goes into the living room and looks out of the window ... "[24] In short space, in brief but pungently expressed prose, Munro has imparted with remarkable efficiency Stella's adverse reaction to David; and by this one next statement of David's, his nature is also summarized: "She [the girlfriend he brought with him] makes me want to hurt her. She hangs on me with her weepy looks.... Sometimes I think the best thing to do would be to give her the big chop. Coup de grace ... "[25]

David and Stella visit her father in his nursing home, an occasion providing Munro with further opportunity to exercise her succinctness in adding layers to her characterizations; for this particular purpose, in this particular instance, she uses an omniscient point of view. "In his father-in-law's eyes David would always be somebody learning how to be a man, somebody who might never learn, might never achieve the steadfastness and control, the decent narrowness of range."[26] From David's perspective comes a beautiful passage—and very telling on *himself*—about why his marriage to Stella didn't work: "This white-haired woman walking beside him [meaning Stella] through the nursing home dragged so much weight with her—a weight not just of his sexual secrets but of his middle-of-the-night speculations about God, his psychosomatic chest pains, his digestive sensitivity, his escape plans, which once included her and involved Africa or Indonesia. All this ordinary and extraordinary life—even such things it was unlikely she knew about—seemed stored up in her. He could never feel any lightness, any secret and victorious expansion, with a woman who knew so much. She was bloated with all she knew."[27] Such remarkable perceptivity into human nature *and* economy of expression.

The next story, "Monsieur le Deux Chapeaux," is a full-fledged Munro story as the "concept" has come to be perceived, defined, and widely appreciated and applauded: longish in number of pages, but comfortably so; with emphasis on character over plot, several different types of characters making appearances, each one thoroughly but concisely realized in Munro's word-perfect sculpting; each character, both male and female, viewed sympathetically in their raiment of foibles; the setting in this particular case minimally described but nevertheless well evoked; and most importantly, in listing the components of the typical—"mature"—Munro story, a circling through levels of time to arrive at a layered delineation of character.

This is a third-person narrative, told from the point of view of the primary character (with some slight violations in this that keep the point of view from being perfectly held) and this character is Colin, a high-school teacher, whose brother, Ross, helps clean up the school grounds; the latter obviously eccentric and even a bit odd—impressions easily gathered by the reader in Munro's very pictorial page-and-a-half introductory scene setting, which sets up the situation and the characters with such sustainability as to carry these impressions throughout the rest of the story. As expected, Colin and Ross's mother refuses to admit how mentally and emotionally challenged Ross is; and Munro, true to her instinct, is sympathetic not only to Ross's condition but also to his mother's and his brother's protectiveness of him.

Colin is married, and he and his wife, Glenna, live in a small fixer-upper house; and in Colin's yard Ross exercises his mechanical "genius" by rebuilding car engines. Through the generous nature of Glenna, Munro is able to direct even more sympathy toward Ross. "There she was... taking Ross and his car seriously...."[28] A friend of Glenna's, Nancy, who teaches French in the lower grades in the public school system, comes to dinner; she, also, is sympathetic with no taint of patronization—to Ross. She tells Ross she and her class had seen him that day trimming the lawn at school—a scene that actually opens the story—wearing two hats; and they had, with utmost affection, dubbed him "Monsieur les Deux Chapeaux." But Nancy is also the bearer of bad tidings to Glenna this evening: mechanically knowledgeable enough is she to recognize that the combination of engine and body that Ross has put together, in rather Frankenstein fashion, has the potential of causing a serious accident.

In a gripping four-page insertion, an event from the brothers' boyhood is featured, which reaffirms the deep-seated bond between Colin and Ross and the former's abiding sense of protectiveness over the latter.

Although at first impression a secondary character, Glenna proves actually to be a pivotal one, and she comes into her own in the story, establishing herself in her distinctiveness as a character—as an individual. "A problem wouldn't just thrust itself on Glenna, and throw her into doubts and agonies. Solutions were waiting like a succession of rooms. There was a way she would see of dealing with things without talking or thinking about them. And all her daily patience and sweetness wouldn't alter that way, or touch it."[29]

The story concludes in two fashions: with Glenna promising Colin she and their little girl will never ride in this car Ross is assembling, and light cast again on the major event from the boys' youth, when a potential accident did not happen. Nevertheless, it was an epiphanous moment for Colin even in his boyhood: "He knew that to watch out for something like that happening—to Ross, and to himself—was going to be his job in life from then on."[30]

In the story "A Queer Streak," it is observable what goes wrong when Munro is not up to her usual stride. The story comprises forty-five pages, and by that fact alone this is—has become—a typical Munro story. But the difference in this story, the problem with this story, is that it seems either an outline for a novel or a condensed one. And that is, of course, what a typical—meaning, *successful* in its typicality—Munro short story is *not*. For that reason, this story is the "problem piece" of the collection. Its other characteristics are not necessarily attributes nor are they flaws; and these characteristics include: third-person narrative told from—and strictly from—the main character's point of view; the mood is actually the overriding characteristic, with the story, the setting, and the characters adding up to the story being reminiscent of Erskine Caldwell, but without his humor; and in conjunction with that, the story has an initial sensationalism we have not witnessed in a Munro story thus far. In that regard, she veers in a direction she fortunately corrects by going beyond the pivotal event—the bizarrely hateful act the narrator's sister performs against her own family—to explore the idea of how the locale from where an individual hails from can, despite moving away, still exert an impact on hopes and achievements.

"Miles City, Montana," however, is a much stronger piece, although not classi-fiable as a masterpiece. The story opens with guns blazing, as it were: "My father came across the field carrying the body of the boy who had been drowned."[31] This first-person narrative, one that is again told from the perspective of time passed, achieves substantiality by the gracefulness with which Munro "stacks" each time level upon the other—three levels of time, to be exact. Essentially, the storyline evolves from the narrator's remembered reactions to the eight-year-old boy who died accidentally and to his horrible death. The benefit of this used, but not overused, technique of adult remembrance of early events—as opposed to having the narrator relating to the event or series of connected episodes as they are transpiring—is, as we have cited before, the availability of a perspective *un*available in an as-it's-happening narration; plus, this method allows Munro's voice to rise to a level of articulation she could not employ otherwise (that is, if the narration was indeed voiced directly from a youthful narrator). An example of this is a passage about the drowning of the boy and the retrieval of his body: "To have to bring back such news, such evidence, to a waiting family, particularly a mother, would have made searches move heavily, but what was happening here was wise. It seemed a worse shame (to hear people talk) that there was no mother, no woman at all—no grandmother or aunt, or even a sister—to receive Steve Gauley and give him his due of grief."[32]

That indicates, of course, one of the story's time levels; the second level fall a couple of decades later, with the narrator now married (but not until the fourth page of the story, when this time level is introduced, is it made clear the narrator is female). She and her then-husband and their two children are returning by car to Ontario from where they currently live, Vancouver, from a visit home. Into the midst of this level of remembrances Munro injects this line about the narrator's ex-husband: "I haven't seen Andrew for years, don't know if he is still thin, has gone completely gray, insists on lettuce, tells the truth, or is hearty and disappointed."[33] By this insertion, but done smoothly and appropriately, the story's "real" time is established: the third level of time upon which the story is structured. Much of the story is given over to the drive from coastal Canada to the interior; and at least Munro's sheer, engaging writing style should be a temporarily forgotten feature of her fiction; here is a reminder: "This is the way you look at the poorest details of the world resurfaced, after you've been driving for a long time—you feel their singleness and precise location and the forlorn coincidence of your being there to see them."[34] The particular focus of this relatively long-followed road-trip is that the narrator's family stops to swim at a pool, and she and her husband panic when they believe one of their daughters has drowned. Thus draws the narrator back to the event and time period that began the story: the drowning of the little boy the narrator knew in her childhood. The situation with her own child in the pool compels her to recall not simply the little boy's death back when she was a girl but also, even more, how she reacted to her parents during this crisis. "I was understanding that they were implicated. Their big, stiff, dressed-up bodies did not stand between me and sudden death, or any kind of death. They gave consent. So it seemed."[35] The story's end is particularly poignant, a heartwarming but not sentimental drawing together of the reason for the narrator's remembrance through the various levels of time: "So we [she and her husband] went on, with the two [children] in the backseat trusting us, because of no choice, and we ourselves trusting to be forgiven, in time, for everything that had first to be seen and condemned by those children: whatever was flippant, arbitrary, careless, callous—all our natural, and particular, mistakes."[36]

"Fits" is a story, a third-person omniscient piece, about an extraordinary event—a murder/suicide—in a small town. Expectedly for Munro, the story also concerns the effect of this event on the community's sensibilities. "The talk turned to reasons. Naturally. There had been no theories put forward at the diner. Nobody knew the reason, nobody could imagine. But by the end of the afternoon there were too many explanations to choose from."[37] Again, as Munro's inclination would have her do, the story is not about the event per se but what the reaction of the neighbor woman who found the bodies says about her character.

Somewhat atypically for Munro, however, "The Moon in the Orange Street Skating Rink" features a male central character. The strongest element is the story's resonance achieved by its realist treatment of memory: that is, memory is imperfect, with blind spots that are past recall. Munro reaches remarkable psychological profundity in this complicated story; the drawback is that with it, something resembling contrivance of plot is here first encountered in her fiction.

"June and Meribeth" also offers an immaculate rendition of psychology; this story develops the theme of the difficult journey presented by trying to find oneself in youth and sending oneself off in the appropriate direction to ensure that such a discovery/self-knowledge will indeed occur. It is an effective story, a strong addition to the collection. On the other hand, the story "Eskimo" suffers from being too much in the main character's head to draw readers completely in.

Sort of boilerplate Munro, in terms of male-female relationships, is found in "Circle of Prayer." This is a story about social practices, namely the pressure on an individual to perform as the community performs; but it is not a compelling piece, difficult to remember what was going on if it is set down in the midst of reading it. "White Dump," which concludes the collection, also derives from a tired premise: domestic issues being aired that have been aired so many times before in Munro's stories. This story's excursions through time and people's experiences do not hold together; the narrative is drawn too diffusely through too many characters' point of view, to the point of perplexity and confusion over whose story this is after all.

## Notes

1. E. D. Blodgett, *Canadian Forum*, 66(32) (October 1986), pp. 32–33.
2. E. D. Blodgett, *Alice Munro*, p. 131.
3. Coral Ann Howells, *Alice Munro*, New York: St. Martin's Press, 1998, p. 85.
4. Alice Munro, *The Progress of Love*, New York: Random/Vintage, 1986, p. 3.
5. Alice Munro, *The Progress of Love*, p. 4.
6. Alice Munro, *The Progress of Love*, p. 7.
7. Alice Munro, *The Progress of Love*, p. 8.
8. Alice Munro, *The Progress of Love*, p. 9.
9. Alice Munro, *The Progress of Love*, p. 9.
10. Alice Munro, *The Progress of Love*, p. 14.
11. Alice Munro, *The Progress of Love*, p. 15.
12. Alice Munro, *The Progress of Love*, p. 15.
13. Alice Munro, *The Progress of Love*, p. 15.
14. Alice Munro, *The Progress of Love*, p. 16.
15. Alice Munro, *The Progress of Love*, p. 17.
16. Alice Munro, *The Progress of Love*, p. 20.
17. Alice Munro, *The Progress of Love*, p. 21.
18. Alice Munro, *The Progress of Love*, p. 22.
19. Alice Munro, *The Progress of Love*, p. 23.
20. Alice Munro, *The Progress of Love*, p. 26.
21. Alice Munro, *The Progress of Love*, p. 26.
22. Alice Munro, *The Progress of Love*, p. 30.
23. Alice Munro, *The Progress of Love*, p. 40.
24. Alice Munro, *The Progress of Love*, p. 42.
25. Alice Munro, *The Progress of Love*, p. 43.
26. Alice Munro, *The Progress of Love*, p. 51.

27. Alice Munro, *The Progress of Love*, p. 54.
28. Alice Munro, *The Progress of Love*, p. 66.
29. Alice Munro, *The Progress of Love*, p. 81.
30. Alice Munro, *The Progress of Love*, p. 83.
31. Alice Munro, *The Progress of Love*, p. 84.
32. Alice Munro, *The Progress of Love*, p. 85.
33. Alice Munro, *The Progress of Love*, p. 92.
34. Alice Munro, *The Progress of Love*, p. 99.
35. Alice Munro, *The Progress of Love*, p. 103.
36. Alice Munro, *The Progress of Love*, p. 105.
37. Alice Munro, *The Progress of Love*, p. 119.

# CHAPTER 7

# REACHING HIGHER PEAKS

Appearing in the United States in 1990, *Friend of My Youth*, Munro's seventh book and sixth collection, gathered ten stories. That all of them had been originally published in either *The Atlantic* or the *New Yorker*—inarguably top-notch periodicals—testifies to Munro's stature at this point in her career. The question for us is, is the book to be looked upon as advancement for her in regard to technical mastery of the form or simply stasis? The title story, which appears first, is not only a high point of the book but also a career peak. It is first-person narrative; the narrator sets a mood of nostalgia and wistfulness from the beginning, the theme upon which the female narrator fashions her recollections is the declined relationship between herself and her mother. The story's opening two lines point to the nature of that relationship, or at least poses questions about it and indicates that answers are to come as the narrative proceeds and the back story is, as would be expected from Munro, eventually filled in. "I used to dream about my mother, and though the details in the dream varied, the surprise in it was always the same. The dream stopped, I suppose because it was too transparent in its hopefulness, too easy in its forgiveness."[1]

This is also a story of loyalty: superficially, the narrator's mother's loyalty to a certain person about whom it would have been quite easy for her to not necessarily turn against in confrontational terms but to join the rest of the community in criticism and even condemnation behind this person's back. Adding to its resonance and appeal, "Friend of My Youth" unfolds surely as a story of inheritance: that a particular tale, about a particular time in the mother's life and the people who populated that time period, is what the narrator's mother left her as a keepsake, which the narrator honors as such. As it has been witnessed, Munro is able to achieve some of her best and most sympathetic characterizations when drawing eccentrics, either male or female. This story stands as further testimony to that ability. Even simply by outstandingly constructed plot does this story engage. These things said, it also has to be said that the best, most intriguing, most artful aspect of this story is its double frame: it is the narrator's remembrances of her mother's remembrance of a certain series of events. Upon further, closer insight, it is actually to be found triple-framed: in addition to the two just-mentioned levels, there is a level upon which the narrator stands to react to the tale as a writer, seeing how it *would* be written in her hands, differing from her mother's remembrance of it and her own remembrances of it being told to her.

This technical presentation is not complicated but is instead carried out with subtlety and seamlessness, Munro permitting the reader to pass through the time levels and back again indeed not unmindful of doing so (what could be the point of that?) but at the same time completely aware of not having to be conscious of "watching one's step" and risking tripping over the time-period joints.

How the narrator dreams about her mother is how the story opens; this preamble is only slightly more than a single page in length, separated from the text that follows by a white space. The writing is especially beautiful, certain passages demanding to be read aloud or at least read to oneself more than once: "I recovered then what in waking life I had lost—my mother's liveliness of face and voice before her throat muscles stiffened and a woeful, impersonal mask fastened itself over her features. How could I have forgotten this, I would think in the dream—the casual humor she had, not ironic but merry, the lightness and impatience and confidence? I would say that I was sorry I hadn't been to see her in such a long time—meaning not that I felt guilty but that I was sorry I had kept a bugbear in my mind, instead of this reality—and the strangest, kindest thing of all to me was her matter-of-fact reply. 'Oh, well,' she said, 'better late than never. I was sure I'd see you someday.'"[2] In other words, the distance between the narrator and her mother is recalled not in bitterness but in a longing for the days when her mother was healthy. (The preamble states that the mother died in her early fifties, when the narrator was only in her early twenties.)

Following the preamble, the time period is when the mother was young and unmarried, a teacher in a one-room school in the area in which she had grown up. The nostalgic mood initially created in the story's preamble is carried over into the main text of the story, set in place by the main body's opening line: "When my mother was a young woman with a soft, mischievous face and shiny, opaque silk stockings on her plump legs (I have seen a photograph of her, with her pupils)..."[3] Never losing sight of evocative scene-setting, Munro quickly offers this precise, even poetic, line to describe the Ottawa Valley, where the narrator's mother taught in school: "It was not a valley at all, if by that you mean a cleft between hills; it was a mixture of flat fields and low rocks and heavy brush and little lakes—a scrambled, disarranged sort of country with no easy harmony about it, not yielding readily to any description."[4] The narrator's mother boarded with a farming family in the vicinity of the school, the Grieveses, who "worked hard and they were far from ignorant, but they were very backward. They didn't have a car or electricity or a telephone or a tractor."[5] They were very religious in a social-restriction kind of way—in other words, the narrator's mother went off "to live in that black board house with its paralytical Sundays and coal-oil lamps and primitive notions."[6] But the time the narrator's mother came to live there, only the sisters Flora and Ellie, and Ellie's husband, Robert Deal, were in residence.

The house had been physically divided in half, Flora living in her half and the married couple in the other. The importance of setting to Munro carries over in this story to the indoors as well, and the well-documented atmosphere within that divided household imparts an appropriately uncomfortable sensation. "Through the washed uncurtained windows came a torrent of unmerciful light. The cleanliness was devastating. My mother slept now on sheets that had been bleached and starched and that gave her a rash.... Flora's hands were raw. But her disposition remained top notch."[7] It was with Flora that the narrator's mother made friends and it was to her that the mother was to remain loyal despite future community disapproval. The bulk of the story comes to be about these characters' immediate past and how it imprints on present-day lives: the present, in this instance, being that Ellie is dying from cancer, and the immediate past is that Ellie's husband was actually Flora's intended husband until he got Ellie pregnant. Prior to Ellie's health being brought low by malignancy, she had suffered a miscarriage and then a second one, and small-town views and mentality are caught in these few words, as the narrator, in recalling the story as her mother recalled it, says about Ellie and her misfortunes, "God dealt out punishment for hurry-up marriages—not just Presbyterians but almost everybody else believed that. God rewarded lust with dead babies, idiots, harelips, and withered limbs and clubfeet."[8]

A nurse is called out to assume care of the dying Ellie on a daily basis, and the nurse turns her nose up at the household's primitivism as compared to the devices and conditions in the real world; and she attempts to enlist the narrator's mother in her mocking and criticizing of the sisters, but the mother continues to stand loyal to her friend Flora. The narrator's mother, however, is engaged to be married (an event that occurred subsequent to her moving into the sisters' house to board)—engaged to the narrator's father, obviously—and she moves out when the time comes for the wedding, saying good-bye to Flora for what turns out to be forever. "The last my mother ever saw of her was this solitary, energetically waving figure in her housecleaning apron and bandana, on the green slope by the black-walled house, in the evening light."[9] Following a white space, the story continues on another time level, but the leap is not considerable: after the narrator's mother's marriage, when she receives a letter from Flora, its news making a delicious plot twist in an already quite compelling storyline. Ellie has died and her husband—as it will be remembered, he was Flora's intended husband before getting Ellie pregnant and having to marry her—has married the nurse! Other people with whom the narrator's mother had been acquainted also write to keep her apprised of events in that always-strange household; from them she learns the nurse made "improvements" in the side of the house in which she now ruled as woman-of-the-house, bringing that part of the residence up to date technology-wise and decoration. As the narrator's mother hears, this created a strange sight. "All these improvements took place on one side of the house only. Flora's side remained just as it was. No electric lights there, no fresh wallpaper or new Venetian blinds. When the house was painted on the outside—cream with dark-green trim—Flora's side was left bare. This strange open statement was greeted at first with pity and disapproval, then with less sympathy, as a sign of Flora's stubbornness and eccentricity (she could have bought her own paint and made it look decent), and finally as a joke. People drove out of their way to see it."[10] The narrator's mother also hears that the former nurse, now married to the late Ellie's husband, "invited them [neighbors and townspeople] to laugh at Flora,"[11] which of course the mother had always refused to participate in.

The narrator's mother writes a letter to Flora, expressing her concern over what she had been hearing. "Back came a letter from Flora saying that she did not know where my mother had been getting her information, but that it seemed she had misunderstood, or listened to malicious people, or jumped to unjustified conclusions.... She wished my mother all happiness in her marriage and hoped that she would soon be too busy with her own responsibilities to worry about the lives of people that she used to know."[12] The narrator expressed her mother's hurt, and her mother and Flora never communicated again. Upon reflecting on the Flora story as potential material for fiction, the narrator guesses her interpretation of Flora would differ from what she believed to be her mother's interpretation: "She would make her into a noble figure, one who accepts defection, treachery, who forgives and stands aside, not once but twice."[13] She believes her mother's interpretation would be seen through the lens of her own physical difficulties that would eventually cause her premature death. The narrator's version has Flora as bad rather than as noble; and, further, the real enigma to her in the whole Flora story is Robert, Flora's intended husband who married Ellie, and then Ellie's nurse. But the narrator realizes how she views Flora is based on how her mother felt about the need for sex: Flora turned away from it, which was "admirable" to the mother but "evil" to the narrator—and this opposition in attitude is a generation gap.

The conclusion of the story is a complete, efficient, satisfying wrapping up. Toward the end of her mother's life, she received a final letter from Flora, who lived in town now and worked in a store. The narrator admits she had thought about Flora since then, despite never having met the women. How she ponders what happened to Flora is intimately tied to how she remembers her mother, which brings the story back to where it began: with the preamble explaining how she dreamed about her mother.

"Oh, What Avails" is a feat of storytelling technique. Falling into three parts (each part designated by a Roman numeral) representing three distinct time periods, it presents itself as a rigorous example of the author's ability to keep a relatively long story (thirty-six pages) from suggesting an unfleshed sense of a condensed novel, boiled down not to its essence but to skeletal skimpiness. This Munro accomplishes by pursuing only two threads through the main character's life. This tight pursuit draws the narrative together as Munro avoids extraneous pathways and even details.

The point of view is the main character, Joan, to which Munro adheres except at the story's end, when she shifts the perspective to that of the second most important character; but, as will be shown, the results of that shift are far from fatal to the story's effectiveness. This story offers great charm in the characters it features, and settings are beautifully drawn. The small Ontario town in which Joan, upon the occasion of her observing it as an adult who has moved away, is evoked thusly: "The town seems crowded, diminished, with so many spruced-up properties, so much deliberate arrangement. The town of her childhood—that haphazard, dreaming Logan—was just Logan going through a phase."[14]

Conditions inside a household—the look and smell of the domestic environment people create for themselves—is a strong element in this story, as had been true in several of Munro's stories previously examined. The correspondence between inside and outside a house is caught by Munro in the story's opening two paragraphs, in prose so clean, direct, and precise that the sentences seem like stage directions: "They are in the dining room. The varnished floor is bare except for the rug in front of the china cabinet. There is not much furniture—a long table, some chairs, the piano, the china cabinet. On the inside of the windows, all the wooden shutters are closed. These shutters are painted a full blue, a grayish blue. Some of the paint on them, and on the window frames, has flaked away. Some of it Joan has encouraged to flake away, using her fingernails. This is a very hot day in Logan. The world beyond the shutters is swimming in white light; the distant trees and hills have turned transparent; dogs seek the vicinity of pumps and the puddles round the drinking fountains."[15]

In the story's third paragraph the understanding is relayed that probably Joan is a girl, not a grown woman. Morris, her brother, is introduced: he is fifteen and wears a pair of glasses that have one dark lens. This first section of the story is titled "Deadeye Dick," and as if on cue, a brief back-story section explains that when Morris was four, an accident caused blindness in one eye, and since, as the story is told from Joan's point of view (not in first person, however, but in third person), an indirectly expressed opinion of Joan on the subject slants the story of Morris's condition distinctly toward her point of view. Her attitude is that their mother did not, but could have, taken Morris to an eye specialist anytime after the accident to tidy up the scar around his eye. Within this white-spaced section, this brief back story, there comes a subtle and undistracting shift in time, which not only adds layering to Joan's opinion of the matter of Morris's blind eye but also indicates that Joan is recalling the entire story in all its various time elements from the true "real" time: from the vantage point of adulthood looking back many years after the event in question (and by now this is certainly to be recognized as a typical storytelling technique of Munro's). In this "real" time, Joan's adult opinion of the matter of Morris's eye arises from her puzzlement over his lack of interest in pursuing further care of it, such as getting an authentic-looking artificial one, now that he is an adult with money to afford such a thing.

Now, this white-space segregated back story gives way to a return to the time level on which the story opened: a hot summer day, with Joan's mother with a friend in the dining room drinking rum and coke. The family dynamics that factor importantly within the household are indicated as having as their core a certain laxity. Their mother "give[s] them [Joan and Morris] the idea of being part of something special."[16] Their grandfather founded the local lumberyard, and even though they have fallen on somewhat hard times, it is the spirit in the house the mother calls important. "None of this is important, none of their privations and difficulties and economics are important. What is important? Jokes and luck."[17]

Across the road from their house are three cement-block houses the mother owns, and one of the tenants is introduced: eccentric and unmannerly. Joan's family calls her Mrs. Carbuncle. She has a daughter, Matilda, on whom Joan has a schoolgirl crush. Munro easily, graphically, catches her appearance thus: "The beauty of Matilda, which prompted this talk, was truly of the captive-princess kind. It was the beauty of storybook illustrations. Long, waving, floating light-brown hair with golden lights in it, which was called blond hair in the day before there were any but the most brazen artificial blonds. Pink-and-white skin, large, mild blue eyes. 'The milk of human kindness' was an expression that came mysteriously into Joan's head when she thought of Matilda. And there was something milky about the blue of Matilda's eyes, and her skin, and her looks altogether. Something milky and cool and kind—something stupid, possibly. Don't all those storybook princess have a tender blur, a veil of stupidity over their blond beauty, an air of unwitting sacrifice, helpless benevolence?"[18] Joan was infatuated even with Matilda's name. "In Joan's mind the name gleamed now like a fold of satin."[19] By the time Joan is in high school, Matilda is out of school and working; and Joan's crush goes the way of all school crushes. Another aspect of how Joan perceives Matilda's beauty can be cited as an example of Munro's understanding of small-town social attitudes: "She saw that such beauty marked you—in Logan, anyway—as a limp might, or a speech impediment. It isolated you—more severely, perhaps, than a mild deformity, because it could be seen as a reproach."[20]

This first section ends with a heartbreaking event. Mrs. Buttler's ("Mrs. Carbuncle's") eccentricity will turn malicious. The situation is this: back in her daughter Matilda's last year in high school (fluidly, the time level is shifted to another time level in this story, with no confusion or grinding of gears), her mother has made her a flowery dress to wear to the school's Christmas dance. No one had asked Matilda to go, though. Joan's mother coerces mild-mannered Morris into asking her. Cruelly, Mrs. Buttler turns Morris away from the door, insisting—shouting—that "We're not so bad off we need some Deadeye Dick to take my daughter to a dance."[21]

Part 2 is called "Frazil Ice." The time is a decade after the above-mentioned incident. Joan has gone home to Logan for a visit; her mother has died and Morris has sold the house, and he wants Joan to help him sort though some boxes of her things. Morris is a successful businessman, owner of a construction company and several apartment buildings. Joan has her own success: living in

Ottawa, married to a well-known journalist. In another specific, accurate citing of small-town mentality, this is offered as an aspect of it with regard to Joan: "Joan is used to being identified as his wife, here and elsewhere. But in Logan this identification carries a special pride ... they are pleased that a girl from this town has got herself attached to a famous, or semifamous, person."[22] (Implicit in this attitude, of course, is an understanding that a "girl" from town could not be successful—be famous—in her own right, and that the path to fame for her *would* be on the arm of a famous man.)

There is a "wrinkle" to Joan's visit: she is expecting every day to receive a letter not from her husband but the man with whom she is having an affair. Munro demonstrates once again her astuteness about the psychology of an affair: "Each day she is disappointed [in not receiving a letter]. Each day a suspicion that she had made a fool of herself—a feeling of being isolated and unwanted—rises closer to the surface. She has taken a man at his word when he didn't mean it. He has thought again."[23] What a devastating, devastatingly authentic line: "He has thought again." This, too: "She has done this, she hardly knows why. She only knows that she cannot go back to the life she was living or to the person she was before she went out that Sunday night to the river."[24] How stale she feels in her marriage. "She feels as if she had been shunted off to some corner of the world where the real life and thoughts, the uproar and energy of the last few years have not penetrated at all."[25]

Joan learns that Matilda is back in town, permanently, after an unsuccessful marriage that had taken her away from town. Ironically in light of the episode when Matilda's mother refused Morris's offer to take her daughter to a dance back in her school days, Morris now functions as Matilda's escort to various functions around town. Joan is astonished that her prosaic, business-minded brother could turn out to have such a romantic side.

A letter from her lover does come, and Joan makes up an excuse to leave Logan and Morris earlier than planned, she understanding that in going to join her lover there is now "an irreparable tear in her life."[26]

Part 3 moves the story forward a dozen years, finding Joan divorced, living in Toronto, where she manages a bookstore. She had a boyfriend—certainly not the lover she went to meet when she was visiting Morris back home in Logan. She visits Morris on occasion; and on one certain visit, they see Matilda on the street, who these days is looking and acting weird—a case of the apple not falling too far from the tree? It seems that not too long ago Morris asked one of his workman to redo her lawn, and she had yelled him off, telling him to "scram," which is exactly the word her mother had used in shouting Morris away when he involuntarily came to their door to take Matilda to the high-school dance. It is a beautiful bringing of things full circle: not a contrivance, not a gimmick, not a cheap shot at being "artistic" on the author's part, but a genuine observation of, not so much the coincidences in life, as the small series of planetary-type rotations everyone's life represents.

Also in Part 3 are isolated—actually stated—the two themes by which the entire story is drawn into a cohesive whole. The first is summarized by Joan toward the end of the story: "Joan thinks of her own history of love with no regret but some amazement."[27] This story has been precisely that: a looking back for her over her love-life, in the process looking back over her love for her brother, Morris, and arriving at a point of appreciation, where "sometimes she gets Morris to talk about the very things that used to seem incomprehensible and boring and sad to her. The peculiar structure of earnings and pensions and mortgages and loans and investments and legacies that Morris sees underlying every human life—that interests her.... It reassures her in some way."[28] The second theme, so closely coupled with the first one as to make them interwoven, is stated thusly: "And in her simply dazzling folly, she had lost his love."[29] "She" refers to Matilda and "his," of course, refers to Morris.

"Five Points" is another superb story, told in the third person. It is another story of an affair: specifically, in Munro's view here, what women squander to have sex and what the path one particular woman takes to and through the course of an affair. Munro does not eschew the physical-sexual side of the affair: "She [the protagonist] loves the sight of Neil's bed—badly made, with a rough plaid blanket and a flat pillow, not a marriage bed or a bed of illness, comfort, or complication. The bed of his lust and sleep, equally strenuous and oblivious. She loves the life of his body, so sure of its rights. She wants to be his territory."[30] What is also indicated in that passage—evidenced in previously discussed stories—is Munro's understanding of the psychology of the affair; and that is a major factor in the success of this story.

Contributing as well to the story's accomplishment is Munro's easy mesh of her own narrator voice—as indicated, the story is told in the third person—and the voice the main character, a voice this woman named Brenda would use as quite natural to her if she were the actual narrator. Essentially, the plot is this: Brenda is married to Cornelius, who is much older than she. They run a second-hand furniture business, now that Cornelius cannot work in the mine any longer, after his accident. She is sleeping with Neil, closer to her own age; Neil works at the mine. That milieu and the men who work there speak sexual excitement to Brenda. "Their casual, good-humored authenticity. She loves the smell of work on their bodies, the language of it they speak, their absorption in it, their disregard of her. She loves to get a man fresh from all that."[31] The frame of the story *is* a story, one that Neil relates to Brenda presumably postcoitally—about where he grew up, in Victoria, British Columbia. His story/remembrance specifically references a store in a neighborhood called Five Points. This is how the older daughter of the couple who run the store is summarized in her physical presence: "Maria, by the age of maybe thirteen, had big, saggy breasts and a rounded-out stomach and thick legs. She wore glasses, and her hair was done in braids around her head. She looked about fifty years old. And she acted it, the way she took over the store.... She looked like she already knew all about running a business."[32] Neil and his buddies—all teenagers—hung around the store because Maria was paying them to have sex with her, and they used the money to buy drugs. Maria spent all the family money, the store went under, and Maria's mother, it was said, was the one who turned her in; whoever it was, Marie was sent to a juvenile detention facility.

This tale Neil tells is juxtaposed against the story of his affair with Brenda, including the point at which, because of the fever pitch and the sneakiness of it and the narrowness and confinement of the context in which one affair partner views the other comes the need to have a fight, even if over trivial issues. But Brenda is smart enough, experienced enough, to understand that the fight between them is a natural turning point in their relationship—but ultimately for the good. It has entered "a new stage." Their relationship's seriousness has intensified. "He has lost some of his sheen for her; he may not get it back. Probably the same goes for her, with him. She feels his heaviness and anger and surprise. She feels that also in herself. She thinks that up till now was easy."[33] The implication is that the affair will continue; and this particular ending is one of Munro's most poignant.

"Hold Me Fast, Don't Let Me Pass" features a strong plot line but not so overwhelming as to interfere with the process of character building. It is related in a third-person point of view—limited, not completely omniscient. The main character is named Hazel, "a widow. She was in her fifties, and she taught biology in the high school in Walley, Ontario. This year she was on a leave of absence."[34] Hazel is taking her leave in Scotland, visiting the places where her late husband had been stationed in World War II. They had planned to make this trip at some point as a couple, but he died before it could be undertaken, and now Hazel is doing it solo as a tribute to him. She is staying at a little hotel where her husband would visit when, on his leave during the war, he came to stay with his mother's cousin, who lived close by. Her husband had also included in his storytelling about those days how he'd met the hotelkeeper's daughter.

Hazel meets a man in the hotel, who "looked like a man who thought so well of himself that he could afford to be a bit slovenly."[35] This man, a local, pays particular and polite attention to her. He offers to drive Hazel out to meet her late husband's cousin, who is very old now. From him she also learns that the woman who owns the hotel is the innkeeper's daughter whom her husband had known back during the war. The hotel owner, however, is posing as a woman much younger than that. As it turns out, it is she who drives Hazel out to see the old lady who is her husband's cousin, and on the way she explains to Hazel that living with this Miss Dobie is a young woman who is sort of a maid and assistant, taken in by Miss Dobie when she has a child out of wedlock (she previously having worked for the mother of the man Hazel met at the hotel.) Hazel is frustrated: no one, including the cousin, who is rather daffy these days, remembers or admits to remembering her husband's being here during the war. Hazel is, however, able to do some reconciling of the present with the past. "She thought that it was a wonder to be here, in the middle of these people's lives, seeing what she's seen of their scheming, their wounds. Jack was not here, Jack was not here after all, but she was."[36]

Another element in the rather exciting plot reveals itself in the final pages: the local man Hazel met in the hotel has a history of involvement with both the hotel owner and the woman who takes care of the old cousin of Hazel's late husband, the implication being that he is the father of her "illegitimate" daughter.

"Oranges and Apples" completes the quintet of most outstanding stories in the collection. Here Munro writes in the third person, strongly suggesting by this point that this is her point-of-view of choice, after having been, in many if not most of the stories in her previous collections, a solid, enthusiastic practitioner of the first-person narration. What is unusual about the story, then, is her employ of a male central character—not unheard of but not customary. Ultimately three time levels are revealed, and the setting is specifically indicated in the opening pages: the year 1955, obviously within a time period for which Munro has shown a partiality. Finally, citing not another typical trait but indicating the story's strongest suits, this story exhibits even finer, more perceptive ability to understand and express the evolution of a character's mindset.

The first section, which extends to three pages in length and is separated from the main body of the narrative by a white space, serves as a prologue, by which are introduced the main characters; also, the prologue features in concentrated space the author's beautiful style, rich in exquisite but easily embraceable metaphors. An example can be cited in the description of the primary character, whose name is Murray, and who has just inherited the family department story in the small town of Walley: "He was an only child, not spoiled but favored, and he felt himself bound by many ties of obligation, decency, and love. As soon as he got home from college, he had to go around greeting all the people who worked in the store, most of whom he'd known since childhood. He had to chat and smile on the streets of Walley, affable as a crown prince."[37] Also, this poetically precise, concise description of Barbara, who clerks in the store, hired by Munro's father right before he died, and with whom Murray falls in love: "A bold black-and-white lily out of the Swamp Irish—Lorna Doone with a rougher tongue and a stronger spice."[38] Finally, these words about Murray's state of mind now that it is filled with thoughts of Barbara: "He was happier than he'd been at any time since he lost his faith. (That was a satisfactory way of putting it. It was more as if he'd come into a closed-off room or opened a drawer and found that his faith had dried up, turned to a mound of dust in the corner.")[39]

The story's actual "present" time is established in the narrative's first paragraph after the white-spaced-separated prologue; obviously, several years have passed, for Murray and Barbara, now married, live at a resort Murray owns twenty-five miles from Walley. What is learned is that the department store failed on him, and he lost it as well as the house in which they lived. In the midst of this fact-fixing about the conditions of the current life Murray leads, a flashback effortlessly occurs, back to the mid-1960s: thus a middle time level to the story, carefully sandwiched between the mid-1950s of the story's prologue and the story's present. The point of this particular time-level visitation obviously is to supply transitional information easing the reader's progression from the prologue's return of Murray from college to claim his place at the store and the "now," his now having lost and, in its place, running a resort. Information about his wife Barbara rises to the surface of this flashback as well (not serious but telling nevertheless): that she has put on weight and spends her time reading serious books.

The event transpiring in the story's present time is this: Murray and Barbara drive into town to visit the doctor, for a potentially serious problem of Barbara's. They drive by a farm where a riding school used to be; and their regard of the former horse farm as they drive by, and their wondering what happened to the husband of the woman who ran the riding school, offers itself as a smooth segue to the mid-level of time again, back to when Murray and Barbara still live in town and he still owns the department store. One day in walked Victor Sawicky, a stunningly handsome Polish man who, with is wife, had just bought a farm at the edge of town; and he announces to Murray that he and his wife intend to board horses and run a riding school. Murray and Victor develop a friendship; Murray appears to have a crush on Victor. But when the four of them—they and their wives—get together, the evening did not go well. "Murray reflected that he had never met a woman who was crazy about horses whom he had liked."[40] Munro's continued insight into Murray's psychology is tracked, from his point of view, through this evening's event; the authenticity of her observations derive from her realistic recording of his attitude toward the outfit Barbara chose for this evening. "One of the things about Barbara that Murray did not understand and was not proud of—as opposed to the things he did not understand but was proud of—would have to be this taste she had for cheaply provocative clothes."[41] And this, as well, about her clothes: "There was something unsure, risky, excessive about them. He was willing to see all sorts of difficult things about Barbara—her uncharitableness, perhaps, or intransigence—but nothing that made her seem a little foolish, or sad."[42]

Victor begins spending more and more time with Murray and Barbara to the point where, convinced his wife intends to poison him, he has to move out, and Murray offers him an apartment behind where they live. At this point comes the almost cliché line: "And one day Murray came home expectedly, in the middle of the afternoon."[43] They aren't having sex, but Victor is spying on Barbara at their pool. But the three-way friendship continues, Murray undergoing a new abandon: more sexually dominant with Barbara, demanding more. "Sometimes he felt in all his trouble a terrible elation. He was being robbed. He was being freed of his life."[44] In fact, Murray pretty much throws Barbara at Victor; and not simply, so it is readable in his actions, to jettison his cares and responsibilities but also in an effort to vicariously experience Victor sexually. What exactly, ultimately, happens between Victor and Barbara is never learned, even by Murray; Victor leaves them as he'd left his wife, slipping away leaving only a note behind.

The ending returns to the story's present time; Murray and Barbara walk along the beach at their lake-side resort, and Barbara's medical scan has turned out to be nothing. The very brief scene is poignantly, even beautifully, drawn. As Murray hears that news, his relief is great. "Easily, without guilt, in the long-married way, he cancels out the message that flashed out when he saw her at the top of the steps [on the beach house, where they are]: Don't disappoint me again."[45]

"Meneseteung" is one of the rare occasions—the only one so far, possibly—when an opening of a Munro story is too obscure; in fact, this story's slow start never recovers itself—that is, the story remains slow-going. It is a story about a town's history and not much more than that; it's only real reason to be read being the fact of its showcasing Munro's descriptive power.

"Pictures of the Ice" is, at nineteen pages, relatively short for a Munro story as is, at this point, generally characterized. It focuses on another male chief character, but he does not occupy the center stage with interesting and sympathetic sides as the male primary characters in the afore-discussed, well-done "Oranges and Apples." This latter story is engaging, but not especially so; it offers no great understanding of character, the primary one not rendered with any great insight, and neither are the ancillary ones. With a general flatness about them, they tend to emerge—what little emerging they do—as cliché representatives of a type rather than ever flowering into distinct individuality. The plot centers on the decision by a retired and now-widower Protestant pastor, with grown children, to marry again—to a woman in Hawaii—which turns out to be simply a story he's telling to get out of people's way.

A female protagonist features in "Goodness and Mercy," which is a third-person narrative about a mother-daughter relationship, recognizable by now as a frequent theme for Munro. The mother is a formerly well-known singer who now is dying, and her daughter has brought her on a passenger-carrying freighter bound for Britain. The setting thus is quite unusual for Munro, in its confinedness, in its stage-set quality; but she demonstrates complete comfort with such limited parameters. Despite its length—twenty-four pages—and a certain poignant tone, it emerges more a sketch of the primary characters than an in-depth portrait.

"Differently" tracks the path taken in two couple's friendship and the two women's extramarital affairs. The story begins flat and confusing—taking the first four pages to get the characters sorted out, who is who and married to whom and *used* to be married to whom—and to the end it remains unengaging, unfortunately never becoming more than a tired exercise of analyzing infidelity.

"Wigtime," although not to be ranked as one of the collections' best, is in fact a good story. It features what Munro does well. It is a story about the reacquaintance of two women who were friends many years ago, as children in the same hometown, who now have encountered one another after the passage of several years. The narrative is in the third person, from a single point of view of one of the women friends (a lapse does occur in the point of view's singularity, but only briefly and with no damage to the narrator's staying on course). The theme of nostalgia for the simpler days of childhood is explored, as is the theme of mature acceptance of what life is *today*.

## Notes

1. Alice Munro, *Friends of My Youth*, New York: Random/Vintage, 1991, p. 3.
2. Alice Munro, *Friends of My Youth*, p. 4.
3. Alice Munro, *Friends of My Youth*, p. 4.
4. Alice Munro, *Friends of My Youth*, p. 5.

5. Alice Munro, *Friends of My Youth*, p. 5.
6. Alice Munro, *Friends of My Youth*, p. 5.
7. Alice Munro, *Friends of My Youth*, p. 7.
8. Alice Munro, *Friends of My Youth*, p. 11.
9. Alice Munro, *Friends of My Youth*, p. 16.
10. Alice Munro, *Friends of My Youth*, p. 17.
11. Alice Munro, *Friends of My Youth*, p. 18.
12. Alice Munro, *Friends of My Youth*, p. 19.
13. Alice Munro, *Friends of My Youth*, p. 19.
14. Alice Munro, *Friends of My Youth*, p. 196.
15. Alice Munro, *Friends of My Youth*, p. 180.
16. Alice Munro, *Friends of My Youth*, p. 182.
17. Alice Munro, *Friends of My Youth*, p. 183.
18. Alice Munro, *Friends of My Youth*, p. 186.
19. Alice Munro, *Friends of My Youth*, p. 187.
20. Alice Munro, *Friends of My Youth*, p. 188.
21. Alice Munro, *Friends of My Youth*, p. 193.
22. Alice Munro, *Friends of My Youth*, p. 195.
23. Alice Munro, *Friends of My Youth*, p. 196.
24. Alice Munro, *Friends of My Youth*, p. 200.
25. Alice Munro, *Friends of My Youth*, p. 201.
26. Alice Munro, *Friends of My Youth*, p.206.
27. Alice Munro, *Friends of My Youth*, p. 207.
28. Alice Munro, *Friends of My Youth*, pp. 207–208.
29. Alice Munro, *Friends of My Youth*, p. 213.
30. Alice Munro, *Friends of My Youth*, p. 41.
31. Alice Munro, *Friends of My Youth*, p. 31.
32. Alice Munro, *Friends of My Youth*, p. 29.
33. Alice Munro, *Friends of My Youth*, p. 49.
34. Alice Munro, *Friends of My Youth*, p. 75.
35. Alice Munro, *Friends of My Youth*, p. 78.
36. Alice Munro, *Friends of My Youth*, p. 101.
37. Alice Munro, *Friends of My Youth*, p. 107.
38. Alice Munro, *Friends of My Youth*, p. 108.
39. Alice Munro, *Friends of My Youth*, p. 108.
40. Alice Munro, *Friends of My Youth*, p. 119.
41. Alice Munro, *Friends of My Youth*, pp. 199–120.
42. Alice Munro, *Friends of My Youth*, p. 120.
43. Alice Munro, *Friends of My Youth*, p. 125.
44. Alice Munro, *Friends of My Youth*, p. 129.
45. Alice Munro, *Friends of My Youth*, p. 135.

CHAPTER 8

# A Plateau

*Open Secrets*, Munro's eighth book and seventh collection of short stories, was published in 1994. Not surprisingly, given her growing reputation, seven of the eight stories were previously published in the *New Yorker*, the single remaining story in the *Paris Review*.

Three of the stories rise to the top of the collection and will be discussed first; two stories are interesting for their technical predicaments, solutions, and weaknesses they present for study; and three stories do not achieve significant success on any level, for various reasons. "Carried Away," at nearly fifty pages in length, leads off the collection and reveals itself within its first two or three pages as a masterpiece. The narrative is divided into four sections, each one titled (but not numbered) and each moving the story forward chronologically. Generally, in Munro's exploration of a character's personal past, she has reached no further back into "world" history than the 1940s. This story, however, breaks new ground for her in that regard to earn the label "historical fiction." Settlement patterns and settler behavior from Old World to New—in Canada, that is—are now brought in as part of Munro's purview.

In the rich layering of this story, Munro creates a particularly absorbing plot. The opening paragraph well sets the stage: "In the dining room of the Commercial Hotel, Louisa opened the letter that had arrived that day from overseas. She ate steak and potatoes, her usual meal, and drank a glass of wine. There were a few travelers in the room, and the dentist who ate there every night because he was a widower. He had shown an interest in her in the beginning but had told her he had never before seen a woman touch wine or spirits."[1]

Implied is that Louisa is unmarried, and that if she doesn't live at the hotel she at least dines there frequently, and that this is an era previous to contemporary times, if a man was noticing Louisa having a glass of wine with dinner in public.

The title of this section is "Letters" and Louisa opens a letter over dinner in the hotel. The letter "was dated six weeks before—January 4, 1917."[2] She is the librarian in the small Ontario town of Carstairs, and the letter is from a local boy—a young man—who is a soldier in the hospital, presumably in Europe, and obviously engaged in Canada's forces in World War I. His name is Jack Agnew and his father lives in Carstairs and works for the Doud family, not at their factory but doing gardening at their house. (The name Doud is a thread extending throughout the collection.) What prompted the wounded soldier to write back home to the town librarian is to share his appreciation for how much better organized and useful the public library became under her direction: "When you came what a change."[3]

Louisa replies to the soldier, her letter sharing background information about herself; it is revealed that, as her habit of dining in the hotel would suggest, she is not native to Carstairs, but with both parents dead, she "just happened to be in this town when I heard the Librarian had died and [she] thought, perhaps that this is the job for [her]."[4] They begin a regular correspondence; and Louisa learns he was a regular visitor to the library, but she can't place him, even though he makes it obvious he was in the habit of watching her closely. (The story's eerie atmosphere is created early.) One particular passage in one of his letters conjures up a poignant, heart-in-mouth feeling; the life-and-death reality of battle is brought home to Louisa in this sharing of his experience: "The other day there was a man who died of a heart attack. It was the News of all time. Did you hear about the man who died of a heart attack? That was all you heard about day and night here. Then everybody would laugh which seems hard-hearted but it just seemed so strange.... Before and after him others have died being shot up or blown up but he is the famous one, to die of a heart attack. Everybody is saying what a long way to come and a lot of expense for the Army to go to, for that."[5]

The soldier's plainspoken eloquence is evidenced in that passage and, also, in this line to Louisa: "You are a cut above the ordinary and it would not surprise me if some officer had spoken for you."[6] The remaining pages (four) of the section "Letters" is taken up by further background on Louisa. She is twenty-five and had recently been in a sanitarium, where she had an affair with a married doctor, over which he lost his job. "Letters had played a part that time, too. After he left, they were still writing to one another. And once or twice after she was released. Then she asked him not to write anymore and he didn't."[7] She began a job of traveling salesperson, which is what brought her to Carstairs and living in the hotel. With her correspondence with the convalescent soldier in Europe, Louisa pays more attention to events as they happen in the course of the war. Munro is beautifully empathetic in understanding "home front" psychology back in such a bygone time: "Now [Louisa] felt what everybody else did—a constant fear and misgiving and at the same time this addictive excitement."[8]

Munro interjects a twist in the story, in the form of Louisa beginning to meet with the Red Cross women in their war-effort knitting sessions, announcing to them she intends to work on a muffler for a soldier-friend overseas. At this point Munro violates the point of view from which the story heretofore had been told—Louisa's, of course—and takes the narrative completely out of Louisa's consciousness and assumes an omniscient perspective, to identify one of the young ladies in the group by name (Grace Horne) and reveal, shockingly to the reader and unbeknownst to Louisa, "She [this young lady] had become engaged to Jack Agnew before he went overseas, but they had agreed not to say anything about it."[9]

The story's second section is titled "Spanish Flu," a term—a factor of life—certainly reminiscent of that era. The point of view alternates between Louisa and Jim Frarey (who is a traveling salesperson like she used to be, and a regular at the hotel where she lives, when he's in town, and who is to be her lover). It is now 1919, the war in Europe is over, and a fresh wave of the flu is sweeping through. Louisa had not heard from Jack Agnew for some time, and despite other institutions—even churches—closing their doors in the face of the epidemic, Louisa keeps the library open, not out of any great sense of community service but in case Jack, the soldier, should walk in sometime soon. She is obsessed with his return, giving little thought to anything else. "It was at this time that she entirely gave up on reading. The covers of books looked like coffins to her, either shabby ornate, and what was inside them might as well have been dust."[10] Louisa did notice, however, a mention made in the newspaper that Jack had married a woman whose name she did not recognize—of course, the reader recognizes the name as the young lady in the Red Cross group. Reminiscent of Elizabeth Bowen's ghost stories about World War II, Louisa closes the library and notices on her desk a note, on which someone had written "I was engaged before I went overseas."[11] Jack obviously had been in the library that evening and left the note when her back was turned and he didn't introduce himself. She and Jim Frarey, the traveling salesman staying in her hotel, after a long conversation about this and other things, have sex, and it is a particularly poignant, nonsleazy, almost euphemistic scene as Munro writes it, worth quoting in full:

> But later in the night Jim Frarey gave a concluding groan and roused himself to deliver a sleepy scolding. "Louisa, Louisa, why didn't you tell me that was the way it was?"
>
> "I told you everything," said Louisa in a faint and drifting voice.
>
> "I got a wrong impression, then," he said. "I never intended for this to make a difference to you."
>
> She said that it hadn't. Now without him pinning her down and steadying her, she felt herself whirling around in an irresistible way, as if the mattress had turned into a child's top and was carrying her off. She tried to explain that the traces of blood on the sheets could be credited to her period, but the words came out with a luxurious nonchalance and could not be fitted together.[12]

The story's third section, "Accidents," moves the story into the 1920s, and is largely about Jack Agnew, but he once again, like a ghost, is a noncorporeal presence. Like his "presence" in Louisa's life via letters and a note left on her desk after his return from overseas, he is ever offstage, his existence definitely felt by Louisa, however. This section begins with Jack's accidental death at the factory where he works—Douds, a major town institution and employer. (The newspaper account mentions that he leaves a widow and a small daughter.) When Arthur Doud, the company head, pays a condolence call on the new widow, she asks him to return a stack of books to the library that Jack had checked out; his widow indicates Jack had gone to the library every Saturday night—once again, a ghostly tone is interjected. Obviously, he's been going there but still unbeknown to Louisa. On the day of the funeral, only two individuals in town did not attend: Jack's father—"He was quite sane but abhorred conversation"[13]—who went out tramping around in the countryside, and Louisa. The tone of ghostliness is given further accent in this chilling paragraph: "Walking in the country that day, he [Jack's father] met another person who was not at the funeral. A woman. She did not try to start any conversation and in fact seemed as fierce in her solitude as himself, whipping the air past her with long fervent strides."[14]

At this point the story's point-of-view is once again shifted, now to factory-owner Arthur Doud, who takes the books back to the library and sees that the librarian—Louisa, of course—is annoyed that they had not been properly checked out. When Arthur explains that they had been in the possession of the man recently killed at the factory, the librarian is noticeably upset, which he believes is due only to the fact that a person now dead had touched the books' pages. Arthur, in fact, his wife having died of Spanish flu, begins paying visits to the library, but to himself he insists he is doing so in his capacity as a civic leader, as a public servant. "By sitting here, reading and reflecting here, instead of at home, he seemed to himself to be providing something. People could count on it."[15] The idea that something will spring up between him and Louisa doesn't at this point, for the reader, seem far-fetched. Visiting the library does Arthur a wealth of psychological good, relieving him of the pressure to maintain appearances in public. "For years after his father's death, he had felt like an imposter. Not steadily, but from time to time he had felt that. And now the feeling was gone. He could sit here and feel that it was gone."[16] Louisa asked him what Jack Agnew looked like; she'd already explained to him (about the library books Jack had had in his possession when he was killed) that she "never saw him, to know who he was."[17] Arthur can't really describe him. He, of course, is unaware of the previous connection between Louisa and Jack—the letters sent from overseas—that is. Arthur is attracted to her, but can't put that into words, either: "He could no more describe the feeling he got from her than you can describe a smell."[18] Unsure of how Louisa feels toward him, he nevertheless suggests marriage.

The fourth and final section of the story is called "Tolpuddle Martyrs." The time is now the mid-1950s. The specific scene is this: Louisa has taken the bus from Carstairs to the much bigger town of London, to consult a heart specialist. She notices in the London newspaper that a ceremony is taking place that afternoon in a local park, and a Jack Agnew from Toronto was to be a featured speaker; and now the story becomes in interior one, taking place only in Louisa's rattled mind: she believing she's in conversation with the Jack Agnew that was, however, never standing before her, nevertheless a strong part of her life for a while. One piece of information she shares with him in this imagined conversation, is something the reader senses is indeed true: that she is Arthur Doud's widow, admitting that back when he used to come into the library, "I wanted to marry him and get into a normal life."[19]

With the brief, one-page conclusion, Munro reaches slightly further back than the point in time at which the story began, to when the previous librarian had just passed away and Louisa was in town on business, her traveling sales business, of which she had grown very tired, and she saw an opportunity. This concluding episode reiterates the story's theme: "She was glad of a fresh start, her spirits were hushed and grateful. She had made fresh starts before and things had not turned out as she had hoped, but she believed in the swift decision, the unforeseen intervention, the uniqueness of her fate."[20]

The second story, "A Real Life," adds an ingredient not found in the first one: charm. The characters are charming, all of them, including the secondary ones. Told in third person, the story opens with a particularly beguiling line: "A man came along and fell in love with Dorrie Beck."[21] As the previous story stood as a reminder, this story does so as well: although Munro's primary objective is development of character, rarely does she neglect the plot aspect of a story. In fact, as this story and the previous one indicate, carefully constructed, deeply compelling plots fall well within her purview—and talent range. This story extends to nearly thirty pages, but Munro eschews her by-now traditional elaborate navigation through time periods.

So, Dorrie Beck is getting married. Dorrie and her recently deceased brother, Albert, lived in a house on the land of Porter and Millicent, and Dorrie continued living there after Albert's death. Dorrie "was a big, firm woman with heavy legs, chestnut brown hair, a broad bashful face, and dark freckles like dots or velvet. A man in the area had named a horse after her."[22] After her brother's death—of heart attack, quite suddenly—Dorrie had grown a bit more eccentric. "Albert always said people living alone are to be pitied," said Dorrie—as if she did not understand she was now one of them."[23] But Millicent valued her as a friend, even more so than she valued her supposed best friend, Muriel, who was unmarried (at over thirty years of age, she of course *should be* married). Muriel was the local piano teacher and also taught piano in the public school system, and Millicent met her when she enrolled her daughter in lessons. Muriel didn't suffer from lack of men in her life; she had plenty, but they were always married. "She found one fairly often but hardly ever one that she could bring to supper."[24] Naturally, these relationships never lasted; they "would all end in misunderstandings, harsh words, unkindness. A warning from the school board. Miss Snow will have to mend her ways. A bad example. A wife on the phone."[25]

One particular evening, Millicent gives a buffet supper on her verandah for the Anglican preacher and a friend of his visiting from out of town. (It is a beautifully, humorously constructed scene, with hints of the pretense and fumbling found on the British television comedy *Keeping Up Appearances*.) Dorrie was invited, more to help clean up afterward than for her company, and Muriel is included on the guest list as well, to entertain on the piano—but the real purpose of *her* presence is some matchmaking on Millicent's part. Dorrie arrives late, explaining that she got delayed by having to shoot a feral cat she suspected of having rabies. The minister's friend, Mr. Spiers, hangs on to every word of hers; he "listened like an old dog."[26] Muriel is not pleased, and Millicent wonders to herself if that is what made Muriel so "saucy" this evening.[27]

A white-spaced break in the narrative brings a marvelous plot twist. Dorrie comes to Millicent's house bearing a bolt of white satin, needing to make a wedding dress—she was to marry Mr. Spiers. She and he had not actually encountered one another in person since the supper party on the verandah; he'd immediately gone to Australia, but letters back and forth had spawned a relationship, which had moved to the point of a marriage proposal. Millicent and Muriel take charge: the former of the requisite wedding luncheon, the latter of the dress itself. Of course, their assumption of these "tasks" into their own hands is obviously all about *them*, about self-inclusion in any event transpiring around them, than it is about doing these things for Dorrie, *for* Dorrie. The rigid, inflexible small-town mindset in which all these people lead their lives rears its nasty head over Dorrie's impending nuptials. "Dorrie was not quite a joke—something protected her from that, either Albert's popularity or her own gruffness and dignity—but the news of her marriage had roused a lot of interest, not exactly of a sympathetic nature. It was being spoken of as a freakish event, mildly scandalous, a possible hoax."[28]

The day of the wedding was set for a Saturday in May; Mr. Spiers was to arrive in town on the Wednesday before and stay with the preacher. In a humorous, poignant, completely realistic scene, with perfectly realized dialogue, Millicent has to reconvince a cold-footed Dorrie of the advisability of this marriage, and Millicent is indeed thinking not of herself—although, truthfully, she has no desire to see all the preparations she had been involved in to go to waste—as she insists to Dorrie she needs a life, which the marriage with provide for her.

The wedding scene, separated out by white spaces, begins in faultless keeping with Dorrie's character: she walks to the her wedding, refusing the car ride that Millicent and Porter offer her, and she does so wearing an old coat that belonged to her late brother over her satin wedding dress. This picture is perfect. The next section takes the story several years into the future, into the 1950s; and in a letter back to Millicent, Dorrie shows herself to have had quite a successful marriage in Australia, which Millicent, crowing about it to her friends, takes credit for—for indeed having made certain Dorrie went ahead and found a life for herself. Millicent hears from her friend Muriel as well, who "inspired" by Dorrie to find a husband, went off to Alberta to do the same, and succeeded. The story draws to a beautiful conclusion with a picture of Millicent, in the story's present time, an old widow, eternally pleased with herself that she in essence forbade Dorrie to lead nothing more than a "life of customs, of seasons . . . in her reasonable eccentricity, her manageable loneliness."[29]

The third superior story in the collection is "Spaceships Have Landed," certainly a provocative title given the commonplace settings and unsensational domestic dramas Munro is in the habit of exploring. In the first sentence, reassuringly, the drama to unfold is grounded in the town of Carstairs, the Ontario community much visited previously in Munro's fiction. By the story's end, its primary theme is seen to be as mundane as the story's title suggests otherwise: mundane, only in terms of being drawn from real life and being universal to nearly everyone's daily life: specifically, young male and female relations, in this instance in the 1950s, a favorite time period for Munro. She favors, too, testing the texture and nature of attitudes *toward* and *of* women. Almost a co-theme is teenage girls' social, physical, and sexual insecurities, which is plumbed to great insight in this story. ("She was not ugly. She knew she was not ugly. How can you even be sure that you are not ugly? But if she was ugly, would Billy Doud have gone out with her in the first place? Billy Doud prided himself on being kind."[30])

Told in the third person, this story is an extremely effective integration of "real" time and backstory. The central event upon which the narrative hangs is revealed in the first seven words of the opening line: "On the night of Eunie Morgan's disappearance . . . "[31] The rest of that opening sentence is, "Rhea was sitting in the bootlegger's house in Carstairs."[32] Rhea had been brought to this place by Billy Doud (by his last name, it can be safely assumed he is of the factory-owning Douds in Carstairs, a family encountered in every story discussed thus far). Billy's friend, Wayne, is present, watching, not participating, in the card game at hand. Wayne catches Rhea's eye "and from then on he watched her, with a slight, tight, persistent smile. This was not the first time Wayne had caught Rhea's eye, but usually he didn't smile."[33] That Rhea is inside this questionable house is unusual; it is not unusual for Billy and Wayne to stop off for a drink, always together, leaving Rhea and Wayne's girlfriend, Lucille, in the car waiting. This night things are different: Lucille is home sick, Billy and Rhea had gone to a dance, and they had met Wayne at the house: the Monk's. Billy lives in town—again, it is to be assumed at this point he is of the town's most notable family—and Rhea on a chicken farm at the town's edge. Mrs. Monk, a cold, distant person, hostess to the booze-and-cards evenings her husband gathers in their house, brings Rhea a soft drink. Rhea ponders the question she always has about Wayne, Billy's friend: does he like her or not? On the few occasions when the two of them have danced together, "he held her as if she were a package he was barely responsible for."[34]

The setting so far in the story has been minimally explicated, and in these terms: "None of these men would be exactly in disgrace for coming here—Monk's was not a disgraceful place. Yet it left a slight stain. It was mentioned as if it explained something. Even if a man flourished. 'He goes to Monk's.' "[35]

Mrs. Monk, the wife of the house, is one of the most beguiling, best quickly sketched-in secondary characters in Munro's entire oeuvre. She rightly holds for Rhea, as the latter sits doing nothing but watching the men drink and play cards, a certain fascination as the "most interesting person in the room."[36] She has "dark, graying hair . . . coiled up at the back of her head, and she didn't wear makeup. She had kept a slender figure, as not many women did in Carstairs. Her clothes were neat and plain, not particularly youthful but not what Rhea thought of as housewifey . . . her expression . . . always the same—not hostile, but grave and preoccupied, as if she had a familiar weight of disillusionment and worry."[37] Her demeanor combined that of an observant servant and an equally conscientious hostess. "She was as watchful as a deaf-mute, and was silent, catching every signal around the table, responding obediently, unsmilingly, to every demand. This brought to Rhea's mind the rumors there were about Mrs. Monk [concerning prostitution, that is]."[38]

Now comes a white space, and the scene abruptly shifts. The name Eunie Morgan is cited again. It will be remembered that her disappearance was mentioned in the story's opening line. As Rhea, Bill, and Wayne occupy themselves at Monk's, the third house down from there is where Eunie lives, with her parents, who have discovered that night that she is not at home. (In reference to their surprising lack of indoor plumbing, given the late time for which an outhouse to still be in use, the exact year in which this story takes place is now indicated as 1953.) Eunie's mother forces her husband to help her go in search of their daughter. Munro draws the two characters together, Eunie and Rhea, with background information. "They were not friends, in the way that Rhea would understand being friends, later on. They never tried to please or comfort each other. They did not share secrets . . . "[39] It was an unsavory friendship; when they got older, at high-school age, Rhea shunned Eunie because of her peculiar looks and rather grating personality. Rhea sees that when Eunie got a job, after quitting school, Eunie blended well with the type of people with whom she worked in the glove factory: noisy and disorderly. "People close to the bottom, like Eunie Morgan, or right at the top, like Billy Doud, showed a similar carelessness, a blunted understanding."[40]

After a white-space jump, how Billy Doud entered Rhea's life is a topic now moved into focus. Rhea, in her last year in high school, got a job—at a shoe store, into which one day walked Billy Doud, now home from college, having obtained his degree, and apprenticing learning how to run the family factory—a piano manufacturing firm. Billy was shopping for boots, but "this was all a ploy, he told her later."[41] He wasn't interested in boots, but in her. She, in turn, found him interesting. "A scent of lovely soap arose, a whiff of talcum. He leaned back in the chair, tall and pale, cool and clean—he himself might have been carved from soap. A high curved forehead, temples already bare, hair with a glint of tinsel, sleepy ivory eyelids."[42] They began dating, which elevated Rhea's prestige in town. She was delighted "at the thought of herself suddenly singled out, so unexpectedly chosen, with the glow of a prizewinner—or a prize—about her now, a grace formerly hidden."[43]

But "Billy brought her honor everywhere but at home. That was not unexpected—home, as Rhea knew it, was where they cut you down to size."[44] Billy, for his part, expressed apparent admiration for Rhea's family, but Rhea—the reader following suit—sees condescension beneath his words. "And all the time Billy Doud said how much he admired Rhea's father. Men like your father, he said. Who work so hard. Just to get along. And never expect any different. And are so decent, and even-tempered, and kindhearted. The world owes a lot to men like that."[45] She and Billy, however, are not having sex, while Billy's friend Wayne and his girlfriend, Lucille, indeed are; and in a statement correlative to the time period in terms of male attitudes toward women, Billy tells Rhea that Wayne intends to marry Lucille, who was good wife material: she is not especially pretty nor very smart but for those very reasons he would not need to worry about the safety of the marriage.

A white space now inaugurates a return to the where the story began: sitting around in Monk's. Wayne, who caught Rhea's eye from across the room, now comes over to sit beside her, the suggestion of his interest in her not difficult to perceive. They converse, they flirt; Rhea feels safe with him, not because he's not a male, a sexual being, but safe because she and he are of the same ilk. She is not out of her league with him as she is with Billy. Together they head off to the bathroom; hanky-panky, as they used to say, ensues, but it is interrupted by Rhea vomiting up the Coke-and-booze Wayne had given her. Mrs. Monk drives her home, and she rather stumbles into bed.

She awakens the next morning hung over and full of thought about Wayne and a comment she recalled him making last evening: "I'd like to fuck you if you weren't so ugly."[46] So, of course, she has to obsess about that; did he really believe she was ugly? *Was* she ugly? She could not confide in her rough father or in her mother, who it is now revealed, is in the hospital. Rhea knows they would not be of any help to her. "You cannot let you parents anywhere near your real humiliations."[47] Rhea goes for a walk, and from the vantage point of an old tree house her brother had built, she spots Eunie Morgan out walking in her pajamas; Rhea is not aware that Eunie's parents had not found her in her bed and how considered her missing. Once again the two elements of this story, the two "plotlines," the two primary characters, are brought together, this time more or less actually crossing paths. Everything about Eunie strikes a note of familiarity with Rhea; she isn't overly concerned or curious about what Eunie is up to. As she watches Eunie, who isn't aware she is being observed, she remembers their earlier days of play and friendship; but she must address the most pressing issue: Wayne. She calls him; he comes over for a discussion. He feels remorse for calling her ugly; she tells him not to marry Lucille but to go to Calgary, where he has a newspaper job waiting for him, and simply leave a good-bye note for Lucille. Rhea volunteers to ride with him as far as Toronto, where she would stay and find a job. "She would always swear it was what she had meant to do."[48] What this sentence does is afford the reader a glance forward to the future, which in effect shifts the story into a new "real" time and renders the entire story more or less as a flashback, apparently narrated from a point in time many years subsequent to the unfolding of events that up to this point had been understood as "now."

A white space brings Eunie back into the picture, the point of view now hers. She returns home from her strange walk to find, in the kitchen waiting for her, not only her parents but also the chief of police: "He disliked anything puzzling or disruptive, anything that might force him to make decisions which could be criticized later or result in his looking like a fool,"[49] and Billy Doud— Eunie's father having called Billy's father, the town's rich man, as one would do in any emergency, but he's forgotten that Mr. Doud was deceased and so Billy came. Eunie tells some fantastic tale suggesting having dealt with aliens from space. Billy Doud thought her story enchanting. She experiences temporary fame, newspaper people and book people coming to see and talk with her. Her fame didn't last, of course, and when writing to Rhea, her father mentioned that Eunie made no money from her experience—a typical small-town, small-minded response to someone undergoing an unusual experience: how much money can be made from it? Authorial stepping in, for two paragraphs, informs the reader that Rhea and Wayne both went to Calgary, where they lived for years to come, married.

Years later, Rhea is back in town, she and Wayne long married and parents of three children, and when visiting the cemetery she spots Lucille's name on a tombstone (Wayne's girlfriend back when the two couples double-dated), and Rhea is made aware of the approach of old age. "There in the cemetery she says out loud, 'I can't get used to it.'"[50] She and Wayne visit the Douds—Billy and Eunie long married as well.

The remaining stories in the collection present themselves not as successfully as the three stories previously discussed. "The Albanian Virgin" is an unusual story; not set in typical Munro country, but rather in mountains, in a place with a name obviously not English and populated by non-English-speaking inhabitants. As the first pages unfold the storyline, a woman is seen to have been traveling in, so it is to be gathered by various references made, the Balkans, but apparently—there is just a feel of this at this point—not in the present day. A white space brings a transition to, indeed, the present, and the narrative shifts from third-person to first, and the "I," the narrator, is a Canadian woman visiting a friend in the hospital. The friend confides she's been spending her time "making up a story, for a movie!"[51] (Although, pretty clearly, she is in no way affiliated with the movie business.) What has been submitted in the first pages of the story *as* the story is now learned to be the story this friend is composing in her head. The pages of the "old" story continue to add up, beautifully written, as this woman traveler seeks to escape from Muslim captors. But the confusion on the correlation between the two storylines becomes increasingly frustrating, the two storylines simply never cohering into one.

The collection's title story is about a girl's disappearance, another story based on that premise (the general incident around which, it will be remembered, the eminently more successful "Spaceships Have Landed" revolved). The story's opening is simply too clever and even too confusing; the story falters at the outset, the reader ungrabbed. A girl by the name of Heather Bell disappeared from the annual hike of a group called the Canadian Girls in Training, led by sixty-something Mary Johnstone, who always leads the hike. The basic—and nearly fatal—problem is that the story suffers from too many storylines and too many characters with pasts and with past stories that, rather than gaining power for the story as a whole, loses for the narrative its focus and power. The time shifts, an important element in Munro's technique of not just storytelling but also character development and advancement, are handled gracefully here;

unfortunately, complication and entanglement of both present and past events leaves this a story the reader is emotionally drawn to but at the same time rebuffed by the almost required need to outline what is going on while reading, to keep matters clear. (This story took its lumps in at least one review of the collection upon its publication. Wendy Lesser, in *The New Republic*, says that the story "falls below its author's usual standards," and that while "not a bad story . . . it is like a pale evocation of all the usual Munro elements." Further, "the subject matter and narrative manner grown from ground that has already been well-tilled so that we are not getting weaker, smaller and less tasty produce from soil that once yielded glorious fruit."[52])

"The Jack Randa Hotel" presents a completely unconvincing character and a plot that, with too many improbable twists, has the feel of a made-for-television script. Additionally, it carries a nasty tone that not only is uncomfortable but also unengaging. "A Wilderness Station" is in epistolary format and qualifies as historical fiction, set almost entirely in the historical past: at least Munro's prose in this case well conjures Canada's frontier environment within the relatively short confines of this story. It is essentially a story about men's misconceptions and prejudices about women—the weaker sex, that is—in the mid-nineteenth century. It is somewhat embracing but not to a remarkable degree. (And this story, as well, is singled out in a full-length study of Munro for its particular lack of success. "The effect of such sloppy narration is to shift the reader's interest away from the event and to focus instead on the storyteller. . . ."[53]) "Vandals" begs the question all short-story writers must face and find a successful answer to: How long will readers go into a narrative unclear about what is going on before they simply give the story up? Munro did not find the answer in this piece.

Short-story collections by their nature, almost by their definition, are uneven; this one is no exception to the—not quite rule—but at least custom. Nonetheless, it coalesces as a cycle of stories more tightly than most of her previous collections; the settings are more clearly defined as the same place, and an almost overarching metaphor is the constant presence in the collection of the Doud family as chief employer and the all-important social place of the Doud family. Thus, for the collection's own good, the weaker stories do not seem to drag down the collection but are supported, as if with arms around the other's shoulders, by the story stars, as if chapters in a novel not as strong but not noticeably so, could be the cast with every independent story in a collection. Is this the advantage of the story cycle? The authors *can* have their cake and eat it, too!

## Notes

1. Alice Munro, *Open Secrets*, New York: Random/Vintage, 1994, p. 3.
2. Alice Munro, *Open Secrets*, p. 4.
3. Alice Munro, *Open Secrets*, p. 4.
4. Alice Munro, *Open Secrets*, p. 6.
5. Alice Munro, *Open Secrets*, p. 8.
6. Alice Munro, *Open Secrets*, p. 9.

7. Alice Munro, *Open Secrets*, p. 9.
8. Alice Munro, *Open Secrets*, p. 11.
9. Alice Munro, *Open Secrets*, p. 13.
10. Alice Munro, *Open Secrets*, p. 17.
11. Alice Munro, *Open Secrets*, p. 18.
12. Alice Munro, *Open Secrets*, p. 20.
13. Alice Munro, *Open Secrets*, p. 25.
14. Alice Munro, *Open Secrets*, p. 25.
15. Alice Munro, *Open Secrets*, p. 31.
16. Alice Munro, *Open Secrets*, p. 33.
17. Alice Munro, *Open Secrets*, p. 37.
18. Alice Munro, *Open Secrets*, p. 40.
19. Alice Munro, *Open Secrets*, p. 48.
20. Alice Munro, *Open Secrets*, p. 51.
21. Alice Munro, *Open Secrets*, p. 52.
22. Alice Munro, *Open Secrets*, p. 54.
23. Alice Munro, *Open Secrets*, p. 55.
24. Alice Munro, *Open Secrets*, p. 58.
25. Alice Munro, *Open Secrets*, p. 59.
26. Alice Munro, *Open Secrets*, p. 66.
27. Alice Munro, *Open Secrets*, p. 64.
28. Alice Munro, *Open Secrets*, pp. 69–70.
29. Alice Munro, *Open Secrets*, p. 80.
30. Alice Munro, *Open Secrets*, p. 250.
31. Alice Munro, *Open Secrets*, p. 226.
32. Alice Munro, *Open Secrets*, p. 226.
33. Alice Munro, *Open Secrets*, p. 228.
34. Alice Munro, *Open Secrets*, p. 230.
35. Alice Munro, *Open Secrets*, p. 231.
36. Alice Munro, *Open Secrets*, p. 231.
37. Alice Munro, *Open Secrets*, p. 230.
38. Alice Munro, *Open Secrets*, p. 231.
39. Alice Munro, *Open Secrets*, p. 237.
40. Alice Munro, *Open Secrets*, p. 239.
41. Alice Munro, *Open Secrets*, p. 240.
42. Alice Munro, *Open Secrets*, p. 240.
43. Alice Munro, *Open Secrets*, p. 240.
44. Alice Munro, *Open Secrets*, p. 241.
45. Alice Munro, *Open Secrets*, p. 241.
46. Alice Munro, *Open Secrets*, p. 250.
47. Alice Munro, *Open Secrets*, p. 251.
48. Alice Munro, *Open Secrets*, p. 253.
49. Alice Munro, *Open Secrets*, p. 255.
50. Alice Munro, *Open Secrets*, p. 259.
51. Alice Munro, *Open Secrets*, p. 86.
52. Wendy Lesser, *New Republic*, 211(October 31, 1994), pp. 51–53.
53. Coral Ann Howells, *Alice Munro*, New York: St. Martin's Press, 1988, p. 127.

# CHAPTER 9

# A STEP UPWARD

Munro's tenth book—her ninth collection of short stories—which is titled *The Love of a Good Woman* and was published in 1998, won the National Book Critics Circle Award for Fiction, indicating not so much the reason for but certainly speaking to it as a reflection of an increased readership and critical appreciation in the United States. Up to the point of this book's appearance, Munro ranked high on the American literary landscape, but this particular story collection emphatically put her on the map. From this point on, Munro will occupy, with Margaret Atwood, the top tier of Canadian fiction writers widely read and highly regarded by American readers and critics.

(Actually, Munro's tenth book was a *Selected Stories*, appearing in 1976, but it gathered stories previously collected—and discussed here—so we shall tarry no further in commenting on it.)

No story in this collection is ineffective; in fact, no story is less than *very* effective. Munro's poise is evermore graceful, her understanding of human behavior increasingly wiser, and her control over her material and the short-story form so second-nature to her that the result is a magnificent ease on her part that allows readers to enter, make comfortable progress through, and exit the narrative with their *own* ease. Despite the provocativeness of some of the themes and situations found in some of the stories, Munro has developed into an extremely hospitable fiction writer: welcoming the reader into her prose to share what she understands about this particular character in this particular situation.

The title story, at nearly eighty pages and thus comprising a fourth of the entire book, is one of the most psychologically complex stories Munro has so far written and one of the most—to use an easy but certainly appropriate word—"beautiful." It is set in Walley, Ontario, a small town near Lake Huron, which Munro has used before; the time is the early 1950s; the story is told from a third-person omniscient point of view; it is divided into a prologue (undesignated as such, but its function as that is quickly realized) and it has four sections, each of which has a Roman numeral and is titled. Munro's process in this story is taking a rather extraordinary event and placing it in an ordinary, even pedestrian, environment and observing how ordinary people react to the event: what it brings out in them, in other words. Reduced to its basic theme, this story is about an affair, common for Munro; but here she delves deeper onto the soulful interior of infidelity and moves this story into a more profound plane of guilt, repentance, and redemption. This is as close to a religious story as Munro has come to write. Munro also explores the "martyr" mentality.

Levels of time are kept to a minimum; on the other hand, Munro's supple yet exact prose style is in full blossom, her loveliness of metaphor, however, never allowing to simply be a brandishing of fancy language without clear meaning ("The wind was warm; it was pulling the clouds apart into threads of old wool...."[1] "Moving her body shook up the information that she was trying to arrange in her head and get used to."[2]). Setting, traditionally a strong element in a Munro story, is the certain, concrete, inescapable, and completely realized foundation of this story. ("This place was called Jutland. There had been a mill once, and some kind of small settlement, but that had all gone by the end of the last century, and the place had never amounted to much at any time. Many people believed that it had been named in honor of the famous sea battle fought during the First World War, but actually everything had been in ruins years before that battle ever took place."[3]). Munro's well-practiced—and in our analysis of all the fiction so far, well-acknowledged—understanding of human nature extends in this story into an understanding of the psychology of teenage boys, of the dying, and of violence. A greatly compelling plot, with nonmanipulative twists and turns, does not compete with Munro's process of character building but enhances it. Lastly, an inventive framing device, which ensures that despite the story's length, the narrative does not sprawl and, in effect, tightens the story's thematic exploration of its several themes and plotlines. The device is this, set in place by the story's first paragraph:

> For the last couple of decades, there has been a museum in Walley, dedicated to preserving photos and butter churns and horse harnesses and on old dentist's chair and a cumbersome apple peeler and such curiosities as the pretty little porcelain-and-glass insulation that were used on telegraph poles.[4]

The second paragraph reveals the existence in this museum of a box of optometrist's instruments belonging to Mr. D. M. Willens, who drowned in the local river in 1951. The plot is given further dimension by the next line: "It [the box of instruments] escaped the catastrophe and was found, presumably by the anonymous donor, who dispatched it to be a feature of our collection."[5]

This paragraph is followed by Section I, called "Jutland," and the time period is exactly established as a Saturday morning in the spring of 1951. Three boys, friends, have come out into the countryside outside their hometown to go swimming, and the isolation of this location is clear: "The turnaround spot came before you got to the ditch, but the whole area was so overrun by nettles, and cow parsnips, and wooly wild hemlock in a wet year, that cars would sometimes have to back out all the way to the proper road."[6] The boys are single-minded in their pursuit of fun, unmindful of detail—*new* details—of their surroundings, as boys will be. "The car tracks to the water's edge on that spring morning were easy to spot but were not taken notice of by these boys, who were thinking only about swimming . . . they would go back to town and say that they had been swimming at Jutland before the snow was off the ground."[7] A murder-mystery tone thus begins to waft off the page, and the tone is heightened when "by this time they were close enough to the water to have had their attention caught by something more extraordinary than car tracks."[8] A Stephen King-esque eeriness, increases which arises with the line, "There was a pale-blue shine to the water that was not a reflection of sky. It was a whole car, down in the pond on a slant, the front wheels and the nose of it poking into the mud on the bottom, and the bump of the trunk nearly breaking the surface. Light blue was in those days an unusual color for a car, and its bulgy shape was unusual, too. They knew it right away. The little English car, the Austin, the only one of its kind surely in the whole country. It belonged to Mr. Willens, the optometrist."[9]

One of Munro's trademark thumbnail sketches of a character, which we have noticed are as piquant as they are concise, is supplied about the optometrist: "He looked like a cartoon when he drove [his blue car], because he was a short but thick man, with heavy shoulders and a large head. He always seemed to be crammed into his little car as if it was a bursting suit of clothes."[10] The boys can now observe the apparently dead Mr. Willens in the car.

The boys now head home, and the story opens to explore the boys' lives individually, Munro rendering them complete individuals and completely individual. The story rightly views them initially within their group mentality and just as appropriately follows up to tell their individual, personal stories of their own unique family dynamics. As it turns out, regardless of the tenor of their home lives and their own kind of relationship with their family, none of the boys revealed what they had seen that afternoon. The three of them reconnect after dinner:

"Did you tell?"
"Did you?"
"Me neither."[11]

They proceed to walk downtown, and in the process they unintentionally pass the optometrist's house and office. Mrs. Willens is out tending to her yard, and seeing her makes recent events disjointed in their mind. "What they knew, what they had seen, seemed actually to be pushed back, to be defeated, by not knowing it."[12] They proceed onward, just occupying time on a Saturday evening; but, of course, later on one of the boys tells a parent what they'd discovered out in the countryside, and the authorities are called. This first section ends by

Munro accomplishing two "procedures": first, establishing a framing device by momentarily flashing forward, by which the entire story is given the slight sepia tone of recollection from memory's vaults; second, stitching a layer of small-town attitude and habits to the story's foundation of setting. These procedures are achieved simultaneously by this brief paragraph: "Something was made of the boys' sitting down and eating their dinners and never saying a word. And then buying a bunch of licorice whips. A new nickname—Deadman—was found and settled on each of them. Jimmy and Bud bore it till they left town, and Cece—who married young and went to work in the elevator—saw it passed on to his two sons. By that time nobody thought of what it referred to."[13]

The story's second section is entitled "Heart Failure" and its connection to the first section is unclear—no, *unknown*—for several pages. A woman named Enid is writing something in a notebook: the term "glonerulonephritis." But a few pages into this section it has now become clear that not only is Enid a nurse taking care of a dying woman in the woman's own house but also that this is the *story's* story: the actual heart of the narrative, which, it is to be assumed, will explain the first section, at least the background to Dr. Willens's strange, fatal accident.

Young Mrs. Quinn will soon succumb to the aforementioned disease; she is in the final stages of her mortal struggle. Mrs. Quinn's husband is someone Enid knew in school. "She felt some embarrassment now because he was one of the boys—in fact, the main one—that she and her girlfriends had teased and tormented. . . . Why did they treat him this way, longing to humiliate him? Simply because they could."[14] (Munro is ever-conscious of the popular versus nonpopular dynamics in school and the resonance of one's social position in schooldays even into adulthood.) The Quinns have two little girls, but the husband appears not to want to spend much time with his wife on her sickbed; and she is quite vocal—even sarcastic—about it to Enid. Munro sensitively enters the mind of a terminally ill person: "Enid thought she knew what this meant, this spite and venom, the energy saved for ranting. Mrs. Quinn was flailing about for an enemy. Sick people grew to resent well people, and sometimes that was true of husbands and wives, or even of mothers and their children. Both husband and children in Mrs. Quinn's case."[15] Despite Enid being used to being detested by her patients for her good health, and being able, under ordinary circumstances, to appreciate the misery they were going through, Mrs. Quinn presents a different case. Enid cannot come up with a reason why, but "she could not conquer her dislike of this doomed, miserable young woman."[16] Enid figured that if Mrs. Quinn cracked under the strain of her illness, "there would be nothing but sullen mischief . . . inside her."[17]

A white space brings a six-page flashback filling in biographical background to Enid, one of the story's few time-shifts. Enid is twenty and nearing completion of her nurse's training. Her father lies dying in the local hospital, and on his deathbed he suggests to her he is not happy with her career choice. Her mother explains that Enid's father has come to decide nursing coarsens a woman, leaving her too familiar with male bodies. Enid does give it up; her father was rich enough she could continue living at home and not work. Years passed. "Children not related to her would grow up calling her Aunt."[18]

Enid is offered the opportunity to take care of ill people at home, as a practical nurse rather than a registered one, and since her promise to her father had been to not work in a hospital, she takes up the assignment. In an ironically humorous line, which, of course, the deliverer does not realize is actually very funny, Enid's mother, in agreeing that such a home-nursing situation would not be a violation of her father's objection, says, "If the only men you get to see are men who are never going to get out of bed again, you have a point."[19]

The years pass . . .

The narrative returns to the story's "real" time, for Munro to explore the relationship between Enid and Mr. Quinn—Rupert—who Enid had known back in her school days. Their current relationship has a much different tone from that which she must endure from his wife; theirs is an increasingly comfortable relationship, prompting a surmise that perhaps something is springing up between them. Mrs. Quinn grows progressively irritable as she declines further physically; but a conversation between her and Enid draws a connection between this section of the story and the first section. As it turns out, Enid's parents' house, in which Enid has always lived and where she lives with her widowed mother, is next door to Mr. Willens, the optometrist; and Mrs. Quinn asked Enid if she went to his funeral, to which Enid responds negatively. An enigmatic line now "thickens" the plot, as it were: "Enid thought of Mr. Willens handing her a rose. His joking gallantry that made the nerves of her teeth ache, as from too much sugar."[20]

Because Mrs. Quinn is worsening, Enid now sleeps on a cot in the patient's room; Enid is now plagued by bad dreams, which can only be described as sex dreams, she waking up sweaty, unrepentant. In other words, she would awaken as if in her dreams she awakened as a sexual being for the first time. Almost immediately after awakening, however, she would return to her true being: experiencing disgust and humiliation at having had such a dream. She would begin her workday, thrusting herself into it, certain that repentance would come from hard work. She was "trying to be good. An angel of mercy. . . ."[21] That she would be dreaming about sex and not in a gentle, romantic fashion, is apt. After all, she's inexperienced and she's in the house with a still-vigorous young man (and he and Enid continue their conversations in the evenings) whose wife will die soon. Such dreams naturally would leave her uncomfortable and feeling guilty, just in and of themselves; add also the factor of the promise she'd made her father on his deathbed that she would give up her quest to be a registered nurse and work in a hospital, to avoid any growing familiarity with the male body. Enid kept the promise to him, yet here she is "indulging" in graphic dreams about the sex act. Unwanted. But *are* they?

At the end of this section, Mrs. Quinn, adding a shocking twist to a plotline already increasingly compelling with its near-murder-mystery breakneck speed, says to Enid that Mr. Willens, the deceased optometrist, had been in her bedroom with her.

Section III is titled "Mistake" and what exactly Mrs. Quinn meant and what exactly happened to Mr. Willens that he and his little car would end up under water is now replayed with the dramatic tension of the denouement of a mystery novel. It seems—Mrs. Quinn is not directly narrating this scene; the narration is in the third-person omniscient—Mr. Willens was giving Mrs. Quinn an eye exam, and this was right before she fell ill, and he was being too touchy, which he apparently had been before. Rupert stormed into the room and beat him to death; and it was Mrs. Quinn who suggested driving his car and his dead body into the river. The very beginning of the story is referenced—remember, the box of optometrist materials in the town museum—when, after an involved process of disposing of Mr. Willens and his car and Mrs. Quinn cleaning up any evidence in the house, Mrs. Quinn realizes "there on the table was sitting the dark-red box with Mr. Willens's things in it and his name on it and it had been sitting there all the time. She didn't remember putting it there or seeing Rupert put it there. She had forgotten all about it."[22] She hid it and never revealed where it was hidden. That is not all; at the end of every eye exam, when Mrs. Quinn asked how much was owed, Mr. Willens would not charge but would virtually rape her on the floor. The last and short paragraph concluding this startling section is not a direct quote to Enid from Mrs. Quinn, but an indirect one: "They said his head got bunged up knocking against the steering wheel. They said he was alive when he went into the water. What a laugh."[23]

The fourth and last section of the story is provocatively titled "Lies." The section's opening reveals Enid distressed over the information Mrs. Quinn has revealed to her. The section title might indicate there is some doubt in Enid's mind, or the omniscient narrative is stating it unequivocally, as to the authenticity of events as Mrs. Quinn has shared them. What definitely *is* a problem is that a crime has been confessed to, authentically or not, and what does Enid do with this information? Enid tends to the two little Quinn children with particular care the next day, wanting "them to hold something in their minds that could throw a redeeming light on whatever came later. On herself, that is, and whatever way she would affect their lives."[24] Redemption is thus spoken of again; Enid's striving for it is an issue with her once more. Apparently, her striving for it is derived from more than just the sex dreams. Does she plan to tell the authorities about Mrs. Quinn's confession? Turn Rupert in? Is that what is implied here? Mrs. Quinn is in her final hours and presently surrenders to her fatal illness, Enid having been, over these last few hours of Mrs. Quinn's life, as hands-off as she ever had been with a dying patient.

Munro accomplishes intense psychological probing in this story. The exception is a clear understanding of Enid's thinking not shared. Consequently, the reader's concentration on Enid's next action is necessary, even to the point of rereading certain passages to completely comprehend her motives. (Munro is being oblique, but one guesses purposefully; complex emotions, full of conflicts, ambiguities, and extreme statements of behavior are in keeping with Enid as she had been portrayed and developed thus far.) Enid drives out to the farm the afternoon of Mrs. Quinn's funeral, but after it is over, when Rupert would be home. She had dressed up, and well. Ambiguity reigns in this line: "When she put these things on she had thought how this might be the last time that she would dress herself and the last clothes she would ever wear."[25] Once inside the house, she "had almost forgotten her excuse, lost touch of the way things were to go."[26] She requests that Rupert take her out in his rowboat into the river, so she may get a photograph of the riverbank. Is she about to sacrifice herself, for redemption for her unclean thoughts and him from his crime? Munro now carefully lays out Enid's thinking at this point, what exactly is her plan, and it does entail her laying her life on the line, and if she does not kill herself then she will have been and will continue to be what she had made of her life: forgetting her own needs and desires to tend to those of others. Consequently, when they are in the boat in the middle of the river she intends to tell Rupert that she cannot swim and second, that she is wondering if it were true he killed Mr. Willens? Further, that she didn't plan to tell anyone, but he definitely should tell, for no one could live with that on their conscience. "If she had got so far, and he had neither denied what she said nor pushed her into the river, Enid would know that she had won the gamble."[27] The gamble with her life, that is.

Before they venture out onto the river, Rupert takes Enid into the room where Mrs. Quinn had lain suffering and died only days ago, and Enid hears Mrs. Quinn saying the word "lies" and wonders if the tale she had told about Mr. Willens is true. The intensity of the story's psychology draws tighter, requiring, once again, that the reader carefully follow Enid's train of thought. She realizes that if she doesn't ask Rupert, and she certainly doesn't absolutely have to, then things will remain as they are now, with everyone believing Mr. Willens had an accident out on that forsaken road; and "as long as that was so, this room and this house and her life held a different possibility, an entirely difficult possibility from the one she had been living with (or glorying in— however you wanted to put it) for the last few days."[28] She realizes silence on her part would bring a "different possibility,"[29] and that "benefits could bloom."[30] "This [letting things slide] was what most people knew. A simple thing that it has taken her so long to understand. This was how to keep the world habitable."[31] Just go along, in other words.

They prepare for going out on the river in the rowboat, with Enid in a completely different frame of mind now. As Rupert searches for boots for her to wear, she thinks about clearing out all the house's accumulation of clutter and how she would establish her own sense of order there. As she dons the boots, Rupert stands next to her, his maleness, his male smell, assails her—positively, not in revulsion, for "there was something new and invasive about the smell of a body so distinctly not in her power or under her care. That was welcome."[32] They get the boat ready, which brings the end of the story, leaving in the reader's mind that Enid will not tell Rupert what she knows. Further, it is not too big a leap to guess she and he will marry.

What does this story have to say about the issue of Munro's attitude toward female and male characters? It has been posited previously in this survey that, essentially, she does not care for her women characters, particularly in the earlier stories, which frequently featured adolescent female narrators, and that the perspective on gender was not so much self-denigrating but, rather, the mother characters often were set up as complainers, whiners, ever-discontented with their lot in life. Further, the traditional female activities in which they engaged proved boring to the young narrator, who found greater comfort in the company of her father, whose work and play were more enjoyable and whose character was more sympathetically drawn.

In the course of our analysis of later stories, we did indeed witness, as Munro moved away from writing stories predominantly about teenage girls in their high-school distress and with quiet-man fathers and snappish mothers, a correlative shift in her view toward the genders, a move toward a middle stance, a more balanced position taken. An evening out of sympathy, a broadening of understanding of both men and women and what they did with their lives. So, the question now is, where does Munro's gender-attitude stand at this point, in this masterpiece of a story? To quickly summarize would be to announce Munro's balance here; she is now presenting characters, both female and male, layered and rounded to consummate reality. Enid, the story's major character, is in some ways enigmatic but is in all ways a real person; the reader is drawn with alacrity to sympathize with her inner turmoil, namely her wrestling with good and bad impulses within her. Mr. Willens, the optometrist, is sleazy, but he needs to be in order to play his role in not only Mrs. Quinn's life, but also whose death is mandatory for Enid's life to take the direction it needs to take for not only redemption but also fulfillment. To have good qualities shown of him is unnecessary in his offstage presence; he is simply the agent of change for Enid. Rupert, on the other hand, is very much a stage presence. In him there are elements of the "traditional" Munro male character: a man of action over talk, physically strong but uncomfortable with emotion; even dangerous in his passions. But Rupert is presented in no less than three full dimensions because of his Munro "traditionalism."

The next story in the collection, titled "Jakarta," also offers itself as an edifying "laboratory" wherein Munro cultivates her attitudes toward the genders and gender roles. This story in particular concerns itself with women's social and domestic roles—specifically, about self-perceptions of their roles—but also, as importantly, how women relate to one another and the demands of young motherhood. The story is also a working out, toward the other end of life's spectrum, of the theme of growing old and acceptance of the death of a spouse. It springs from a certain time period, or more precisely, the atmosphere in the world at large during a certain time period: the settling into place of the cold war, when capitalism versus Marxism was party conversation among educated people and the word "pinko" still got tossed around. Unfortunately, the story is somewhat oblique; the ending might as well have trailed off with an actual ellipses. A certain tone permeates the story: a nostalgic one, a wistful one, of better days in the past.

In Section I, although it is not actually numbered or titled (Sections II and III will be so designated by Roman numerals), Kath and Sonje are grown women friends, who, with their husbands, and with Kath's baby, are staying in old vacation cabins on the beach, in the vicinity of Vancouver. Kath and Sonje keep themselves separate, when out on the beach, from a group of other young mothers, whom they refer collectively to as the "Monicas," even though only one of the women is actually named that. Munro sets up this situation to resemble school society, a certain segment of the social order in school in which two girls do not aspire to popularity but exclude themselves and protect their identity from the clique that socially dominates but whose members seem to eschew individuality. The Monicas are, in Kath and Sonje's eyes, guilty of "turn[ing] the whole beach into a platform. Their burdens, their strung-out progeny and maternal poundage, their authority, can annihilate the bright water."[33] Kath, from whose perspective the first section of the story is told, resists full devotion to maternity and its processes, "so as not to sink into a sledge of animal function."[34] Kath and Sonje, as information comes to the fore in a relatively brief filling in of backstory, had known each other in earlier years and just happened to both be in residence in this "colony" of vacation houses; they both used to work at the public library in Vancouver, and in a sure sign of the times, Kath was required to quit when she was six months pregnant, "lest the sight of you should disturb the patrons."[35]

Sonje had quit the library job because of a scandal; the newspaper had reported that her journalist husband had made a trip to China, and when it was found out that she and he were American, not Canadian, suspicions arose, and "there was concern that in her job she might be promoting Communist books and influencing children who used the library."[36] Again, this is an example of the kind of sociopolitical thinking that went on in those times. From Kath's point of view, now that they had encountered each other again, shouldn't Sonje be planning on a baby. It was the usual progression of life: marriage, then parenthood. But Kath has a somewhat progressive streak, which shows up one day when Sonje states that her happiness depends on her husband, and Kath, who doesn't verbally reply, nevertheless doesn't see herself that way nor does she desire to.

The story's second section, so designated by a roman numeral, propels the storyline forward in time, and this section is told in third person from the point of view of Kent, Kath's husband. Kent is married to his third wife now, Deborah, and the scene sees them in the United States, in Oregon, looking up Sonje and Cottar. (So it happened, at the end of that summer during which the couples had occupied neighboring cabins, Sonje had come down to this Oregon town to take care of Cottar's mother while he went off on another journalist assignment.) They get directions locally, and outside the house to which they were directed they see an old woman gardening. It wasn't the mother but Sonje herself. "He had made the usual mistake, of not realizing how many years—decades—had gone by. And how truly ancient the mother would have to be by now. How old Sonje would be, how old he was himself."[37] And Sonje makes an identifying mistake, too: guessing (incorrectly of course) that Deborah is his daughter by Kath.

Cottar, she reveals, has been dead for more than thirty years, dying of a tropical disease in Jakarta, Indonesia, and buried there.

Section III quickly pulls the story back to the time and place in which the first section was set, and again it is told from Kath's point of view. Sonje and

Cottar are having a farewell party at the end of that summer, before he goes off to Indonesia and she to Oregon to take care of his mother. All the people in their beach neighborhood were asked, all the "Monicas" and their spouses; and it was a heady gathering. "Everybody in the room was so certain of everything. When they paused for breath it was just to draw on an everlasting stream of pure virtue, pure certainty."[38] The party unfolds over the course of several pages. Kathy is kissed by a strange man and she loves the thrill of the experience. Section IV of the story, from Kath's perspective, jumps back to the future time of the second section, and Sonje is "ranting" about her husband Cottar's death, having always felt there were mysterious, untold circumstances surrounding it, and that he might even still be alive. Obviously, her devotion to him had cost her some degree of rationality.

"Cortes Island" is unfolded absolutely effortlessly; Munro's material could not rest more easily in her steady hands. This story is a return to first-person narration, about a young married woman in the 1950s facing choices about traditional domesticity or something less conventional: "Chess [her husband] and I both came from homes where unmarried sex was held to be disgusting and unforgivable, and married sex was apparently never mentioned and soon forgotten. . . . It seemed as if their main itch had been for houses, property, power mowers, and home freezers and retaining walls."[39] A curtain was hung separating the alcove where they had a bed, from the kitchen, the curtain symbolic of the narrator's need to separate her "private" self from her married life, for behind the curtain she read books and wrote in notebooks: in essence, the need for a room of one's own. But her view of the male side of the working world arose from traditional values of her own: "He [her husband, Chess] worked hard, not asking that the work he did fit in with any interests he might have had or have any purpose to it that he might once have honored. . . . But then, I thought, it's what men do."[40]

The narrator herself seeks a job, but her notions of male-female differences color her attitude: she believes herself incapable of learning anything new, lacking confidence that as a woman she can function comfortably in the world outside the home. One of the story's most interesting dynamics is the narrator's relation with the woman upstairs, the mother of the man who owns the building; and, by the way, this man always has a cough: "Each cough was a discreet independent statement, defining his presence in the basement as a necessary intrusion. He did not apologize for being there, but he did not move around in the place as if he owned it."[41] Anyway, his mother, living upstairs from the narrator with her invalid husband, is the ultimate snoop, which she attempts to pass off as neighborliness. "Her appetite for friendliness, for company, took no account of resistance."[42] When the narrator seeks to find employment, the upstairs neighbor offers her the job of sitting with her stroke-victim husband for a few afternoons a week, so she could do some volunteer work. From the word "go," as they say, the reader, but not the neighbor, has the uneasy sense that this isn't going to go well; and, indeed, it doesn't. The husband allows the narrator access to some information about his wife and his shared past that is quite disturbing; but the babysitting for him is over, when she is offered a job working in a library: a traditional female job back then, but one that the narrator grows comfortable with and from it finds herself and a place for herself: "I moved with a sense of release and purpose."[43] She and her husband move out of the apartment into a much nicer place. "We fell in love with each other in a new way, in love with our new status, our emergence into adult life from the basement that had been only a very temporary way station."[44]

The woman upstairs turns vicious when they move out; it's obvious the woman knows that the secrets of her past had been exposed. The narrator, in the last two paragraphs of the story, admits—and it's almost a beautiful admission—that the old man, the invalid, often inhabited her dreams, because in her mind, based on what he'd informed her when she was babysitting with him, he was a swashbuckling character who had murdered a man and run off with his wife: a romantic figure, in other words.

The other particularly outstanding story, in this collection of generally outstanding ones, is called "The Children Stay." Thematically, this story falls into the category of "outsiderness," a common one for Munro. Additionally, not a unique situation for her, this is a story of an affair and woman's interpretation of her marriage as stifling. Time—that looming factor in any Munro story, its employ not only a construction device but also a character exploration method for her—is presented relatively straightforwardly here, with no elaborate shifting from one time level to another. Another feature of this story is also a common Munro technique: despite time shifts not being the *ascendant* trait, the story's "real" time is indeed framed by a future perspective. The story's opening line is, "Thirty years ago, a family was spending a holiday together on the coast of Vancouver Island."[45]

That Munro consistently finds the telling statement about an affair that most clearly elucidates what the experience is making this particular *experience* bears further citing: "When she had started to quote Jeffrey, Pauline had felt a giving-way in her womb or the bottom of her stomach, a shock that had traveled oddly upwards and hit her vocal chords."[46]

"Save the Reaper" is a compelling story populated by a variety of characters. Two tones mix here: one of nostalgia (that times past were better, and a tone of tension), the kind of tension deriving from an actual life-threatening circumstance. The story begins with a relatively considerable amount (for Munro, that is) of backstory about characters, in which relevant—indeed, emphasis here on *relevant*, and not excessive and extraneous—information about them is told. In the long run, it does not prove sluggish to the narrative flow getting underway. The specific plot situation is this: a grandmother is driving her two young grandchildren down country roads, playing a car game with them. She is essentially killing time. Some rather scary events ensue. When the grandmother relates the incident to her daughter and her daughter's husband, she leaves lots of details out. Her little grandson flashes her "a flat look, a moment of conspiratorial blankness, a buried smile, that passed before there could be any need for recognition of it."[47] The subsequent few lines not only summarize this story but also serve as a brief position paper on Munro's chief preoccupation in her fiction: "What did this mean? Only that he [her grandson] had begun the private work of storing and secreting, deciding on his own what should be preserved and how, and what these things were going to mean to him, in his unknown future."[48]

"Rich As Stink" suffers from vagueness of point and of characterization. It's about, essentially, a girl going to spend the summer with her mother and her mother's boyfriend; she lives with her father during the school year. But the relationship between the mother and this man remains muddy, as does his with his wife, who is the mother's neighbor and landlord. An accident that summer causes the girl grievous bodily harm, which has considerable emotional impact on her mother and boyfriend and the boyfriend's wife.

"Before the Change" is in epistolary form, which is off-putting from the very beginning; there is a resultant artificiality to the story, not simply because of the epistolary form but due to Munro's own execution of it: the writer of the letters tells her correspondent information he obviously already knows, or in narrating events to him that he was involved in. The story is about abortion, certainly a more hot-button sociological and political issue than Munro has touched before; and her description of the abortion procedure is quite graphic. The backbone of the story is the narrator letter writer's relationship with her father, who is a physician, and the truth of his "special cases" dawns on her. The doctor is drawn darkly, not as a compassionate person; his allowance of "special cases" to come to him for treatment arise, we gather, more for revenue than sympathy for the plight of others.

"My Mother's Dream" concludes the collection; it is a story about, on a general level, women devoting themselves to the care and well-being of a heroic male. On the same general level, it is about a mother-daughter conflict, but with a different take on it for Munro: an infant daughter and her mother. It is told in the first person, but which, in this case, proves an awkward technique, for the narrator knows more than she should about things happening before she was born and when she was quite young.

From the *Yale Review* response to this collection is this concluding line: "Munro knows her characters intimately, yet she is at peace with the fact their lives will, and should, retain a fundamental mysterious quality."[49]

## Notes

1. Alice Munro, *The Love of a Good Woman*, New York: Random/Vintage, 1998, p. 8.
2. Alice Munro, *The Love of a Good Woman*, p. 63.
3. Alice Munro, *The Love of a Good Woman*, p. 4.
4. Alice Munro, *The Love of a Good Woman*, p. 3.
5. Alice Munro, *The Love of a Good Woman*, p. 3.
6. Alice Munro, *The Love of a Good Woman*, p. 5.
7. Alice Munro, *The Love of a Good Woman*, p. 5.
8. Alice Munro, *The Love of a Good Woman*, p. 6.
9. Alice Munro, *The Love of a Good Woman*, p. 6.

10. Alice Munro, *The Love of a Good Woman*, p. 6.
11. Alice Munro, *The Love of a Good Woman*, p. 22.
12. Alice Munro, *The Love of a Good Woman*, p. 24.
13. Alice Munro, *The Love of a Good Woman*, pp. 30–31.
14. Alice Munro, *The Love of a Good Woman*, p. 33.
15. Alice Munro, *The Love of a Good Woman*, p. 36.
16. Alice Munro, *The Love of a Good Woman*, p. 38.
17. Alice Munro, *The Love of a Good Woman*, p. 38.
18. Alice Munro, *The Love of a Good Woman*, p. 41.
19. Alice Munro, *The Love of a Good Woman*, p. 43.
20. Alice Munro, *The Love of a Good Woman*, p. 50.
21. Alice Munro, *The Love of a Good Woman*, p. 52.
22. Alice Munro, *The Love of a Good Woman*, p. 62.
23. Alice Munro, *The Love of a Good Woman*, p. 62.
24. Alice Munro, *The Love of a Good Woman*, p. 64.
25. Alice Munro, *The Love of a Good Woman*, p. 70.
26. Alice Munro, *The Love of a Good Woman*, p. 71.
27. Alice Munro, *The Love of a Good Woman*, p. 72.
28. Alice Munro, *The Love of a Good Woman*, p. 75.
29. Alice Munro, *The Love of a Good Woman*, p. 75.
30. Alice Munro, *The Love of a Good Woman*, p. 76.
31. Alice Munro, *The Love of a Good Woman*, p. 76.
32. Alice Munro, *The Love of a Good Woman*, p. 77.
33. Alice Munro, *The Love of a Good Woman*, p. 80.
34. Alice Munro, *The Love of a Good Woman*, p. 80.
35. Alice Munro, *The Love of a Good Woman*, p. 81.
36. Alice Munro, *The Love of a Good Woman*, p. 82.
37. Alice Munro, *The Love of a Good Woman*, p. 87.
38. Alice Munro, *The Love of a Good Woman*, p. 95.
39. Alice Munro, *The Love of a Good Woman*, p. 123.
40. Alice Munro, *The Love of a Good Woman*, p. 125.
41. Alice Munro, *The Love of a Good Woman*, pp. 117–118.
42. Alice Munro, *The Love of a Good Woman*, p. 119.
43. Alice Munro, *The Love of a Good Woman*, p. 140.
44. Alice Munro, *The Love of a Good Woman*, p. 142.
45. Alice Munro, *The Love of a Good Woman*, p. 181.
46. Alice Munro, *The Love of a Good Woman*, p. 197.
47. Alice Munro, *The Love of a Good Woman*, p. 180.
48. Alice Munro, *The Love of a Good Woman*, p. 180.
49. Michael Frank, *Yale Review*, 87(2) (April 1999), p. 157.

CHAPTER 10

# HER BEST BOOK YET

Munro's tenth short-story book, titled (unfortunately) *Hateship, Friendship, Courtship, Loveship, Marriage*, was published in 2001. The author's previous collection, *The Love of a Good Woman*, placed her securely within critical and popular estimation as a foremost practitioner of the short story in English. By her tenth book she took a step even higher in the international fictional pantheon to now be regarded simply as one of the world's best fiction writers, period. *Hateship, Friendship, Courtship, Loveship, Marriage* is her best book to date ("to date" including the two collections that have appeared after it). It presents more superior stories—superior to herself as well as to other short-story writers—than any other collection of hers. At least four of the stories (out of a total of nine) can claim perfection, one of which is perhaps the most flawless short story ever written in English.

The flawless story is "What Is Remembered." The title summarizes Munro's fundamental fiction "theory": how individuals recall events in their lives or in the lives of others. The secondary theme is a tried one for Munro: when a woman is interested in a man who is not her husband. Munro identifies and fathoms the actions and mental processes and emotional thrills and despair associated with infidelity. This line snaps with electricity as the main character, a young married woman named Meriel, and the physician she has just met at the funeral of her husband's best friend, have suddenly intersected each others' lives: "A stealthy, considering, almost married glance, its masquerade and its bland intimacy arousing to those who were after all not married."[1]

"What Is Remembered" is a relatively straightforward narrative, but the psychological probing is deep and intense in its exposure of the rawness of human behavior. That said about relative straightforwardness, it remains Munro's most immediate, most obvious, and most admirable presentation of her abiding interest in levels of time. This story is a prime example of, an effortless encapsulation of, the concept—so obviously subscribed to by Munro—of the present being the child of the past: how no thought or action really takes place only in the present time but has provenance in the past, with direct implications for the future course of someone's life or at least the future course of their way of thinking. This time-level structure she has perfected, and it is perfect in "What Is Remembered." With a system of flash-forwards and framing devices, the structure is complicated but not confusing.

The story's first line, "In a hotel room in Vancouver, Meriel as a young woman is putting on her short white summer gloves,"[2] not only identifies the main character and the story's setting but also, with the phrase "as a young woman," suggests the view of events from the distance of time. She and her husband, Pierre, are going to a funeral, having come over to the mainland the previous evening from where they live on Vancouver Island. The funeral is for Pierre's best friend since childhood—Pierre in his late twenties now—who had been killed in a motorcycle accident. From Meriel's perspective, the difference in male and female roles in the 1950s is this: "What a lot they [young husbands] had to learn, so quickly. How to kowtow to bosses and how to manage wives. How to be as authoritative about mortgages, retaining walls, lawn grass, drains, politics, as well as the jobs that had to maintain their families for the next quarter of a century."[3] Pierre and Meriel, after the funeral, part company, he to return home directly but she sidetracking to visit an old friend of her mother's who lives in a nursing home. The doctor who took care of Pierre's friend after his accident, who attended the funeral, graciously offers to drive Meriel to her destination so she won't need to rely on a bus. The visit with the old woman in the nursing home goes well; during the course of this visit, Meriel and the doctor establish "something." Munro's subtle, almost elegant, movements in time to stress a point, or to finalize a point, is shown in consummate shrewdness in this simple but resonant line, about Meriel and the lady she came to visit (whom she has always called "Aunt"): "She had a feeling that she would never see Aunt Muriel again, and she never did."[4]

She and the doctor are not interested in parting company just yet, and he suggests a walk in a park; once there, though, their desire is expressed, a brilliant succinctness and directness, without their naming what is happening between them: "'Take me somewhere else,' she said. He looked her in the face. He said, 'Yes.'"[5] In an interesting sort of twist, which adds a richer burnish to the character of Meriel, she thinks as the doctor takes her to the apartment where he's staying these few hours he's in town for the funeral that, although the apartment building is fine, "a small decent building, three or four stories high,"[6] she "would have preferred another scene, and that was the one she substituted, in her memory."[7]

A combination of the romance of what she was embarking on and the illicitness of it compels her to want the scene to be taking place in a hotel that used to be fashionable but has now gone to seed. "Nothing actually dirty or disrespectable, just an atmosphere of long accommodation of private woes and sins."[8] Why did she need, or desire, this setting to be different than the actual one? "It was for the moment of exposure, the piercing sense of shame and pride that took over her body as she walked though the (pretend) lobby. . . . "[9]

As in old movies, before they were allowed to depict graphic sex scenes, Munro now draws a curtain on the couple, leaving us to know what went on; after a white space, the story continues with Meriel taking the ferry, as planned, back to Vancouver Island. A beautiful summary of the major theme of the story is thus expressed: "The job she had to do, as she saw it [while on the hour-and-a-half ferry ride], was to remember everything—and by 'remember' she meant experience it in her mind, one more time—then store it away forever. This day's experience set in order, none of it left ragged or lying about, all of it gathered in like treasure and finished with, set aside."[10]

As part of the frame of the story that makes it clear it was an event that took place in the past, is this simple statement: Meriel's marriage to Pierre would last and she will never see the doctor again. Cut, dried, quite effective. A white space brings a short elaboration on the rest of Meriel's marriage: she and Pierre, during what turned out to be his fatal illness, are discussing a book about two lovers, but what Meriel is really referring to in this conversation is her experience with the doctor. She eventually sees a notice in a newspaper of the doctor's accidental death, and the story ends with Meriel pondering the role he had played in her life; or rather, the role the memory of him had played.

The collection's title story, despite the cumbersomeness of the title, is a long (more than fifty pages) but lithe piece that, while not as sleek and fleet as the previously discussed story, nevertheless could be called the collection's flagship; after all, it is the longest, it is the first in order of appearance, it lends its title to the collection as a whole, and proves to be a completely enveloping reading experience. This is, in essence, the story of a weak, manipulative man and a strong woman who, oppositely, get things done. Consequently, Munro has reversed traditional gender roles as well as reversed her traditional "allegiance" to male characters. Here, she stands fully in the camp of the story's protagonist, the strong female character—who bears, ironically, masculine traits. Perhaps Joanna, then, is a compromise character for Munro: a strong, masculine female.

The story is told in third person, Munro moving from one character's perspective to another—but the point-of-view shifts occur in sections, not in dizzying one-line shifts. The ancillary characters are well and distinctly drawn. The story's opening two words, "Years ago,"[11] indicate that the story actually took place prior to the time in which it is being narrated, which is being framed by a "real" time that—as this technique in Munro's hands always does—divides the narrative into at least two time periods as well as revealing the story is not simply set in the past. Her next phrase, "before the trains stopped running on so many of the branch lines,"[12] again moves the reader's consciousness backward in time. Within the first paragraph, which is only four lines long, the plot is launched: a woman walks into a railway station and asks the agent for details about shipping furniture. In Munro's trademark thumbnail sketching, the agent "often tried a little teasing with women, especially the plain ones who seemed to appreciate it."[13] And this of the woman asking about shipping furniture: "Her teeth were crowded to the front of her mouth as if they were ready for an argument."[14] The woman explains her situation to the agent; she wants to send a considerable load of furniture to a tiny place in Saskatchewan and she'll be needing a ticket for herself as well, to the same destination: Glynia by name. The ticket man again, for all his brief appearance at the story's beginning, is wrought by Munro with care, humor, and individuality. As he and the woman discuss her plan, he, being a man, reacts to her as a woman: "She might have been under forty, but what did it matter? No beauty queen, ever. He turned all business."[15] He reflects on not knowing who this woman is who is shipping furniture west, when he assumed he knew everyone in town; she and he had never had contact through any of the town' institutions: school, church, restaurants, or stores. She reminds him of a nun he'd seen on television talking about her missionary work. "This nun had smiled once in a while to show that her religion was supposed to make people happy, but most of the time she looked out at her audience as if she believed that other people were mainly in the world for her to boss around."[16]

At this point the story shifts point of view: to the woman, whose name is Joanna. She is off to the local dress shop, called Milady's, to buy an outfit, the occasion for which has yet to be clarified. Obviously, though, this is all part of her preparation for going away. In an instance of insightful atmospheric observation, Munro sees this irony, which she refracts through Joanna's consciousness, of course, about the window display of the dress shop: "Big gaudy paper maple leaves were scattered round the mannequins' feet and pasted here and there on the window. At the time of year when most people's concern was to rake up leaves and burn them, here they were the chosen thing."[17] The six-page scene of Joanna in the dress shop is immaculately rendered: funny, poignant, realistic, and character revealing. Upon stepping into the store, Joanna encounters a full-length mirror and surmises: "They did that on purpose, of course. They set the mirror there so you could get a proper notion of your deficiencies, right away, and then—they hoped—you would jump to the conclusion that your had to buy something to altar the picture."[18] The shop owner approaches, her "girdle so tight her nylons rasped."[19] Joanna indicates a suit she would like to try on. "This was what she'd come prepared for, after all. Clean underwear and fresh talcum powder under her arms."[20] Another garment is brought out, and Joanna approves of it; and she admits to the store owner she is to be married in it. But some ambiguity exists, reinforced by this line: "Her face was hotly flushed because marriage had not, in fact, been mentioned. Not even in the last letter. She had revealed to this woman what she was counting on and that had perhaps been an unlucky thing to do."[21] The store owner's patronizing friendliness is well summarized in this utterance: "Well, I can say my day has not been wasted. I've provided the dress for somebody to be a happy bride in. That's enough to justify my existence."[22]

In the following section, plot information is helpfully supplied. Joanna is house-keeper to a Mr. McCauley, an insurance salesman who apparently does very little business these days. His wife is dead, and his daughter Sabitha, whom Joanna "was the nearest thing [she] had to a mother"[23] since the death of her actual one, has just been taken away to be raised by her late mother's cousin in Toronto. But now, not all is clarified. Joanna—the story's point of view being hers—considers herself a fool for having indicated to the dress shop owner that she was to be married, when "he hadn't mention it."[24] Who is "he"? "His" identity is still unknown. Joanna has been sending "him" letters, and the last one informed him that his furniture is being sent to him via train; and apparently other letters had been dispatched to him previously, these not directly to him, as had been the one concerning the furniture shipment, but rather slipped in with letters Sabitha sent to him.

Joanna leaves her employer Mr. McCauley a note informing him that she has left town and has shipped Mr. Boudreau's furniture to him. (Is this Mr. Boudreau "he"?) Mr. McCauley finds out from a telephone conversation with the station agent where Joanna has gone; and in a telling sense of "small-townness," interjected into the narrative, the station agent maintains to Mr. McCauley, with a couple of people in the station overhearing him, that if he'd known who she was and that she had in essence stolen the furniture, he would have stopped her from fleeing. "This assertion was heard and repeated and believed.... Most people who repeated his words believed that he could and would have stopped her—they believed in the authority of station agents and of upright-waling fine old men in three-piece suits like Mr. McCauley."[25] The point of view now shifts, importantly so for the edification of the reader, to Mr. McCauley's. He was careless in his approach to Joanna, unmindful of her as an individual, and her turning up missing amazes him because she took the furniture with her; and here the story opens up—from his continued perspective—to disseminate even more vital plot information. Ken Boudreau, to whom the furniture is being sent, is Mr. McCauley's son-in-law, husband of Mr. McCauley's deceased daughter, and he now owns a hotel out West; and he had written asking that the furniture be sold and the money for it forwarded to him or that Mr. McCauley advance him some money against the furniture being sold. Mr. McCauley sent him a check but now Joanna has gone with the furniture, so Mr. Boudreau has money *and* his furniture, because Joanna has interfered. Mr. McCauley in his way misses Joanna, but not personally, only because she took care of the house and household. "He belonged to a generation in which there were men who were said not to be able even to boil water, and he was one of them."[26] He is suffering from a keen sense of abandonment: first, his wife dying; second, his daughter eloping; and now Joanna running away with furniture not hers. In his new state, he's become jabbery; people passing him on the street now get an earful of his woes, and considering he used to be so gentlemanly, so reluctant to impart such information, his new opening up is discomfiting for the community. "He should have been the last person to air wrongs or asked for sympathy ... yet here he was, pulling out some letter, asking if it wasn't a shame the way the fellow had taken money from him over and over again, and even now when he'd taken pity on him once more the fellow had connived with the housekeeper to steal furniture."[27] (Of course, in technical terms, right at this point in the story the point of view is being violated: it had been Mr. McCauley's but suddenly snatched from him to an omniscient point of view, but not casually or accidentally on the author's part, but for good, effective use; and, besides, the point of view quickly recovers itself, returning to Mr. McCauley's.) He is becoming, ironically, given the narcissism seen in him, more aware of his surrounding now that he is alone, deserted by the most recent of his female deserters. In the shoe repair shop, where he had been many times before, "the sounds and smells and precise activities of the place had been familiar to Mr. McCauley for years but never identified or reflected upon before."[28] As it turns out, the shoes repairman's daughter was a friend of Mr. McCauley's granddaughter, Sabatha, who, so it will be remembered, has been taken away for a better life by Mr. McCauley's late wife's cousin. With another shift in point of view, the story now comes to rest for the time being in the shoe repairman's household. The shoe repairman mentions to his wife the new tenor of Mr. McCauley's behavior; and interjecting another whiff of small-townness, the shoe repairman's wife reacts to her husband's observation thus: "'Maybe a little stroke,' she said. Since her own operation—for gallstones—she spoke knowledgably and with a placid satisfaction about the afflictions of other people."[29] Their daughter, Edith, is uncomfortable hearing about Joanna's flight out West; and now the story moves—as if it were a living creature—to its most crucial resting place, where past events are tied together to answer the story's mysteries that have so far impeded complete understanding. It comes to rest on the shoulders of the friends Edith and Sabatha. "It had all begun . . . "[30] so this section of the story begins, these four words indicating a flashback, and at the same time a promise of resolution of the lingering questions.

On the way to school one day, Sabatha indicates to Edith she needed to mail a letter to her father at the post office. Edith, so it is explained in authorial commentary, is a sharp, observant child; she notes how fat the envelope is. Sabatha reveals she wrote only one page, and Edith surmises that Joanna has included something. They do not post the letter after all, but take it to Edith's house and steam it open; the upshot is, they get involved in a correspondence between Joanna and Sabatha's father, forging letters and leading Joanna to believe Sabatha's father is interested in her.

A white space returns the story to Joanna and her point of view. She has now arrived at her destination in Saskatchewan, to find the town to not really *be* one, the station only an enclosed shelter. She does, however, find a man to drive her to the hotel in "town." In one bedroom she finds the man she came to marry, Ken Boudreau, who is quite ill. She makes herself at home and tends to his illness. The next day, Ken awakens feeling much better, and a white space brings his point of view of events now to the fore. He recognizes Joanna but doesn't remember her name; by opening her purse behind her back, he learns it again. He also finds her bankbook, and the balance "added a sleek upholstery to the name Joanna Parry."[31]

A return to Joanna's point of view brings a resolution to the story. Ken had mentioned he would like to go on farther west, to British Columbia, and being a take-charge individual, Joanna makes it happen, promising him things will turn out all right. He being basically a weak person, pretty much an advantage taker of other people rather than a director of his own fortune, Ken "understood that she did know, and that it was, it would be, all right."[32]

The story's final section is a typical Munro wrapping up: sending the story ahead into the future, to put a cap on how things turned out—in this case, seen from Edith's point of view, when Mr. McCauley died two years after Joanna left town, a notice in the paper indicating he was survived by his granddaughter and his son-in-law, Ken Boudreau, who was married to Joanna and they had a baby boy, Omar. Edith no longer fears being found out about the forgery she and Sabatha practiced; she does reflect on this irony that "where, on the list of things she planned to achieve in her life, was there any mention of her being responsible for the existence on earth of a person named Omar?"[33]

In the story "Floating Bridge," Munro once again demonstrates an under-standing of and sympathy for the seriously ill; in technique, she once again draws on time shifts to emphasize—give grounding—to a character's present situa-tion. In this case, its employ—the use of time for creating simultaneous depth of character and increased understanding of that character—is in the form of a relatively brief flashback. But the important aspect of it, in addition to what it flashes back to, of course, is that Munro positions it at the start of the story. In other words, the story begins with a two-page flashback. This technique accom-plishes its purpose so fluidly it draws no attention to itself *as* a technique; with its perfect suitability, it insinuates itself into the reader's consciousness as the only correct way for this story to begin. That the "flash" is backward is obvious from the first line: "One time she had left him."[34] As the flashback is developed, it supplies, first, that the "she" in question is Jinny, and the "him" is her husband, Neal, and his crime had been minor. Nevertheless she had walked to a nearby bus shelter for a couple hours; it was a nonserious running away from home, like a child's, simply to make a point, but her brief absence had gone unnoticed by Neal. Jinny sits in the bus shelter pondering the ramifications of truly running away. "But the life she was carrying herself into might not give her anybody to be angry at, or anybody who owed her anything, anybody who could possibly be rewarded or punished or truly affected by what she might do. Her feelings might become of no importance to anybody but herself, and yet they would be bulging up inside her, squeezing her heart and breath."[35]

A white space brings the story into its real time, and quickly it becomes obvious Jinny is suffering from, and being treated for, cancer; she had just been to another visit to her oncologist, and she leaves with news, wondering when to inform Neal—importantly, leaving the reader to wonder if the news is good or bad, whether she is worsening or getting better. The setting is explicit: summer in Ontario. Neal is there in their van to pick her up, and he had along with him a girl from where he works, which is a correctional family for young offenders. The girl is going to be helping them out around the house while Jinny is ill. In one paragraph Munro demonstrates both keen psychological understanding: "... [I]t wasn't time to give him her news if news is what you'd call it. When Neal was around other people, even one person other than Jinny, his behavior changed, becoming more animated, enthusiastic, ingratiating. Jinny was not bothered by that anymore—they had been together for twenty-one years"[36] and a continued ability to, in thumbnail fashion, describe a character, when physical appearance *reflects* character: "Like Neal's antique appearance—the bandana headband, the rough gray ponytail, the little gold earring that caught the light like the gold rims 'round his teeth' and his shaggy outlaw clothes."[37]

This girl who will be helping out lives with foster parents, and upon being picked up at the doctor's office Jinny learns they need to drive to the hospital, where the girl's sister works, to pick something up for her; but as it turns out, the sister forgot to bring the item, so Neal now insists they drive out to the girl's foster parents' house to retrieve it. This brief description, from Jinny's point of view, from which the entire story is told, sizes up the girl and Jinny's rather irritated reaction to her: "Helen's presence was like that of a domestic cat that should never be brought along in any vehicle, being too high-strung to have sense, too apt to spring between the seats."[38] To get there, they drive through neighborhoods Jinny had never been to before, a literal descent in the socioeconomic scale of things, a world apart from Jinny's, which of course the girl Helen represents to her.

This visit is the locus of the story, the main event, the very raison d'etre of the narrative. It is beautifully executed, with the even, elegant choreographing of a ballet. Expectedly, the property they visit is run-down, and as expectedly, there is a small pack of barking, threatening dogs about the place. The people live in a trailer and everyone but Jinny goes inside; she remains outdoors. She notices tree leaves yellowing and some already fallen. Symbolic of what she is facing in terms of her extreme illness? With the narrative unfolding through her consciousness, she indicates no specific perception of the leaves thusly, but their autumnal state certainly strikes a note in the story's overall somber tone. While she remains outdoors, while the others are inside, a young man bicycles up, a teenager, who explains that he is the son of the house; and Jinny reacts to his physical presence, triggered by her class snobbery, which, although never directly expressed, is present nevertheless, in this fashion: "Slim and graceful and cocky, with an ingenuous enthusiasm that would probably not get him as far as he hoped."[39]

The point of the story emerges in perfect clarity when she goes on a drive with the boy. He promises her, "I'm going to show you something like I bet you never seen before."[40] (The diction of the characters, those other than Jinny and Neal's, rings with impeccable accuracy, even though, of course, the narrative is all filtered through Jinny's consciousness.) Thus the story gets summarized in that one brief, highly significant line; for not only is she shown specifically what the boy is referring to—a floating bridge—but also, when he kisses her, a life new to her. Backdropped by her illness (although, a few pages earlier, while Jinny waited outside ruminating on things, it is revealed that the news from the doctor that she hesitated sharing with Neal was actually positive), which has reconfigured her life and altered its tone, she had encountered lifestyles this day quite unlike her own, and an event—kissing the boy—that came with its own uniqueness. "It seemed to her that this was the fist time ever that she had participated in a kiss that was an event in itself. The whole story, all by itself."[41] For the boy, too, it was a new experience in his vast *in*experience: the first time he'd ever kissed a married woman.

Rarely does Munro end a story so cogently, so tightly wrapped up, but she does so in the story's last line: "A swish of tender hilarity, getting the better of all her sores and hollows, for the time given."[42] "For the time given"—at once beautiful and chilling.

The aptness of the title "Family Furnishings" is obvious once this story is recognized as, on its primary thematic level, being about the use of family stories as material for fiction writing: a story obviously close, at least in its theme, to Munro's own heart. A companion theme is the almost clichéd situation of not being able to go home again, articulately expressed by the narrator in this way: "There was a danger whenever I was on home ground. It was the danger of seeing my life through other eyes than my own."[43] An ancillary theme is one Munro has had business with on many previous occasions: the antagonism felt by an adolescent girl for her mother, and correlative to that, the mother's sense of and behavior based on superiority over the father's family. A first-person narration, this story is set primarily in the 1950s Ontario, the tone and subject as well as setting reminiscent of Munro's early stories; it is heavily based on small-town and rural social attitudes and customs of the time. (Family get-together dinners proceeding in this way: "There was hardly any idea of a general conversation, and in fact there was a feeling that conversation that passed beyond certain understood limits might be a disruption, a showing-off."[44]

"Comfort" suffers from sensationalism, from a lack of nuance, as if Munro strains acceptability and credibility when dealing with large social issues outside family situations. Her main characters here are aging, and the story deals with forced retirement and suicide. "Nettles" is woven from Munro basics, a first-person reminiscence piece; the adolescent female lives on a small farm, on which her father raises foxes and mink (an industry that father characters have participated in in earlier stories; and smoothly shifted moments in time. What is new—not appearing on the list of Munro basics, that is—is the theme of loss, and the plot revolving around a big coincidence.

The last of the especially successful stories in this collection (six of the nine can be labeled excellent) is "Post and Beam." This story, too, could be considered a return to Munro "basics," in that the major theme is the pull of family on an individual's current situation. This is a deeply psychological story, but there is nothing confusing or murky in Munro's fathoming of character; in structure, in the author's firm hands at play, the story is however straightforward for Munro. The plot premise is this: Lorna and Brendan are a relatively young married couple with children, who have gotten reacquainted with Lionel—no, simply *acquainted* for Lorna—who had been Brendan's student at the university. The plot twist in the story is achieved by another advent: that of Polly, Lorna's cousin who comes to visit.

Polly is kind of a bumpkin, irritating to Lorna as well as Brendan, and she gets very emotional when she detects they don't want her in their house. But Polly and Lionel both morph into something Lorna doesn't know. This condition does have an effect on her: leading her to see that no big adventuresome changes were awaiting her in life, but husband and children and a nice house were what constitutes, and will always constitute, the source of her happiness.

"Queenie" and "The Bear Came Over the Mountain" are lesser stories. The former concerns a husband who is a domestic tyrant, he being one of the most disagreeable male characters Munro has created; but, then, the primary female character, the title character, is not far from disagreeable herself. But the story is chiefly about the narrator, a young woman who goes to live with her older stepsister and her tyrant of a husband, and the time there becomes her transition time: the dawning of her independence as a grownup, the establishment of her own life.

"The Bear Came Over the Mountain" demonstrates, once again, Munro's understanding of and empathy for people who are seriously ill. A story of ironic twists, the primary irony is, however, in the theme upon which it is constructed: that memory should be such a major aspect of Munro's fiction, and in this story an elderly woman suffers the loss of hers. It boils down to the history of a long-term marriage: that in and of itself is unusual for Munro's married characters. Again, it is a story with force, but not with the force of many of the other stories in the collection.

## Notes

1. Alice Munro, *Hateship, Friendship, Courtship, Loveship, Marriage*, New York: Random/Vintage, 2001, p. 233.

2. Alice Munro, *Hateship, Friendship, Courtship, Loveship, Marriage*, p. 219.

3. Alice Munro, *Hateship, Friendship, Courtship, Loveship, Marriage*, p. 222.

4. Alice Munro, *Hateship, Friendship, Courtship, Loveship, Marriage*, p. 233.

5. Alice Munro, *Hateship, Friendship, Courtship, Loveship, Marriage*, p. 235.

6. Alice Munro, *Hateship, Friendship, Courtship, Loveship, Marriage*, p. 236.

7. Alice Munro, *Hateship, Friendship, Courtship, Loveship, Marriage*, p. 236.

8. Alice Munro, *Hateship, Friendship, Courtship, Loveship, Marriage*, p. 236.

9. Alice Munro, *Hateship, Friendship, Courtship, Loveship, Marriage*, p. 236.

10. Alice Munro, *Hateship, Friendship, Courtship, Loveship, Marriage*, p. 237.

11. Alice Munro, *Hateship, Friendship, Courtship, Loveship, Marriage*, p. 3.

12. Alice Munro, *Hateship, Friendship, Courtship, Loveship, Marriage*, p. 3.

13. Alice Munro, *Hateship, Friendship, Courtship, Loveship, Marriage*, p. 3.

14. Alice Munro, *Hateship, Friendship, Courtship, Loveship, Marriage*, p. 3.

15. Alice Munro, *Hateship, Friendship, Courtship, Loveship, Marriage*, p. 4.

16. Alice Munro, *Hateship, Friendship, Courtship, Loveship, Marriage*, p. 7.

17. Alice Munro, *Hateship, Friendship, Courtship, Loveship, Marriage*, p. 7.

18. Alice Munro, *Hateship, Friendship, Courtship, Loveship, Marriage*, p. 8.

19. Alice Munro, *Hateship, Friendship, Courtship, Loveship, Marriage*, p. 8.

20. Alice Munro, *Hateship, Friendship, Courtship, Loveship, Marriage*, p. 9.

21. Alice Munro, *Hateship, Friendship, Courtship, Loveship, Marriage*, p. 12.

22. Alice Munro, *Hateship, Friendship, Courtship, Loveship, Marriage*, p. 12.

23. Alice Munro, *Hateship, Friendship, Courtship, Loveship, Marriage*, p. 16.

24. Alice Munro, *Hateship, Friendship, Courtship, Loveship, Marriage*, p. 14.

25. Alice Munro, *Hateship, Friendship, Courtship, Loveship, Marriage*, p. 19.

26. Alice Munro, *Hateship, Friendship, Courtship, Loveship, Marriage*, p. 22.
27. Alice Munro, *Hateship, Friendship, Courtship, Loveship, Marriage*, p. 24.
28. Alice Munro, *Hateship, Friendship, Courtship, Loveship, Marriage*, p. 25.
29. Alice Munro, *Hateship, Friendship, Courtship, Loveship, Marriage*, p. 27.
30. Alice Munro, *Hateship, Friendship, Courtship, Loveship, Marriage*, p. 28.
31. Alice Munro, *Hateship, Friendship, Courtship, Loveship, Marriage*, p. 48.
32. Alice Munro, *Hateship, Friendship, Courtship, Loveship, Marriage*, p. 52.
33. Alice Munro, *Hateship, Friendship, Courtship, Loveship, Marriage*, p. 54.
34. Alice Munro, *Hateship, Friendship, Courtship, Loveship, Marriage*, p. 55.
35. Alice Munro, *Hateship, Friendship, Courtship, Loveship, Marriage*, p. 56.
36. Alice Munro, *Hateship, Friendship, Courtship, Loveship, Marriage*, p. 57.
37. Alice Munro, *Hateship, Friendship, Courtship, Loveship, Marriage*, p. 58.
38. Alice Munro, *Hateship, Friendship, Courtship, Loveship, Marriage*, p. 67.
39. Alice Munro, *Hateship, Friendship, Courtship, Loveship, Marriage*, p. 78.
40. Alice Munro, *Hateship, Friendship, Courtship, Loveship, Marriage*, p. 82.
41. Alice Munro, *Hateship, Friendship, Courtship, Loveship, Marriage*, p. 84.
42. Alice Munro, *Hateship, Friendship, Courtship, Loveship, Marriage*, p. 85.
43. Alice Munro, *Hateship, Friendship, Courtship, Loveship, Marriage*, p. 114.
44. Alice Munro, *Hateship, Friendship, Courtship, Loveship, Marriage*, p. 90.

# CHAPTER 11

# A Slight Step Backward

Munro's next collection of stories, titled simply *Runaway* (in sharp contrast to the far more elaborate title of the previous collection), was published in 2004. It is not the powerhouse the previous collection was. (The book was greeted upon publication with this jab from the *New York Times*: "Unfortunately, her latest collection of stories . . . does not represent Ms. Munro's artistry at its best."[1] ) The crown jewel of the collection might expectedly be the three-story cycle, "Chance," "Soon," and "Silence," which dominates in terms of number of pages: 100 of the collection's total of 335. A short-story cycle has inherent attractiveness, even a cycle comprised of only three stories: demonstrating how stories can work together for enhanced impact and depth in their total effect and at the same time avoiding the crowdedness often felt in novel chapters; at the same time appealing to readers who tire of the usual stop-start of a standard story collection wherein the component stories have little in the way of linkages.

So, the question: Why isn't this collection's three-story cycle the most appealing aspect, in what ways do the other stories, those not cohorts in the cycle, step ahead in effectiveness?

(As a brief digression, it should be pointed out that all the titles of the included stories in the collection are simple to the point of sheerness; all being simply one word, all immaculate summaries of the major theme upon which each story rests. Yet the titles/theme statements are not giveaways, the story not "spoiled" for the reader by the title. This is not a gimmick of Munro's, but rather a unifying device that does not—as it should not—compromise the integrity and individuality of the stories as separate entities.)

"Chance" introduces the character of Juliet, in her early twenties, around whom the three-story cycle revolves, the title referring to a chance Juliet takes. While on a break from her teaching duties at a private school in Vancouver, beckoned by a letter she receives, she goes up the coast to visit a man she'd met in a strange circumstance. A flashback adjusts the story back six months prior, to answer questions about this man and circumstances: when Juliet was traveling by train to assume her new teaching position, which was only temporary, which suited her since she was in the process of working on her Ph.D. in classics. "In the town where she grew up her sort of intelligence was often put in the same category as a lisp or a second thumb, and people had been quick to point out the expected accompanying drawbacks—her inability to run a sewing machine or tie up a neat parcel, or notice that her slip was showing. What would become of her, was the question."[2]

On the other hand, the sexism of academe at the time (which Munro clearly states in the story's first line, 1965) is also indicated as a force on Juliet. Her classics professors were pleased to have someone interested in ancient languages, but less pleased with a girl than a young man. "If she got married . . . she would waste all her hard work and theirs,"[3] but if she did *not* get married, she would end up "bleak and isolated"[4] and so, according to this strange, partisan way of thinking, "she would not be able to defend the oddity of her choice of classics, to accept what people would see as its irrelevance, or dreariness, to slough that off the way a man could. Odd choices were simply easier for men, most of whom would find women glad to marry them. Not so the other way around."[5]

This train ride taking her to a temporary respite from academic life—a temporary teaching position—comes to define itself as a turning point in her life, an event determining the outcome of her life. A stranger sits down next to her, whom she rebuffs, who then, at a stop later in the journey, throws himself to death in front of the train; and Juliet suffers great remorse for her rudeness, assuming she was the precipitant of his action. She meets another man on the train and they share coffee and conversation, and Juliet learns—the reader learning as well—about Eric, who is a fisherman with an invalid wife.

A white space returns the story to its real time: Juliet taking a break to go visit Eric where he lives, somewhat summoned there by the letter he sent her care-of the school in which she is teaching. Juliet arrives by bus in the little town to find his wife has just died and that there are other women in his life—but exactly in what capacity? But no Eric on the scene yet, and like alternating scenes in a movie, a white space ushers in a return to Juliet and Eric on the train to Vancouver when they had just met; their mutual attraction is made obvious. Continuing the movie-like sensation, again a white space which again takes the story back to Eric's house, without Eric at home; but soon he arrives, having been informed by his network of women of *Juliet's* arrival. The story just simply peters out, with indications that Juliet stayed for quite some time; the implication is that ellipses actually stand at the story's end, as if the narrative thread will be picked up by the next story, which to a degree compromises the integrity of *this* story.

"Soon" carries Juliet's life-story further; it reworks a trio of interrelated themes that are favorites of Munro's: small-town narrow-mindedness and the difficulties, presented because of that, of going home again; remembrance of the past and how a person's present is a product of the past; and mother-daughter relation-ships. The story opens with a three-page section amounting to a prologue, in which certain situations important to the rest of the story are established: Juliet is expecting a child, and she is now good friends with one of the women with whom Eric had been involved before Juliet's advent. The exact circumstance transpiring in this brief section is this: Juliet purchasing a painting for her par-ents' Christmas present. A white space ushers in the story's "main element": it is now 1969, a few years after the events of the previous story, and Juliet's daugh-ter, Penelope, is just over a year old; and mother and baby are on an extended visit to Juliet's parents back in Ontario. Her parents are in decline and have a young local woman helping around the house. (There to be realized once more is how often Munro's mother characters are seriously ill.) Her father taught in the public schools for three decades and abruptly quit. "His methods could be seen to undercut authority."[6] (Another realization is there to be taken in: that in Munro's fiction, nontraditional teaching is always punished, which is another aspect, of course, of small-town narrow-mindedness.) It is revealed in conversa-tion between Juliet and her father that she and Eric, despite having parented a child, remain unmarried; and therein lies the major rub in the story. Evidence of what her parents really think of her—that she is an embarrassment—comes in increments; the first instalment comes in the form of a discussion with her mother about the painting that she had sent them (the painting she is seen purchasing in the opening scene). Juliet finds it leaning against a wall, and her mother explains to her (out of earshot of her father) that the painting was indeed hanging up but the father took it down for no known reason; that probably he felt it would disturb the hired girl with its modernnesss. "He might be afraid it would make her feel—oh, sort of contemptuous of us. You know—that we were weird. He wouldn't like for Irene to think we were that kind of people."[7] In two long paragraphs of narration from Juliet's point of view, the history of her adolescent shift in alle-giance is documented: from being close to her mother, doing mother-daughter things, to wanting nothing more to do with her mother, wanting only stimu-lating conversations with her father. (This attitude is certainly in keeping with Munro's abiding sentiment that fathers are nicer, more interesting people than mothers.)

Juliet's innate rebelliousness against small-town constraints is encapsulated in this statement: "But occasionally—and now, especially, here at home, it was the fact of her unmarried state that gave her some flesh of accomplishment, a silly surge of bliss."[8] She has another conversation with her father in which it is revealed that he might have quit his long-held teaching position because of town attitudes toward Juliet's unmarried status; the father posits, indicating that while he may suffer from it, he is in the middle of the town's conservatism: "Unfortunately your mother and I don't live where you live. Here is where we live."[9] A devastating realization now occurs to Juliet: that when her parents told her the passenger train bringing her home didn't make a stop in their town anymore and they picked her up in another town down the line, which was not the truth: they simply didn't want to be seen picking her up in her hometown.

Juliet is also increasingly aware that her father's feelings for the hired girl might be inappropriate: lustful, in fact. And she has an argument with the preacher, who has called on her mother, about religion. All this is adding up to her desire to get back home: where she currently lives with Eric, that is. A page-long addendum ends the story; Munro has a habit, quite observable on previous occasions, wanting to wrap things up by a glance into the future, or a final view of the present that bookends the storyline that had been set in previous times. In this case, it is strictly a narration, not exposition by actual scene; mentioned is Juliet's final return to her parents' home occasioned by her mother's funeral not long after her previous visit ("Soon," the story's title, reflects just how short her mother had to live). Then her father remarried and he and his second wife took long trips in a trailer they bought, visiting Juliet and her family twice; and with the mother gone, she gets along with her father very well, as does he with her. Implications are that away from their small hometown, her father relaxed and expanded. But years later, Juliet discovers a letter she had sent to Eric during that tense summer visit when her mother as still alive, which she sees was a strange cover-up, with its rather benign tone, of how she was really reacting to conditions between herself and her parents, "contrasting with the pain of her memories."[10] She now realizes "some shift must have taken place, at that time, which she had not remembered. Some shift concerning where home was. Not at Whale Bay with Eric but back where it had been before, all her life before. Because it's what happens at home that you try to protect, as best you can, for as long as you can."[11]

"Silence" completes the trilogy, the three-part cycle. The title indicates what Juliet—who remains, in this conclusion of the trio, the central character—is receiving from her now-grownup daughter, Penelope, who has run off to live in some sort of alternative community. Juliet is now a relatively famous television personality and Eric is dead, drowned while out fishing—which was his livelihood, it will be remembered, not simply his avocation. Thus most of the story is consumed with Juliet attempting to reestablish communication with the very absent Penelope, over the course of several years; the story's real time is consequently quite expansive, which leads to the story's major problem: too much narration and thus a lack of narrative tension—in a word, undramatic. The story's limpness comes to a soft head in this concluding paragraph, which summarizes what Juliet has learned from her particular experience of motherhood: "She keeps on hoping for a word from Penelope, but not in any strenuous way. She hopes as people who know better hope for undeserved blessings, spontaneous remission, things of that sort."[12]

"Powers" is the least successful story in the collection; careful examination is instructive in learning what goes wrong when Munro is not at her best. The title refers to powers of the extrasensory kind. The story will not be remembered for originality in handling this tricky, too-easy-to-fall-into-cliché theme, but for the sensational, contrived, and overly coincidental way she *does* handle it. A young woman, Nancy, still living at home, gets engaged to a doctor, and the doctor's cousin comes to town for a visit and will be the groom's best man. Nancy takes her fiancé's cousin to visit an eccentric young woman Nancy knew in school, who has "powers." The cousin continues to visit this person and later writes an article about her; and behind Nancy's back the cousin and the friend run off to get married and try to involve themselves in scientific research into her powers but instead, descend into side-show practices to make a living. (The only emotional pull of this story on the reader is the ignorance Munro delivers to Nancy, ignorance of her own jealousy over her new husband's cousins' apparent attraction to this friend of hers rather than to herself; the reader, not *she*, sees it coming.) This early part of the story is set in the late 1920s, and then the narrative jumps ahead to the late 1960s. Nancy is visiting a private hospital in Michigan, where her friend with the powers is institutionalized; her husband is quite incapacitated, and she hasn't communicated with her friend in many years. This institution has written to Nancy about the possibility of her taking her friend home with her; the friend is capable of living on the "outside" as long as someone cares for her. But Nancy has just come to visit, not to take her old friend away; during this visit, however, the friend insists that the man she ran off with, Nancy's husband's cousin, is dead, which Nancy isn't certain is the truth.

A new section removes the story to a new place and a time a few years hence. Nancy (now a widow) is visiting Vancouver, a city she had never been to before, and she just happens to run into, on the street, her husband's cousin, who obviously is not dead after all; and he, as well, just happens to be visiting the city. They spend time together, Nancy learning about his life with her childhood friend with the powers, and Nancy is struck by how much he is not the same person she remembers. "So Nancy had missed Ollie a lot without ever figuring out just what it is was that she missed. Something troublesome burning in her like a low-grade fever, something she couldn't get the better of."[13] Nothing will ever arise between them; and that is what the story is about: *them* and what is between them.

Woven upon a thematic framework of the frictional rub between provincialism and sophistication, and rendered in mixed format—epistolary, diary entries, as well as straight narrative—and featuring alternating points of view, the story fails to achieve cohesion, leaving a sensation of wobbliness.

That is the opposite sense given by the collection's title story, a masterpiece. "Runaway" is forty-five pages long but cannot be accused of wobbling on unsteady feet. The title is literal: a young wife runs away from her husband (and an animal runs away from *her*, the creature and its act of running away Munro endows with both rich and natural symbolic value, explained later). This story represents one of Munro's deepest psychological penetrations. It is, primarily, a story about a marriage in serious dysfunction. It is related in a tight, limited third-person point of view, from the alternating perspectives of only two characters. The tone of personal frustration is quickly established and is maintained throughout, well connecting the story's theme and the atmosphere fairly wafting off its pages. Munro creates in this story two sympathetic female characters and a male character who is indeed *not* sympathetic, which is a reversal of her usual practice. As indicated earlier in this paragraph, the author's psychological understanding of these three characters, chiefly the young woman who is the runaway, is particularly on target, but also—this said in all seriousness—her psychological understanding extends to the animal world as well, without embarrassing anthropomorphizing.

The primary character is immediately given a name: Carla. The setting is rural. From inside her barn, as the story opens, Carla hears a car going by and approaching and assumes it's her neighbor, Mrs. Jamieson, who is newly home from a European vacation. By Mrs. Jamieson having been to Greece, and that the road takes an incline to accommodate an elevation "that around here they call a hill,"[14] sets up a question: are these people really farmers, or are they outsiders recently come to experience what they imagine to be authentic rural life?

The second paragraph poses another yet-to-be answered question. Carla is hoping it is not actually Mrs. Jamieson driving by. But why? But it is indeed she, as Carla is able to affirm by a quick glimpse at the road. Carla is hoping Clark—husband, so assumed at this point—will not see that their neighbor is home from vacation. Again, why?

To this initial element of mystery is soon joined a tone of oppressiveness that will linger throughout the story, first set in place by this line: "This was the summer of rain and more rain."[15] That Carla lives not in solid economic surroundings is indicated when, still in reference to the rain, it falls not on a comfortable farmhouse but "loud on the roof of the mobile home."[16] The constant rain is affecting their business, which is boarding horses and offering riding lessons and trail rides.

The second level of oppressiveness, the most serious and damaging to Carla's psychology—the constant rain simply an appropriate backdrop for what is the nature of her married life—is brought to the fore in these two lines: "Clark had fights not just with the people he owned money to. His friendliness, compelling at first, could suddenly turn sour."[17] And, too, this brief exchange between him and Carla:

"You flare up," said Carla.
"That's what men do."[18]

Clark extends his grumpy nature to one of the horses in their care, by the name of Lizzie; her owner complains to Clark about the dampness of the mare's quarters and he takes it out on her horse—not physically, but by simply ignoring her, when up to this point he had been treating Lizzie as his personal pet. As indicated previously, Munro extends her understanding of psychology to the animal world in this story, with completely realistic, unsentimental results, observing that, "Lizzie's feelings were hurt, in consequence—she was balking when exercised and kicked up a fuss when her hoofs had to be picked out, as they did every day, lest they develop a fungus. Carla had to watch out for nips."[19] Thus a picture is established of Carla's husband's inability to get along equably with either people or animals. That inability will come to threaten both human and animal, in the latter case, Flora, the little goat Carla and Clark keep around as a pet. As the story opens, Flora has run away. For the two nights Flora has been away, Carla has dreamed of her—dreaming of her own escape?

A brief flashback indicates Carla is living in reduced circumstances: until her marriage she would not have used the term "mobile home" in reference to a trailer nor had she paid any attention to the kinds of mobile homes are available and how they can be fixed up individually. A return to the story's real time continues to build up the picture of Clark's difficult nature as well as Carla's unhappiness; specifically cited are Clark's bad moods creating an oppressive atmosphere within the confined mobile home, as he is consumed with his computer. That situation creates an indelible picture of their relationship: Clark has his back turned to Clara. The horses, when they in turn sense Carla's unhappiness, won't look at her, either. But the goat Flora, ever the symbol of playful innocence in sharp contrast to Clark's growing image in Carla's eyes as subjugator, is also the opposite of the horses: in the face of Clara's unhappiness, Flora does not shun her but, rather, attempts to cajole her into a better mood.

Telling, too, is Flora's transference of her affection for Clark to Carla. Clark was, as explained at this point in a two-paragraph narration, the one who had brought her home and had been the object of Flora's affection at the beginning. Flora is a playful personality but nevertheless an animal governed by instinctive reactions, comes to find Clara more suitable to her liking than Clark. The question suspended over the narrative, as if a super title not observable by Carla or Clark, is whether since Carla doesn't appear to like Clark much anymore either, will she also—the story's title reverberates—join Flora in flight from this disharmonious domestic situation?

A dialogue between Clark and Clara ensues, the purpose—or at least effect—of which is two-fold: to contribute to the impression of his irritability and near-abrasive tone in communicating with her, and to move the story onto a quite different plane, one of even intense psychology that for the author is a gamble. In other words, the story could not have foundered on the rocks of melodrama. Clark informs Clara that Mrs. Jamieson, their neighbor, had phoned and would like Carla to come clean her house, which apparently she has been in the practice of doing. Carla, however, indicates reluctance to go this time, while Clark insists she must. In a four-page back story—in which a lesser author, with less sense and forethought and plain talent for grasping realism in her characterizations than Munro possesses—Carla and Clark's separate and united agendas vis à vis Mrs. Jamieson are aired. Carl had been helping around the Jamieson house when Mr. Jamieson, though ill and bedridden, was still alive; and when he passed away, Carla and Clark read in the local paper that, unbeknown to them, the poet (Mr. Jamieson) had not too long before his death been awarded a significant financial prize for his poetry. Clark's response to this information, when he and Carla learn it, is ambiguous. "We could've made him pay."[20] Unlike the reader, Carla understands what he means. Clark proceeds to talk, saying that although the dead poet can't be forced to pay them money, his widow, if threatened with the exposure of her late husband's behavior, could be forced to give them some money. Clark, Carla reflects, "sometimes got notions like this that were not practicable, which might even be illegal. He talked about them with growing excitement and then—she wasn't sure why—he dropped them. If the rain had stopped, if this had turned into something like a normal summer, he might have let this idea go the way of the others. But that had not happened, and during the last month he had harped on the scheme as if it was perfectly feasible and serious."[21]

The exact nature of the scheme still eludes the reader. Fortunately, the answer now arrives, explained over the next two pages. Clark's plan is to extort money from Mrs. Jamieson by telling her some indecent information about her husband; but a previous deceit already exits: Clark's scheme of Carla having made up the stories of Mr. Jamieson's inappropriate sexual advances toward her—made them up for titillation purposes to get Clark out of his foul mood. Clear, now, is the reason for Carla's reluctance to go to Mrs. Jamieson's to clean up: Clark wants the scheme set in motion immediately. In a half-page scene, separated off by white spaces, floating into the story before Carla heads to her neighbor's house, she is outside walking, keenly feeling the absence of her little goat Flora; the crux of the story now arises in summary: "It was almost a relief, though, to feel the single pain of missing Flora, of missing Flora perhaps forever, compared to the mess she had got into concerning Mr. Jamieson, and her seesaw misery with Clark. At least Flora's leaving was not an account of anything she—Carla—had done wrong."[22]

At this point Mrs. Jamieson's point of view comes to reign. She is now referred to as Sylvia. Basically the story is handed over the "victim," as it were, of Clark's nasty temperament and Carla's desperate need to sway him out of his meanness. By telling the story now through Sylvia's consciousness, Munro is in effect seeking a second opinion on Carla and what her course of action *should* be, should it be continued appeasement and self-sacrifice, or something radically different? Sylvia's view of Carla emerges quickly in the first paragraph. She is eager to see Carla, in such contradiction to Carla's dread of seeing Sylvia. This relationship is made obviously one-sided; further narrative, refracted though Sylvia's mind and memory, does more than simply hint at just how strong Sylvia's feelings are for Carla. Specifically, she recalls a harmless kiss Carla had planted on Sylvia's head after they had been working hard around the house together; harmless, yet it "had been in Sylvia's mind ever since. . . . Sylvia saw it as a bright blossom, its petals spreading inside her with tumultuous heat, like a menopausal flash."[23] When Carla does come over to Sylvia's following the latter's return from Greece, Carla's advent causes this reaction in Sylvia: "The long-limbed, uncomfortable, dazzling girl was sitting there at last, in the room that had been filled with thoughts of her."[24] And, further, Sylvia has brought a gift back for Carla, and in a brief, graceful flashback to Sylvia while actually in Greece, she indicates to the two lady friends with whom she is traveling *for* whom she intends to give the present she had purchased. Her friends, in a way suggesting they know more about what is going on than Sylvia is admitting to or even realizing, use the word "crush."

But—and the narrative continues to unfold through Sylvia's point of view—she observes (more like senses) a change now in Carla. She finds Carla "sullen." Sylvia mentions to her the goats she observed in Greece, which of course reminded Sylvia of Carla's little goat, about which she asks; and Carla informs her that little Flora is missing. The question, the mention of little Flora, precipitates a gush of tears, which Sylvia encourages Carla to let loose with; but Sylvia's true mindset about Carla's crying jag is an interesting psychological twist: "And Sylvia could not help feeling how, with every moment of this show of misery, the girl made herself more ordinary . . . "[25] Sylvia comprehends Carla's breakdown is not necessarily just over the loss of her goat, which Carla admits to. She goes on to confess she cannot tolerate Clark's attitude toward her any longer, at which point Sylvia rather manipulates Carla into realizing that she, like Flora, needs to take flight. Sylvia's encouragement quite arouses Carla to take action—to leave Clark this very day; and Sylvia even comes up with a place for Carla to flee to: with a friend of hers in Toronto, with whom Sylvia will arrange things.

It is decided that Carla can't even go back home for a minute, and Sylvia gives her a better outfit of clothes to wear on the bus trip. Carla writes a brief note of good-bye, which Sylvia deposits in Carla and Clark's mailbox after leaving Carla off at the bus station. Sylvia's reaction to seeing her off combines maternal and romantic elements: but both aspects of her reaction boil down to her having been spurned, as Carla reacts like a spoiled child. "She kept seeing Carla, Carla stepping onto the bus. Her thanks had been sincere but already almost casual, her wave jaunty. She had got used to her salvation."[26]

The story now, by necessity, returns to Carla's point of view. She is rationalizing her flight as "Mrs. Jamieson's presence has surrounded her with some kind of remarkable safety and sanity and had made her escape seem the most rational thing you could imagine, in fact the only self-respecting thing that a person in Carla's shoes could do."[27] This section, as Carla travels on the bus, is actually not an action scene but an interior one, as an important aspect of Carla's past, the nature of which connects with her current situation, is recalled by her, *to* herself. The fact emerges that she has experienced a previous incident of leaving everything behind. Ironically, she had left her parents and their conventional and comfortable lifestyle behind, to run off with Clark. Her naïveté, so obvious in the present time, was apparently a characteristic of hers back then as well; she sensed no red flag back then, when driving away with him in a truck, "his concern about the truck's behavior, his curt answers, his narrowed eyes, even his slight irritation at her giddy delight—all of that thrilled her. . . . She saw him as the architect of the life ahead of them, herself as captive, her submission both proper and exquisite."[28]

But her mind doesn't dwell entirely on the past; as the bus ride takes her further on her flight, she imagines her new future. She is, because her default position is being in denial about Clark, or at least fooling herself into believing things will change, that *he* will change, now losing heart and courage over her running away from home. Her moral weakness rises to the surface of her skin like a bruise; she can't imagine taking charge of her own life. Yes, it would be a life with "nobody glowering over her, nobody's mood infecting her with misery,"[29] but, then, "What would she care about? How would she know that she was alive?"[30] It comes as no surprise, then, that she removes herself from the bus long before arriving in Toronto and telephones Clark to come retrieve her.

Again, almost by necessity, to give the story all its rich sides that make it so remarkable, the point of view now shifts back to Sylvia. This section does not actually involve Carla's presence, but is *about* her. The appropriateness of her absence from the stage becomes clear when it is realized that the point of this piece of the story is how Carla is being used as a commodity between Sylvia and Clark, in a tug of war. She is an object onto which they each have projected their owns needs, rather than seeing her in her own true light and recognizing what is best for her. In an eerie encounter, Clark goes to Sylvia's house at night, purposely frightening her by his sudden appearance at her French doors. He says to his nemesis, "My wife Carla is home in bed. Asleep in bed. Where she belongs"[31] His demeanor—simply his *presence*—is threatening. The possibility that he could do bodily harm to Sylvia hangs in the night air. Sylvia sees him clearly, though:

> He was both a handsome man and a silly looking man. Tall, lean, well-built, but with a slouch that seemed artificial. A contrived, self-conscious air of menace. A lock of dark hair falling over his forehead, a vain little mustache, eyes that appeared both hopeful and mocking, a boyish smile perpetually on the verge of sulk.[32]

Clark indicates his displeasure over what he terms her interference in his marriage, and he more-or-less forces an apology from her. It is obvious she simply wants him gone. But all of a sudden out of the darkness, stepping right up to them, is the lost goat, Flora. In their discussion of how and where she might have gone on *her* flight, the tension between Clark and Sylvia is reduced: in the face of the goat's playful innocence, animosity seems unnecessary.

The rest of the story is related from Carla's perspective; again, the reasoning for this is faultless, since Carla's reaction to being back with Clark and how he treats her now is what there is left of the story to tell. When Clark returns from Sylvia's, he explains to Carla they had had a good talk; and his manipulativeness, and Carla's lack of realization of it, surfaces again when he tells her: "When I read your note, it was just like I went hollow inside. It's true. If you ever went away, I'd feel like I didn't have anything left in me."[33]

The weather clears and their horse business picks up; Clark and Carla appear to have a new affection between them, but the sense exists—again, recognized by the reader while undetected by Clara—that it is only temporary; that Clark, once Carla is firmly back in his grasp, will return to his irritable, even angry, ways. In a chilling exchange, Clark says to a woman who boards her horse at their establishment that Flora the goat has run off again; his nonchalance leaves the reader wondering, suspecting. . . .

Carla receives a letter from Sylvia in which she apologizes for her interference in Carla's life, and she goes on at some length about how Flora's innocence that evening of her return erased any tension or misunderstanding between herself and Clark. "We parted almost as friends,"[34] she posits; and that he has now fooled her, too, completes the picture of this Svengali-like character. Carla destroys the letter, experiencing a sensation of a "murderous needle somewhere in her lungs."[35] She senses that while Flora might be freer now, enjoying the freedom that Carla could have had but gave up, she doesn't trust that Clark didn't destroy Flora like he really wants to destroy her. She is more astute than had seemed.

"Passion" fits snugly into Munro's oeuvre by, first, being a memory piece told in third person from a single point of view, and second, by theme: the changes that the passage of time brings as well as "outsiderness" and the issue of nontraditional female roles when the girl protagonist actually wants to be an insider and traditional. The particular spin this story gives is that the girl is actually a local resident and the group she feels outside of is a family who has a summer home in the area. The girl, now a grown woman, goes in search of that actual house and in the process recalls her affiliation with the family, especially with two sons of the family.

"Trespasses" is a sensational story that never succeeds in drawing the reader in. (Stylistically, at least, it is among the best in the collection—ironically.) There is a sinister tone maintained throughout, and there is obviously something going on—or something that *has* gone on—that the reader, like the main character, a schoolgirl who lives with her mother and father in a small town, does not understand that needs to be learned about. Still, even given these hooks, the story remains outside the reader's complete interest.

"Tricks" is a particularly poignant, even romantic, but certainly not sloppily melodramatic story woven around a common Munro theme: a young woman feeling at odds with her small-town surroundings and the people living there. She can see more stimulating things over the horizon, which draws her to, every summer, take the train to Stratford (Ontario, that is) to see a Shakespeare play. The summer in question—the summer in which this story takes places—Robin loses her purse and, to get back home, must rely on the kindness of a man she meets. The next summer she hopes to meet him again, and she does, but he is so rude she is greatly disturbed. A second section moves the story forward in time, several years into the future in fact; and by way of her nursing (her occupation) she learns that the man she had spotted the second time, so many years ago, was actually the twin of the man who had been so nice to her, and the twin was rude obviously because he had no idea who she was.

## Notes

1. Michiko Kakutani, *The New York Times* (December 7, 2004), p. 1.
2. Alice Munro, *Runaway*, New York: Random/Vintage, 2004, p. 53.
3. Alice Munro, *Runaway*, p. 53.
4. Alice Munro, *Runaway*, p. 53.
5. Alice Munro, *Runaway*, p. 53.
6. Alice Munro, *Runaway*, p. 93.

7. Alice Munro, *Runaway*, p. 99.
8. Alice Munro, *Runaway*, p. 102.
9. Alice Munro, *Runaway*, p. 105.
10. Alice Munro, *Runaway*, p. 125.
11. Alice Munro, *Runaway*, p. 125.
12. Alice Munro, *Runaway*, p. 158.
13. Alice Munro, *Runaway*, p. 320.
14. Alice Munro, *Runaway*, p. 3.
15. Alice Munro, *Runaway*, p. 4.
16. Alice Munro, *Runaway*, p. 4.
17. Alice Munro, *Runaway*, p. 6.
18. Alice Munro, *Runaway*, p. 6.
19. Alice Munro, *Runaway*, p. 7.
20. Alice Munro, *Runaway*, p. 13.
21. Alice Munro, *Runaway*, p. 13.
22. Alice Munro, *Runaway*, p. 16.
23. Alice Munro, *Runaway*, p. 18.
24. Alice Munro, *Runaway*, p. 18.
25. Alice Munro, *Runaway*, p. 22.
26. Alice Munro, *Runaway*, p. 30.
27. Alice Munro, *Runaway*, p. 31.
28. Alice Munro, *Runaway*, p. 32.
29. Alice Munro, *Runaway*, p. 74.
30. Alice Munro, *Runaway*, p. 34.
31. Alice Munro, *Runaway*, p. 37.
32. Alice Munro, *Runaway*, p. 37.
33. Alice Munro, *Runaway*, p. 42.
34. Alice Munro, *Runaway*, p. 45.
35. Alice Munro, *Runaway*, p. 46.

CHAPTER 12

# A SLIP BACKWARD

Munro's most recent collection, and last to date, is *The View from Castle Rock*, published in 2006. It is a problematic book (which I called, in my pre-publication advance review, "both frustrating and exhilarating"[1]), in which Munro attempts the invention of, as she essentially invented her own kind of short story over the course of her several collections, something else anew: not simply historical fiction on a smaller scale than the usual novel-length treatment of the historical past. She has done that before, and has successfully accomplished it. These new "stories" warrant the quotes with which I surround the word. Also let it be said at the outset that Munro has incorporated her own family's history into her fiction before; in fact, that is an integral part of her fiction, especially in the stories from the first half of her career. But now in this book, at least in what is designated "Part 1" Munro goes well beyond the "simple" integration of her family history into fiction and reaches into the realm of memoir, *absolute* memoir, and not just autobiographical fiction. She boldly abandons the conventions of fiction to color every "story" in Part 1, a too-much-like-memoir factor, with far too much undigested family history. In these instances, which can only be described as startling, Munro as author steps in *as the author*. As I went on to say in my pre-publication review, Munro's "intrusions into the prose not as narrator but as actual author prove distracting and erode the veil of suspension of disbelief."[2] Granted, other reviews, upon the book's release, pointed out the unusualness of the collection but with more temperance than I, as in this review by the distinguished American short-story writer Deborah Eisenberg: "This amalgam of history, fiction, and memoir is unlike any historical fiction or autobiographical fiction that I have ever encountered. It is more on the order of a flowing exploration, which begins in obscurity, brings vividly into the light assorted pioneers and settlers of Munro's own life, probing possibilities and happening upon continuities."[3] Then again, some reviewers barely batted an eye over the unconventionality of these pieces in their desire to applaud Munro—but with a sense of simply applauding her for *being* her, not really pausing to look hard at this particular gathering of her work.

The question poses itself in the reader's mind, particularly in the mind of the reader who has closely followed Munro over the course of her career: Are the pieces in Part 1 simply memoir/family history that Munro has been interested in writing lately and it was a publisher decision to keep calling what she writes "fiction" because that is what her reputation and commercial success has been based on, and consequently there were publisher worries about possible disadvantages of a collection of memoir essays in terms of critical and commercial reception?

On the other hand, is this a case of splitting hairs? Does what to call the pieces ultimately matter to readers? Do what critics have to say about identifying these so-called stories carry much weight except among themselves? Is my pre-publication review of the collection, in which I, as I have previously quoted, took issue with the form and technique found therein; but I concluded that "only purists will howl over the issue of authorial intrusion, and the vast number of fiction readers will be completely absorbed."[4]

But to argue the other side again, as if making up one's mind about these stories is troublesome—which it is—if we enter the actual prose of the book, we are faced first with a Foreword, and not only is this the first occasion of a Munro collection be preceded by such, but also the connotation—irresistible to perceive, difficult to ignore or pretend one's reaction is otherwise—is that what follows *is* nonfiction. Munro uses this Foreword to explain that approximately a decade prior to this writing, she took a keener interest in her father's family and went to Scotland to spend time investigating past generations. Interestingly, in her choice of words, she relates, "I put all this material together over the years, and almost without my noticing what was happening, it began to shape itself, here and there, into something like stories."[5] She elaborates to a certain extent; but the Foreword, although only two pages in length, remains confusing and even muddled. She talks about, simultaneous to collecting family history, writing a "special set of stories."[6] "I was doing something closer to what a memoir does—exploring a life, my own life, but not in an austere or rigorously factual way."[7] And in a few sentences more, she avers, "these are *stories*"[8] [emphasis hers]. The tone of the Foreword is irritating: less an introduction than a self-defense. But its muddiness in explaining what she means to do in these stories seems to indicate *she* is unsure what to call them.

There are five "stories" in Part 1—as I have indicated—the problematic section of the book, of the two sections into which the book is divided. They are all beautifully written, no doubt, in her trademark vivid, lush, yet limpid style; and on that basis, when read for beautiful sentences, they are a pleasure. The first one is titled "No Advantages," and it in and of itself represents the problem with all five of the pieces in Part 1: too much breathless recitation of her family's history back in Scotland and her own pursuit in learning it (standing before the reader as very much the author, not simply in first-person narration). In essence, this piece is a series of biographical sketches of some of her Scottish forebears, one minute rising to the "occasion" of fictional technique, bringing much revivification to these individuals, but then showing the author's inability to resist intruding *as author*. Overall, there is simply too much narration to arrest the reader's attention except for brief moments here and there; and the novella-length (at sixty pages) title story, which appeared previously in *The New Yorker* as fiction, does indeed take on some of the appurtenances of fiction. It is the story of the immigration of Munro's family from Scotland to Canada, thus serving as sort of a preface to the rest of the collection. Here, the family comes to the New World (and all the "stories" that follow it in the book are about the experiences of this family in Canada over the next several generations.) Told from multiple points of view, the narrative frequently breaks open into scenes and dialogue: that is, it is *not* simply a recitation of information reading nearly like nonfiction. This story of the immigration of Munro's family to Canada is specifically about the family's shipboard experiences, often it is rising to colorful, dramatic conjuring of what life on sailing ships was like, its physical hardships and the mental stress of facing permanent relocation. Munro's characterizations—her establishment of the identities of each individual family member—show, once again, an abiding ability to do so. Then, within four pages of the story's end, Munro ruins it— there is no other way to say it—by stepping in, once again, as author, saying such things as "except for Walter's journal, and the letters, the story is full of my invention."[9] From that point to the story's end, she resorts to a recitation of literal family history. It is like the glass has shattered. The gripping story she told could indeed have stood alone; why the need to tack on actual family history at the end? For the reader, it is like watching a dramatic piece being played out well on stage, by actors, but having to endure the playwright sitting in the front row and turning around to the audience to explain certain contents of the play he has written. Either it stands on its own, or it doesn't.

The third piece, "Illinois," continues the immigrant-pioneer adventures of the author's Scots-originating family, but it threatens to not even get off the ground, to gain any buoyancy. The story's opening paragraphs read like straight family history, with Munro herself present and accounted for, acting once again as hostess to the saga of her family; fortunately, by the second page it opens into fiction, with dramatic scenes and dialogue. The story is about, as all the stories are in Part 1, family members finding their destiny, fortune, or at least preservation in the North American wilds of the early nineteenth century; and this story specifically concerns a band of the family who had immigrated to the state of Illinois in the United States, returning to the original family landing place, Ontario. By the story's fifth page, personal conflict among the members of the journeying group, dramatized well, elevates the narrative to the realms of fiction, where it remains till the last line.

"The Wilds of Morris Township" suffers acutely from too much undigested, straight-from-research family history, and Munro once again is like the playwright commenting to the audience on his own play while it is being performed. Well into the story—too far—an actual drama of frontier life (a man building his own house) unfolds like a late-blooming flower, the scent it gives off definitely that of fiction. Alas, in four short paragraphs that end the story—the four sentences together form a section unto itself, separated off by a white space—the dramatic, even beautiful air of fiction is allowed to be seen as illusory, as a mirage, when Munro the author—again, not as narrator—speaks as herself, concluding the story by tying it, however briefly, to real facts. As if the balloon cannot be let off to sail free; it must be tethered to the ground—the ground of actual fact, character, and event.

Munro's prose style in "Working for a Living" is exceptional in its vividness and clarity. This fifth story concludes the section comprising Part 1. If nothing else, to credit Munro with sustained brilliance in her actual process of sentence writing—word choice and arrangement—is to be reminded that although the structure or even the philosophy behind (of what constitutes fiction or not, that is) these pieces are open to criticism, the power of her writing as *writing* cannot be criticized. A few examples serve as sufficient proof of the above stated insistence on the potential of her writing abilities in that regard:

> He had a streak of pride which might look like humility, making him scared and touchy, ready to bow out. I know that every well. He made a mystery there, a hostile structure of rules and secrets, far beyond anything that really existed. He felt nearby the fierce breath of ridicule, he overestimated the competition, and the family caution, the country wisdom, came to him then: stay out of it."[10]
>
> But the people in town had Saturday or Wednesday afternoons and the whole of Sundays off and that was enough to make them soft. The farmers had not one holiday in their lives. Not even the Scots Presbyterians; cows don't recognize the Sabbath."[11]
>
> . . . [T]he masculine approach to the land was managerial, dictatorial. Only women were allowed to care about landscape and not to think always of this subjugation and productivity."[12]

Even with a strong narrative voice in first person, the story opens giving off a sense of fiction; but even this piece, beginning thusly—so promising—falls victim to its seeming, too many times, like straight family history. The material is perfect support for an actual Munro story: truly fiction, that is. It is about a country boy—the narrator's father, the narrator a female closely resembling other Munro female narrators—who passes the entrance examination to continue his schooling in town. The outsider theme—obviously from discussions of previous stories, a common Munro theme—strongly surges through this story: the father an outsider—a country boy—attending a school in town. The different take for Munro here on the outsider theme is that it is usually the female narrator recalling her own outsiderness back in school days. However, in this story, as the outsider theme is worked out, there are two sides to it: her father being an outsider by being a country boy going to school in town, one; and two, country people's attitude toward town people, to which the father-character subscribes: "And farmers saw people who lived in towns as having an easy life and being unlikely to survive in situations calling for fortitude, self-reliance, hard work."[13] The narrator's father does not remain in school; he drops out to become the farmer he was rather destined to become. But he takes up trapping, and in common with Munro's usual young *female* protagonists growing up rurally, he thus selects his own type of life, on his own terms, rather than simply falling into line as to what was programed for him.

The narrative then suffers a blow: authorial intrusion again. Munro seems, once again, to be replacing the narrator with herself. This story completes Part 1, with its highly observable, problematic mix of fiction and nonfiction. Part 2 contains six stories; fortunately, in these Munro adheres more closely to fiction technique and, relievedly, creates a sincerely fictional tone. The first story in this more traditional section is "Fathers," which essentially concerns the narrator's experiences with two very different types of fathers, as well as her own father. The first-person narration arises from familiar Munro territory: rural Ontario in the immediate post–World War II period. Also familiar is Munro's adeptness in capturing and humanizing the eccentricities of rural people: that is, not finding them grotesque in body and moral fiber, to be used simply in making humor. The first father passing under Munro's scrutiny is Bunt Newcombe, notorious in the region for his mistreatment of his animals as well as his family. In describing his suffering wife, Munro offers a beautiful articulation of one aspect of social times past: "Nowadays Mrs. Newcombe might be seen as a serious case, terminally depressed, and her husband with his brutish ways might be looked on with concern and compassion. *These people need help.* In those days they were just taken as they were and allowed to live out their lives without anyone giving a thought to intervention."[14] This passage as well: "But there was a feeling that some people were born to make others miserable and some let themselves in for being made miserable. It was simply destiny and there was nothing to be done about it."[15]

By the third page that the story is to be related in the first person is declared; and nothing in the declaration would lead to the assumption that the "I" is anything other than the traditional Munro narrator—a *character* in the story, that is, rather than Munro participating in the prose as *writer* herself. The narrator enters the narrative after three pages of omniscient narration about Bunt Newcombe and his oppressed family, including five daughters and one son; the narrator is an "acquaintance" of one of the daughters, Dahlia. The narrator and this Newcombe daughter walked to high school together, from their farms into town. The fact that schoolgirls are conscious of social order is a fact made obvious by this statement by the narrator: "Walking together did not mean that we became exactly friends . . . Dahlia's senior dignity and a matter-of-factness about her that ruled out silly conversation."[16] Their companionship is severed when Dahlia moves in with her married sister in town; but after a long period of their not encountering one another, Dahlia one day asked the narrator to walk home again with her: she still lives with her sister in town but wants to go out to the farm just to look around. Dahlia's proficiency as a basketball player had elevated her appreciation at school, and further indication of Munro's understanding of school mentality is made manifest in this passage: "I think that she must have started high school with all the business of her family dragging behind her. It was a small enough town so that all of us started that way, with favorable factors to live up to or some shadow to live down. But now she had been allowed, to a large extent, to slip free."[17]

As she and the narrator walk, Dahlia further explains her interest in going out to the farm: specifically, to see if her father is beating up her brother; she intends to spy, not necessarily confront. To the narrator's bold question whether her father ever beat her, Dahlia answers affirmatively. That times have changed in regard to the countenance of abusive husbands and fathers is almost a "lesson" of this story. Dahlia insists to the narrator that if she had her hands on a gun she would easily kill him; the narrator, as precocious as Munro's young, adolescent female narrators tend to be, sees that probably Dahlia wouldn't be capable of murdering her father and that she desired the narrator simply "to see her hating him."[18]

A white space in the narrative ushers in the next father about whom the narrator is concerned. The focus here is on another local family, the husband and wife operating a new wallpapering business, and the daughter, Frances, who (chronologically speaking, at a time prior to the narrator's friendship with Dahlia) was rather forced on the narrator by her concerned mother. The narrator isn't thrilled by this forced daily walk to school with the very uncool Frances; but some conversation does occur on their walks home. One day, Frances' mother asked the narrator to dinner the following Sunday, since the family would be moving away soon; and for the narrator the family's move away meant that "the boredom of Frances would be lifted, no further obligation would be involved and no intimacy enforced."[19] The meal turns out to be lovely, the food excellent, and France's father involving himself in playing host and in serving the food. In other words, the narrator participates in a level of sophistication heretofore unknown to her. Nevertheless, she is a reflection of her own milieu: she refrains from telling her parents about how good the food was and the other interesting aspects of the occasion, because she was made uncomfortable by the "way the two adults put themselves at the service of two children."[20] It is, plainly, a domestic atmosphere she is quite unused to.

The purpose of this flashback to this friend and her peculiar—to the narrator, that is—father is revealed after a white space and the narrator returns to the situation "at hand": the narrator's renewed acquaintance with Dahlia, who showed up one day to walk with the narrator out to her farm, to, as she openly admits, to spy on her abusive father and see what he is up to now. It becomes clear—the story drags to a degree at this point—that both of these parental situations, namely, the nature of the fathers—are drawing the narrator into a realization about how she related to her own father. In contrast to how she kept quiet about what went on in her "friend" Frances' house, the narrator opens up about Dahlia; she reveals that at this stage in her adolescence, "I had become the entertainer around home."[21] She is playing to her family, carving out a role for herself, as if she were an outsider in this group. In telling her family of Dahlia's hatred of her father, "it seems strange to me now that we could conduct this conversation so easily, without it seeming ever to enter our heads that my father had beaten me, at times, and that I had screamed out not that I wanted to kill him, but that I had wanted to die."[22] As an adult looking back on these events, the narrator realizes that she did not, at the time, see any comparison between that family and hers, who were "decent people."[23] She recalls her father as "a man of honor and competence and humor, and he was the parent I sorely wanted to please."[24] Interestingly, even the narrator did not, back then, look beneath respectable public behavior in her own family to question inappropriate domestic behavior; about her own father's physical abuse of her, she admits (now as the adult looking back) that she threw the onus on herself: "I did not hate him, could not consider hating him. Instead, I saw what he hated in me. A shaky arrogance in my nature, something brazen yet cowardly, that woke in him this fury."[25]

Ironically, this story is good but certainly not among Munro's best. Its effectiveness is enhanced by it being the first real "story" in this collection. However, the next story, "Lying Under the Apple Tree," is a superior one, superior on its own terms not simply because of the troublesome nature of the collection to which it belongs. It features Munro "basics": the first-person narrator is an adolescent female; a setting of rural Ontario; and the primary theme being social image within the school environment and the narrator's sense of her outsider status there.

The opening two paragraphs are scene-set with particular stylistic beauty, introducing a character by the name of Miriam McAlpin, who, on her farm, kept horses for people, and in one of her pastures were three old apple trees, which had been allowed to grow in their own fashion with no pruning. The narrator, who steps into the frame in the story's third paragraph, has use of a found bicycle, which her younger sister implores her *not* to ride to school because of the social damage that could result. But the narrator did ride the bike in the opposite direction: further out into the countryside, to indulge in her passion for nature and for reading poetry, both of which she realizes would leave her open to criticism from her peers. In the open countryside, however, she is free to be the person she wants to be; with the bicycle, she "could ride on Sunday afternoons into territory that seemed waiting for the kind of homage [she] ached to offer."[26] Her desire is to lie under the blossoming apple trees in Miriam McAlpin's pasture; she imagined it like kneeling in church, which she had once experienced in a Catholic church but had been chastised for doing because she wasn't of that faith—reinforcement of her outsider status, of course. The narrator proceeds to lie under the blossoming branches but gets caught by the owner of the land upon which the apple trees grew, who was "well known for her tendency to bawl people out."[27] She nastily demands the narrator leave the premises; the two men who are with her leer at the narrator. "The slight dull droop and thickening of their features, as the level of sludge rose in their heads."[28] (The stable boy also joins the scene, who appears to be uninterested in what is going on; but he now figures importantly in the story.)

She recognizes him standing on a downtown street corner as the trombone player in a group of Salvation Army members. He and she establish contact. He is of a Salvation Army family, in which usual entertainment is forbidden: no movies or dances, so bicycle riding became his and the narrator's arrangement for being together. Close physical contact ensues, and she is made aware that she is not as certain about the male body as she had believed herself to be, especially when it comes to a man's sexual arousal. "I had heard a lot of jokes, and I had seen animals coupling, but somehow, when education is informal, gaps can occur."[29]

At one point in their burgeoning relationship, she is invited to his house for an evening meal, and she doesn't inform her mother of the plan. The reason for her actually telling an untruth about where she is going that evening stems from her mother's social consciousness, which itself derives from strict and narrow small-town values: "Once you went into certain houses as an equal and a friend— and this was true even if they were in a way perfectly respectable houses—you showed that the value you put on yourself was not very high, and often that others would value you accordingly."[30] The psychology at the supper table— specifically, what the narrator experiences in her thought processes during the course of the meal—is particularly authentically rendered. She admits to herself that she is falsely under this roof and at the table, and that the only significance of she and he being together is to eventually have sex, not be taken as a couple in any sort of romantic, long-term fashion. "It never crossed my mind that a young couple in our situation did indeed belong right here, that we were entered on the first stage of a life that would turn us, soon enough, into the Father and the Mother."[31]

After the meal, the narrator is walked home by the young man, but first they adjourn to Miriam McAlpin's barn to finally consummate their relationship; but having heard a disturbance, she shoots off her shotgun in their direction. The narrator remains hidden while the young man steps forward to reveal himself and in the process he uses an endearment with her that reveals to the stunned narrator the true nature of the employer-employee relationship.

After a white space, the story is concluded—a leap in the future, and the narrator never seeing him again after that night. In an odd but effective construction technique, a subsequent white space sends the narrative back to that evening; when she returned home, she grabbed a book to read. "Because it was in books that I would find, for the next few years, my lovers. They were men, not boys."[32]

The collection's remaining four stories are—in a word, ordinary. "Hired Girl" features a young female protagonist, but instead of, as was the case with the previous story, turning out to be a case for Munro to return to her basics, this one suggests, with its lack of compellingness, a sense of rehash of old Munro themes and plot situations. "The Ticket" simply refuses to move in a successful direction. It is perambulatory to no good effect, simply frustratingly rambling, as if Munro had for the time being lost the knack of bringing her digressions back to a central point. "Home" is a story about when a person does go home again; "home" grabs you back into operating within old family roles but it lacks both steam and poignancy. "What Do You Want to Know For?" suffers from its two storylines being too disparate; also, echoing the "stories" in problematic Part 1, it tastes too much of memoir.

## Notes

1. Brad Hooper, *Booklist*, 103(1) (September 1, 2006), p. 8.
2. Brad Hooper, *Booklist*, p. 8.
3. Deborah Eisenberg, "New Fiction," *The Atlantic Monthly* (December 2006), p. 128.
4. Brad Hooper, *Booklist*, p. 8.
5. Alice Munro, *The View from Castle Rock*, New York: Knopf, 2006, p. 1.
6. Alice Munro, *The View from Castle Rock*, p. 2.
7. Alice Munro, *The View from Castle Rock*, p. 2.
8. Alice Munro, *The View from Castle Rock*, p. 2.
9. Alice Munro, *The View from Castle Rock*, p. 84.
10. Alice Munro, *The View from Castle Rock*, p. 128.
11. Alice Munro, *The View from Castle Rock*, p. 129.
12. Alice Munro, *The View from Castle Rock*, p. 130.
13. Alice Munro, *The View from Castle Rock*, p. 129.
14. Alice Munro, *The View from Castle Rock*, p. 175.
15. Alice Munro, *The View from Castle Rock*, p. 175.
16. Alice Munro, *The View from Castle Rock*, p. 176.
17. Alice Munro, *The View from Castle Rock*, p. 177.
18. Alice Munro, *The View from Castle Rock*, p. 182.
19. Alice Munro, *The View from Castle Rock*, p. 187.
20. Alice Munro, *The View from Castle Rock*, p. 192.
21. Alice Munro, *The View from Castle Rock*, p. 193.
22. Alice Munro, *The View from Castle Rock*, p. 194.
23. Alice Munro, *The View from Castle Rock*, p. 195.
24. Alice Munro, *The View from Castle Rock*, p. 195.
25. Alice Munro, *The View from Castle Rock*, p. 195.
26. Alice Munro, *The View from Castle Rock*, p. 199.
27. Alice Munro, *The View from Castle Rock*, p. 202.
28. Alice Munro, *The View from Castle Rock*, p. 202.
29. Alice Munro, *The View from Castle Rock*, p. 212.
30. Alice Munro, *The View from Castle Rock*, p. 214.
31. Alice Munro, *The View from Castle Rock*, p. 218.
32. Alice Munro, *The View from Castle Rock*, p. 226.

# Conclusion

In June 2006 it was reported in the press that Alice Munro had indicated (by way of an essay included in an anthology of essays by Canadian and international writers, which was sponsored by PEN Canada) that she had decided to retire from writing "in the interests of a manageable life."[1] Later, reports circulated that she had subsequently taken back these words—this threat?—indicating that her announcement to retire had been issued by her prematurely.[2] So, now where are we with regard to this situation? Are we really faced with a cessation of Munro stories? Only time and the appearance, or nonappearance, of further fiction will tell. Given the memoir-nature of her latest collection, suggesting a loss of interest in true fiction, she may well be deciding to pull up fiction-writing stakes.

If Munro does close down shop soon, with no new fiction forthcoming, which is a situation actually affording a good opportunity (not usual with regard to a living author), for critics to estimate her entire oeuvre as an intact body, as a closed and ended commodity. It can be analyzed as a completed progression. Her contribution to the world of letters can be judged in final terms. That is the basis, then, upon which I conclude my study of her work. What is there, already published and available, is all that there will be. Final conclusions about her body of work can be responsibly drawn.

Except for supplying a brief biographical profile of Munro at the beginning of this study, the purpose of which was to familiarize readers unfamiliar with her life and work (with a short context for developing an appreciation of that body of work), I have not been interested in the details of her life. That means I have not been concerned in my book-by-book analysis with drawing parallels between her life and her fiction. I do not read her own life into her stories; I read the stories as they exist on the page, not below the surface of the page into the well of Munro's personal experiences. I do not know what these are, aside from basic facts, and I am uninterested in them—at least uninterested in them as informers upon her fiction. As I say, what is on the page is my interest and purview. I see her characters as they stand on the pages, as they exist, and move within the narrative at hand, and I observe the situations into which Munro places them simply as that, not as extensions of, reflections of, various workings out of Munro's own life situations.

Munro has modified the short story to suit her own interests, needs, and capabilities, and the short-story genre will remain modified from her efforts. There will always be, now, the Munro-type of short story; and it will be referred to as such. And I do not mean a brand of short story that is simply idiosyncratic to her, which was exercised by her alone. No, I mean a permanent opening of the genre to possibilities—expansion possibilities, primarily—that authors after her can explore for their own purposes.

Munro has not simply taken care of the short story; it has not been up to her, nor has she been inclined to shoulder the responsibility, to maintain its conventions, set them down again intact, after her use of them is done, and send the short story on its way in a healthy condition but still in a traditional form. She has broadened the scope of what defines a short story but by following only the strictest procedures in opening the story form while *keeping* it the short-story form, not calling her product short stories when they are in fact underdeveloped novels. I insist upon this: she writes short stories, not short novels.

It is the resonance of what is on the page that gives her stories the experience of a novel; there is nothing condensed in her stories, only expanded by the universalities she touches upon in the particulars of her stories. That is the essence of a Munro short story, the fundamental process of her technique and the gist of her reader's appeal.

Many instances have been cited in the course of my analysis of her work of her use of first-person narrative; one finds, particularly in the first half of her oeuvre, this is almost exclusively her narrative technique. It is a choice for a reason; it makes no difference whether the narrator proves prejudiced, naive, uninformed, or one-sided, for the point of this narrative technique is to eliminate detachment, to make her stories as personal as possible, to bring her characters to the reader as real as they can be. But not only has Munro claimed the first-person narrative voice as her own, but she has also, as she has adapted the short-story structure to her own needs and interests, adapted it well to suit her purposes. She often uses the technique of first-person narrator narrating from the perspective of many years after the events being recalled as her way of having the narrator reconcile his or her (most often the latter, of course) past to his or her present: not only to see it through the clarifying lens of many years standing between the past and present, but also to help read the past as meaningful provenance of the present.

Of course, no adequately comprehensive discussion of Munro's fiction can fail to bring into the light her use of, her abiding interest in, the past: not so much the historical past, although that occasionally does play a role, at least as a backdrop to her characters' *personal* past. To be specific—to be accurate—her stories are not so much set in the past as they are remembrance pieces "about" the past, glances backward functioning to explore the present. Conversely, very little in a Munro story is about *just* the present; the past is always present in her stories, which, of course is a main reason for the depths to which her fiction goes in exploration of character. The result is her fiction's intense resonance, the profound analysis of a character that at once defines the character as an individual, yet binds that character to the general human condition with whom all readers can connect.

A corollary theme to the theme of the influence of the past on the present, around which many of her stories are constructed, is the "outsider" consciousness. As observed on numerous occasions, Munro's stories, protagonists frequently feel, are outside the mainstream in socioeconomic and, in the case of schoolgirls, "coolness" terms. The outsider theme is often played out in gender situations: girls and women who don't want to practice/perform traditional female roles. They are not so much in rebellion against accepted practices as simply uninterested. They stand outside, looking in, but not willing to be part of the accepted "crowd." A sub theme, a logical extension of it, or even a refinement of it, is the functioning of the adolescent female narrator as a bridge between the traditional male and female spheres of interest and endeavor; these situations—these that spring from this particular sub theme—offer some of the most intriguing, resonant, reader-appealing stories in all her oeuvre, for who cannot identify with an adolescent lack of desire to fit into neat and tidy boxes? Or, better stated: who, even if they did not experience such lack of interest in resisting the traces of tradition when they were adolescents, cannot understand Munro's characters going through such a psychological process? That is a strong testament to her ability to create characters perfectly comprehensible even to readers with whom they share not much in terms of gender, background, or life pursuits.

That brings us to the major conclusion that must be drawn—given the course that this critical survey has taken—about Munro as a fiction writer. She has moved the boundaries, the dimensions, the techniques in composing the short story beyond traditional methods and expectations, yes. But as I stated in the Introduction, all of that was in service to a higher, more personal objective for her: to achieve a deeper understanding of her characters. Her "invention," if you will, of the Munro short story was not intentional as a goal unto itself; it simply was the by-product of her magnificently achieved goal of building a character within the parameters of the short-story form.

## Notes

1. Richard Helm, "Munro Giving Up the Writing Life," *The Edmonton Journal* (June 20, 2006) (Online).

2. Mona Simpson, "True North," *The Atlantic Monthly* (December 2006), p. 128.

# Bibliography

## Editions of Alice Munro's Works Cited in the Text

*The Beggar Maid*. New York: Random/Vintage, 1991.
*Dance of the Happy Shades and Other Stories*. New York: Random/Vintage, 1998.
*Friends of My Youth*. New York: Random/Vintage, 1991.
*Hateship, Friendship, Courtship, Loveship, Marriage*. New York: Random/Vintage, 2001.
*Lives of Girls and Women*. New York: Random/Vintage, 2001.
*The Love of a Good Woman*. New York: Random/Vintage, 1998.
*The Moons of Jupiter*. New York: Random/Vintage, 1996.
*Open Secrets*. New York: Random/Vintage, 1994.
*The Progress of Love*. New York: Random/Vintage, 1986.
*Runaway*. New York: Random/Vintage, 2004.
*Selected Stories*. New York: Random/Vintage, 1996.
*Something I've Been Meaning to Tell You*. New York: Random/Vintage, 2004.
*The View from Castle Rock*. New York: Knopf, 2006.

## Secondary Sources

Baum, Rosalie Murphy. "Artist and Woman: Young Lives in Lawrence and Munro." *North Dakota Quarterly* 52(3) (1984).
Birkets, Sven. "The Tether of Origins: Alice Munro's *The Beggar Maid: Stories of Flo and Rose*." *Reading Life: Books for the Ages*. St. Paul, MN: Graywolf, 2007.
Blodgett, E. D. *Alice Munro*. Farmington Hills, MI: Twayne, 1988.
Carrington, Ildiko de Papp. "Controlling Memory: Mothers and Daughters, Fathers and Daughters." In *Controlling the Uncontrollable: The Fiction of Alice Munro*. DeKalb, IL: Northern Illinois University Press, 1989.
*Contemporary Literary Criticism*. Farmington Hills, MI: Thompson/Gale, Vol. 222, 2006.

*Dictionary of Literary Biography.* Vol. 53: Canadian Writers since 1960. Farmington Hills, MI: Gale, 1986.

Eisenberg, Deborah. "New Fiction." *The Atlantic Monthly.* December 2006.

Fowler, Rowena. "The Art of Alice Munro: *The Beggar Maid* and *Lives of Girls and Women.*" *Critique* 25(4) (Summer 1984).

Howells, Coral Ann. *Alice Munro.* New York: St. Martin's Press, 1998.

Hoy, Helen. "Rose and Janet": Alice Munro's Metafiction." *Canadian Literature* 121 (Summer, 1989).

Lynch, Gerald. "No Honey, I'm Home: Place Over Love in Alice Munro's Short Story Cycle: "Who Do You Think You Are?" *Canadian Literature* 160, 1999.

Merkin, Daphne. "Northern Exposures." *The New York Times Magazine.* October 24, 2004.

Miller, Judith Maclean. "Deconstructing Silence: The Mystery of Alice Munro." *Antigonish Review* 129, 2002.

Munro, Sheila. *Lives of Mothers and Daughters: Growing Up with Alice Munro.* Toronto, Canada: McClelland & Stewart, 2001.

Parker, Peter, and Kermode, Frank. *A Reader's Guide to Twentieth-Century Writers.* Oxford, UK: Oxford University Press, 1996.

Schiff, James. "A Conversation with John Updike." *Southern Review* 38(2) (Spring 2002).

Smythe, Karen. "Ad Elegies: The Ethics of Epiphany in Munrovian Elegy." *University of Toronto Quarterly* 60(4) (Summer 1991).

Solotaroff, Ted. "Life Stories. *Nation* 259(18) (November 28, 1994).

Stitch, Klaus, P. "The Cather Connection in Alice Munro's 'Dulse.'" *Modern Language Studies* 19(4) (Autumn, 1989).

Sutten, Brian. "Munro's 'How I Met My Husband.'" *Explicator* 63(2) (Winter, 2005).

*World Literature Today* 79(2) (May–August 2005).

# INDEX

**About the Author**

BRAD HOOPER is the Adult Books Editor at Booklist. Before coming to Booklist, he was a reference librarian at Cleveland Public Library. He is the author of *The Short-Story Readers' Advisory* (2000), *The Fiction of Ellen Gilchrist* (Praeger, 2005), and *Read On ... Historical Fiction* (2006).